Man's Nature and Nature's Man

MAN'S
NATURE
and NATURE'S
MAN

The Ecology of Human Communities

Lee R. Dice

GREENWOOD PRESS, PUBLISHERS
WESTPORT, CONNECTICUT

The Library of Congress has catalogued this publication as follows:

Library of Congress Cataloging in Publication Data

Dice, Lee Raymond, 1887-
    Man's nature and nature's man.

    Bibliography: p.
    1. Human ecology. I. Title.
[HM206.D5 1973]   301.31   72-9607
ISBN 0-8371-6594-6

Designed by George Lenox

Originally published in 1955 by the University of Michigan Press,
Ann Arbor

Reprinted with the permission of the University of Michigan Press

Reprinted from an original copy in the collections of the University
of Michigan

Reprinted by Greenwood Press, Inc.

First Greenwood reprinting 1973
Second Greenwood reprinting 1977

Library of Congress catalog card number 72-9607

ISBN 0-8371-6594-6

Printed in the United States of America

Preface

In preparing my book *Natural Communities,* I had planned to include a chapter on human communities. It soon became evident, however, that an adequate treatment of this important topic would require much more space than could be given in even a very long chapter. After much reworking, therefore, the material then prepared is now presented as a separate book.

No originality is claimed for any of the conclusions here reached. So much has been written about human societies that almost every possible idea has been expounded at some time by somebody. Nor do I attempt to trace the history of each important concept, or to credit the originator of every idea. I have, however, tried to give sufficient references so that the reader, if he so desires, may expand his knowledge of topics that especially interest him.

Few attempts have been made so far to describe human communities from the point of view of their resources, physical habitat, human populations, associated plants and animals, and ecologic interrelations, including community regulatory mechanisms. Practical methods for describing and measuring the various ecologic features of human communities in quantitative terms are still largely lacking, especially for the complex interrelations within an industrial community.

Practical methods for the measurement and analysis of human communities of every grade of complexity can certainly be devised. This will, however, not be easy nor can it be accomplished without many rigorous field studies, each carefully planned to improve in methods on those previously made. If this book arouses interest in these problems it will have succeeded in its purpose.

George G. Simpson has kindly granted permission to quote in Chapter III a passage which he originally published in volume 31 of the *Journal* of the Washington Academy of Sciences. The manuscript has been read by Francis C. Evans and by J. N. Spuhler, whose criticisms have been of much value.

L. R. D.

February 22, 1955
Ann Arbor, Michigan

Contents

Introduction: The Frame of Reference

CHAPTER I

The major thesis of this book is that man is able to exist only as a member of some community in which associated species of plants and animals supply him with food and other essential supplies and services. Man, in turn, has profound effects upon his plant and animal associates. These interrelations between man and other kinds of organisms are of great significance for human welfare.

Community

According to the definition here employed, any aggregation of ecologically related individuals belonging to two or more different species constitutes an ecologic community (Dice, 1952: 15). Every individual, whether man or another kind of organism, has numerous ecologic relations with individuals belonging to other species. Man, for example, uses parts of various kinds of plants and animals for food, for clothing, and for other purposes. He may in turn be used as a source of food by mosquitoes, by parasites of numerous kinds, and more rarely by large carnivores. Ecologic relations between the members of a community may include association not only for food, but also for shelter, transportation, and various other purposes.

Those species of plants and animals that live together may usually be assumed to have direct or indirect ecologic relations with one another. Every fairly permanent aggregation of individuals belonging to several diverse species may consequently be considered to be a community.

This definition of community is somewhat more restricted than the loose usage of everyday speech. It is related to, but broader than, the definition employed by sociologists (MacIver, 1917: 22; Hawley, 1950: 223; Quinn, 1950: 48), who usually direct their attention to man alone.

The term community as used by ecologists may refer to an assemblage of organisms of any size or ecologic rank. Even the smallest communities are usually composed of a considerable number of individual organisms belonging to several species. At the extreme, all the organisms of the whole world, considered together, form a single enormous community.

Ecosystem

Ecologists use the term ecosystem to refer to a community together with its habitat. An ecosystem, then, is an aggregation of associated species of plants and animals, together with the physical features of their habitat. Ecosystems, like communities, can be of any size or ecologic rank. Thus, a drop of pond water together with the organisms that live therein constitutes a small ecosystem. At the extreme, the whole earth and all its plant and animal inhabitants together constitute a world ecosystem. The concept of ecosystem emphasizes the interrelations between the group of organisms that form a community, and the soil, water, climate, and other physical features of its environment.

Matter and energy are constantly being interchanged between the community and its habitat. Not only is the community closely dependent upon and controlled by its habitat, but the habitat in its turn is modified in many ways by the activities of the organisms that compose the community. The community and its habitat together constitute, therefore, an interacting system.

Human community

In the study of any particular community, attention may be directed chiefly to certain kinds among its member organisms. Should our attention center on the plants, for instance, we may speak of a plant community, even though we recognize that animals also are present. Just so, we speak of a human community when our attention is directed chiefly to man and to his relationships with the various species associated with him in a particular situation.

No fundamental ecologic difference exists between a human community and any other special type of animal community. Every complete community must contain green plants to furnish a basic supply of food for the other member organisms. Every community now in existence also contains herbivores. Most communities contain in addition various kinds of carnivores and parasites.

Society

A distinction must be made between a community and a society. A society, according to the definition used in this work, is an aggregation of individuals belonging to a single species who are cooperating directly or indirectly with one another. A group of cooperating men, for example, constitutes a human society. The individual persons in a human society may cooperate with one another to obtain food, to defend themselves against their enemies, to provide themselves with shelter, or in other ways.

When attention is centered entirely on the human individuals in a given habitat, rather than on their plant or animal asso-

ciates, the group may rightly be called a society. When attention is directed both to the human population and to populations of other species associated with man, then the combined
aggregation, whether concrete or abstract, is properly called a
community. In common usage, however, the terms society and
community, insofar as they apply to aggregations that include
men, are used somewhat interchangeably. To avoid confusion,
we shall refer to an aggregation of socially related individuals
belonging to the same species as a social group rather than as
a society.

Culture

The term culture in its anthropologic sense may be defined as
learned behavior shared by the members of a social group, and
transmitted from generation to generation (Wissler, 1929: 15;
Linton, 1945: 30; Kroeber and Kluckhohn, 1952). The customs,
technology, and art of a people constitute essential parts of its
culture; but its beliefs also are included under the term, because they often control important features of social behavior
(Dixon, 1928: 3; Wissler, 1938b; Linton, 1945: 32). Thus used,
the term culture covers a very wide field. In this book, emphasis will be placed mostly on those customs and procedures
that govern the securing and utilization of food, shelter, and
other necessities for life, and on the organization and regulation of communities. This emphasis does not indicate a failure
to recognize the fact that the non-material aspects of culture
are an important part of the adjustment of each human society
to its local environment, or that religion and art may to a considerable degree affect community survival and evolution.

No distinction will here be made between those elements of
human behavior that are inherited as instincts, and those that
are acquired during the life of the individual. That learned
social behavior is a special property of man, and is entirely

lacking in the societies of other species of animals, is an assumption made by many social scientists. Actually, many kinds of social animals other than man learn numerous features of their behavior during their lifetime. Many animals, if they are subjected to influences different from those usual for their kind, will acquire new and often peculiar types of behavior. A bird, under such conditions, may imitate the songs of another species. Every domesticated animal has learned certain features of behavior which are different from those of its wild relatives. A duckling raised away from water by a domestic hen, for instance, not only fails to learn to paddle, but, as I can relate from my own observation, appears to be terrified if forcibly placed on the water of a pond.

Man is an animal with an unusually complex culture, which must be learned by each individual during his lifetime. Learned behavior plays a much more important role in the culture of a human society than in any other. Still, the difference in culture between a human society and a society of any other animal, though tremendously great, is one of degree, and not a difference between learned and unlearned behavior.

Inherited differences between individuals may be presumed to control in part the things each person will learn best, and the position he will occupy in his society. It is possible, also, that inherited differences in temperament and special abilities among tribes and races may in part affect the type of culture they evolve; but actual information on this point is scanty.

Adaptation

Every individual organism, in order to survive, must have characters that adapt it to the habitat in which it lives. The conditions in every habitat, however, are continually changing. In order to go on living, every organism must thus be able to adjust itself constantly to the changes in its environment. This problem of constant adjustment is the principal problem of life.

Each community of organisms must likewise be adapted to its habitat. A type of community that would thrive in a rainy climate, for example, could probably not exist in an arid region. Communities, furthermore, must be able to adjust themselves to the continual fluctuations in the physical factors of their habitats. Each community, consequently, must have regulatory mechanisms that operate to prevent fluctuations in its composition from reaching an unviable extreme.

Complexity of human communities

The various parts of a human community often are complexly interrelated. Man's domestic animals, for example, sometimes come into competition with wild animals for food supplies. Man will then usually make attempts to reduce the numbers of these wild animals by a variety of control measures. At times, however, the competing wild animals are game or fur-bearing species that are themselves sources of sport, fur, or food for man. Their elimination, then, may mean the loss of a valuable natural resource.

The diversity of human interests included within a single community may be illustrated by an actual occurrence. In the mountains of eastern Oregon, domestic livestock come into competition for summer forage with the introduced American elk (Pickford and Reid, 1943). The range will support only a certain amount of pasturing. If elk increase, then fewer domestic cattle, sheep, goats, and horses can be supported. In this particular situation, many diverse economic and sociologic relations are involved. The interests of foresters, livestock raisers, farmers, sportsmen, and nature lovers are all affected. Even the local merchants, manufacturers, truckers, teachers, preachers, lawyers, and other city dwellers are concerned. The interests of the whole county, and to a lesser extent those of the state and nation must also be considered. The adjustment of these complex and sometimes conflicting interests is the province of the political administrator. In the past, the reconciliation of such conflicts has all too often been attempted without an adequate consideration of the ecology of the area. Administrators, however, are becoming increasingly aware of the importance of scientific advice from range managers, soil conservationists, foresters, wildlife managers, and other kinds of practical ecologists.

Human history is in major part a consideration of the ecologic relations of human societies of the past to their habitats. In recognition of this relationship, historians are coming to place less emphasis on national heroes, royal dynasties, and battles, and to devote more attention to density of population, natural resources, food productivity, routes of trade, the degree of development of technology and science, competition among communities, and other ecologic factors (Barnes, 1925, 1940; Childe, 1953). Rulers, edicts, laws, wars, and treaties may have temporary effects on the course of history—but the major trends of human history may be assumed to be controlled primarily by the ecologic relations within and between particular human communities.

SELECTED REFERENCES

Allee, W. C., A. E. Emerson, O. Park, T. Park, and K. P. Schmidt. 1949. Principles of animal ecology. Philadelphia: W. B. Saunders Co.
Dice, Lee R. 1952. Natural communities. Ann Arbor: University of Michigan Press.

Kroeber, A. L. 1948. Anthropology: race, language, culture, psychology, prehistory. New York: Harcourt, Brace and Co.

Odum, Eugene P. 1953. Fundamentals of ecology. Chap. 8. Philadelphia: W. B. Saunders Co.

Sears, Paul B. 1939. Life and environment; the interrelations of living things. Teachers College, Columbia University.

Essentials of Human Existence

CHAPTER II

Any kind of organism, in order to thrive, must find in its habitat certain essentials for its existence. The essentials for the existence of man may be listed as (1) a tolerable climate, (2) suitable kinds and quantities of food, (3) shelter from extremes of the physical factors of habitat and from dangerous organisms, and (4) conditions suitable for reproduction.

Climate

Each of the species of plants and animals that inhabit the world is able to live only within a narrow range of temperature, barometric pressure, and other features of climate. Man is able to adjust himself to a far wider range of physical conditions than most other kinds of animals, but there are limits to his adaptability beyond which he can survive only for a short time.

Temperature

Man is a warm-blooded animal, a character he shares with other mammals and with the birds. He cannot for long endure an increase or decrease of his body temperature of more than a few degrees. With the help of clothing, of shelters of various kinds, and of fire, and by physiologic acclimation man nevertheless is able to live in very cold climates. Eskimos, for example, thrive in climates where the temperature averages below zero for several months of the year. At the other extreme, man can exist in hot deserts and in humid tropical forests, again by practicing appropriate types of behavior.

Barometric pressure

The human body is able to endure a wide range of atmospheric pressure. Men are able to live below sea level and at high elevations in the mountains. At high altitudes, the limiting factor is the low amount of oxygen in the air. By an increase in the proportion of hemoglobin in the blood, an increase in the depth of respiration, and by other means, most men are able to adapt themselves to the low oxygen supply of fairly high altitudes. The Aymara Indians of the Lake Titicaca region of the Andes, with altitudes of 12,500 feet and more, have unusually capacious chests, and are able to carry on activities that require vigorous physical exertion (La Barre, 1948: 45). Their large chests, and their ability to thrive at high altitudes, are probably in part due to hereditary adaptation, and in part are a response to an existence from birth with a low oxygen supply. There is a limit, however, beyond which the oxygen supply is too low for acclimation.

Rate of evaporation

The amount of humidity in the air affects man chiefly by its relation to the rate of evaporation of water from his body. In hot weather, man's body temperature is held down to a tolerable level mainly by the evaporation of moisture from his skin and lungs. The effectiveness of this heat regulating mechanism depends on the rate of evaporation.

The rate of evaporation of water from a moist surface is influenced by temperature, relative humidity of the air, rate of wind movement, and barometric pressure. While the daily fluctuations in barometric pressure at any given altitude have only a slight influence on the rate of evaporation, the other three factors all have important effects.

Under very dry conditions, a man can endure very high air temperatures, even those exceeding the temperature of his body and reaching 110° F or more. By evaporating moisture from his lungs and skin, he can keep himself cool enough to live. In very moist air, on the contrary, evaporation from the skin cannot cool the body. Thus, hot and moist climates are less comfortable and less healthy than hot and dry climates.

Food

Every animal must have food in order to live. Man is an omnivore, able to use a wide variety of foods. Certain hunting and fishing peoples, such as the Eskimo, live almost exclusively on foods of animal origin, while certain agricultural peoples are mostly vegetarian. The great majority of people, however, live on a mixture of foods of both vegetable and animal origin.

The food that supports a human community is supplied either directly or indirectly by green plants. Food such as beefsteak or cheese is derived from green plants indirectly, through a food chain consisting of the plants, the cow, and man himself. The animal link in the food chain is absent when man eats the plant itself, for example, in a lettuce salad. Food chains can be much more complex. When he eats a mackerel, for example, man is the last link in a food chain that began in microscopic green plants such as the diatoms, and then passed through several food links that probably included one or more kinds of small crustaceans and perhaps several sizes of fish, before the mackerel. No matter how complex the food chain, however, its base is always the green plants. With a few negligible exceptions, the only organisms able to transform the energy in the sun's rays into stored food energy are green plants.

Energy

Any system composed of organisms constantly consumes energy. Every plant and every animal needs energy just to remain alive. In the food chains that begin with the green plants, and include herbivores, carnivores, parasites, and saprophytes, each link consumes a certain amount of energy. All the energy that keeps a community alive is derived originally from the sun.

Communities of organisms are always open systems constantly receiving energy from outside (Lotka, 1948). Every human community is dependent for its existence upon the energy which comes from the sun and which in part has been transformed by green plants into food suitable for animals.

Man gets on poorly when he is exposed naked to the inclemencies of his physical environment, or to the attacks of insects and wild beasts. Primitive man learned early to wear clothing, build habitations, and use fire to protect himself against extreme cold and against dangerous animals. By the use of suitable shelter (including now air-conditioning), man is able to thrive in climates where life would otherwise be difficult or impossible for him.

Reproduction

No organism can thrive in a region where conditions are unsuitable for reproduction.

The most critical period in man's life is infancy. Adults can exist for a time in many situations which are unendurable for young children. In most parts of the world, infants more than adults need protection by clothing and shelter. In many parts of the humid tropics, white children survive only with difficulty, though the native children do not seem to suffer. Until techniques are developed for rearing white children successfully in such climates, or until white children acquire an hereditary adaptability, the white race will be unable to colonize such regions.

Fluctuations in the habitat

The features of the physical and biotic habitat that affect man are continually fluctuating. The daily change from night to day, and the seasonal changes, produce important effects on man's welfare.

Critical periods

The struggle for survival often becomes particularly acute during certain seasons which constitute critical periods. In the cold, temperate, and frigid zones, winter is usually such a critical period, a period when primitive tribes often suffered severely from cold and food shortage, and when even modern man may undergo acute discomfort. In hot climates, on the other hand, summer may be the most difficult season to survive.

Critical periods do not always occur in cycles, but may come at irregular intervals. During the 1930's, for example, severe droughts affected large parts of the Great Plains of North America and brought disaster to many local human communities. Similarly, floods may cause damage to communities that adjoin a large river.

Certain types of critical periods, such as storms, may occur only rarely and last but a short time, and yet they may cause profound local changes. A tornado is an example of a temporary but potentially very damaging feature of the physical habitat. An unseasonable frost, though not as spectacular, may cause much and widespread damage.

Man's ability to adjust to the environment

Each individual man is able to adjust to a wide diversity of foods. Man is able to live on a diet wholly vegetarian, wholly of fish or flesh, or composed of various food combinations. Similarly, man is able to adjust to widely diverse types of climate. The ability to adjust to high altitudes, after a period of acclimation, has already been mentioned. Similarly, man is able to become acclimated both to hot and to cold climates. A striking instance of the effects of this acclimation can be observed whenever a short period of unseasonably cool weather occurs in summer. We are much more uncomfortable in such a cool period than during much colder weather in the winter, when we have become adjusted to the cold.

Individuals vary to some degree in their ability to adjust to extremes of climate. Some races or sub-races of man may possibly also be better able to adjust to certain types of climate than other races; but conclusive evidence on this point has not yet been presented. Great civilizations have arisen in hot-dry deserts (if water has been available for irrigation), in hot-damp tropics, and in temperate regions. No high civilization has arisen in the frigid zone, but certain peoples, such as the Eskimo, have become well adapted to life in the arctics. The diversity of climate under which various tribes and races live demonstrates the high adaptability of man (Wulsin, 1949).

Although each individual man is thus to a considerable degree able to adjust to the conditions of his habitat, his power of acclimation has definite limits. Civilized man actually adjusts to changes in weather and in climate mostly by changes in his behavior, by the use of clothing, shelter, and fire, and by other special devices of culture.

Man's dependence on his habitat

Although man is able to adjust himself so that he can endure a wide variety of habitats, yet he is greatly affected by the climate and other conditions of his physical environment. Every farmer and stockman is well aware that the vicissitudes of the weather greatly affect his chance of success. Even among persons who live in steam-heated houses, the weather is one of the common topics of conversation.

Changes in certain of the biotic elements of a human community may affect man's welfare no less profoundly than changes in the physical habitat. Thus, a plague of crop-devouring insects, or an outbreak of disease in man's cultivated plants, among his domestic animals, or in the human population, may greatly disrupt the communities affected.

We may conclude, then, that the conditions of the physical and biotic habitat, and their regular and irregular fluctuations, affect both directly and indirectly the welfare of every human being.

SELECTED REFERENCES

Cannon, Walter B. 1939. The wisdom of the body. Rev. ed. New York: W. W. Norton and Company.

Huntington, Ellsworth. 1945. Mainsprings of civilization. New York: John Wiley and Sons.

Wulsin, Frederick R. 1949. Adaptations to climate among non-European peoples. *In* Physiology of heat regulation and the science of clothing, edited by L. H. Newburgh. Philadelphia: W. B. Saunders Co. Pp. 3–69.

Man and His Plant and Animal Associates

CHAPTER III

From the point of view of the biologist, man is only one among the numerous kinds of plants and animals that exist on the earth. Although from our own selfish point of view man is a very interesting and very important organism, he really is only a part within the total web of life (Laura Thompson, 1949a). His very existence depends upon his continued close association with other organisms.

All human life is dependent upon plants and animals for food and other essentials. No man can continue to live for any appreciable length of time when he is deprived of food. He thrives best when he is also provided with clothing, shelter, and other materials that are obtained directly or indirectly from plants and various kinds of animals.

The iron, copper, coal, petroleum, and other materials stored in the ground are essential for our present industrial operations, but none of them can sustain life. Coal and petroleum actually are the products of plants and animals that lived in past geologic time. When these stored fuels are exhausted, man will be dependent upon current plant and animal products for a still greater proportion of his biological and industrial needs than at present (Gabrielson, 1941: 1–4).

Primitive man is directly dependent for food and shelter on the products of wild plants and animals (Ekblaw, 1921). In a description of the plants used by the Indians of the Missouri River region, for instance, Gilmore (1919) lists about 200 species, of which approximately one-third were used for food, more than one-third for medicine, and the rest for tent poles, fibers, dyes, "tobacco," and so on (Clements and Chaney, 1936: 32–33).

Early in his history, man developed special tools for capturing or gathering his food, processing and storing food and other materials, constructing habitations, and defending himself against dangerous animals or men of other tribes. The tools used by primitive European man to capture animals, for example, include a variety of types of spears, harpoons, arrows, traps, snares, and other devices (Clark, 1952). Such special tools may enable man to succeed where otherwise he could not, but they do not make him independent of his animal and plant associates.

Civilized man produces much of the food and other materials necessary for his existence in cultivated fields, pastures, plantations, and in feeding yards where environmental conditions are more or less artificially controlled. But in spite of man's best efforts to grow only one kind of cultivated plant in a particular field, other unwelcome associates persist. Weeds compete with the crop plants for space, food, and sunshine. Parasites and diseases attack the growing plants. Sucking insects may drain crop plants of their nutrient sap, herbivores may devour them. Beneficial parasites may in turn attack the primary plant parasites or the herbivores. Carnivores may prey upon the herbivores, and be attacked themselves by parasites or larger carnivores. Domestic animals, too, are subject to attack by parasites, by diseases, and sometimes by predators. Man himself often serves as the host of many kinds of parasites. An artificial com-

munity, therefore, may have all the diverse ecologic interrelations of a natural community, in addition to those complexities
that are introduced by the activities of man.

Crops grown in cultivated fields produce a large amount of
food, fodder, and other materials for modern man's use. Many
of the biological resources of the world today, however, are
still produced naturally, with little or no control by man. Much
wild game is harvested annually, even in economically well organized regions. Approximately 13,633,000 pounds of meat, for
example, were obtained from wild animals in the state of Michigan during the hunting season of 1941–42 (Burt, 1946: 9).
Nearly all our supplies of fish are obtained from uncultivated
waters. The total catch in 1943 of fishing products taken in
the waters of the United States and Alaska is estimated at
4,202 million pounds (Anderson and Power, 1947). Most of
the world's furs come from wild animals. Many important plant
products, such as lumber, are secured in considerable part from
wild plants. The pasture lands of the world are populated
mostly by wild plants.

A large proportion of the food and other essentials of the
native populations in extensive parts of the world is obtained
from uncultivated plants and wild animals. Consequently, the
natural communities of the world are of enormous importance
to the welfare of man. Even those natural communities that are
not of direct use to man are at times of indirect importance to
him. For instance, a marsh that harbors mosquitoes may affect
the comfort and health of the people in nearby communities.

Man's relations to endemic disease

An illustration of the close interrelations between man and certain native organisms is offered by endemic disease. Disease
may be a serious hazard to agricultural crops, to domestic animals, or even to man himself. Malaria, for example, is caused

by a protozoan parasite (*Plasmodium*) that is transmitted by the bite of an infected mosquito. Only certain kinds of mosquitoes are able to transmit the disease. These mosquito species affect the welfare of man wherever they occur in the same community with him.

Numerous kinds of wild animals are known to serve as reservoirs or alternate hosts for diseases that may affect man or his domestic animals. Thus, certain of the wild ungulates of Africa serve as hosts for a protozoan parasite (*Trypanosoma*), which is transferred by the bite of a particular insect, the tse-tse fly (*Glossina*), to domestic animals and sometimes to man, causing sleeping sickness. The ecologic relations are complex, for several species of trypanosomes are involved, as well as several species of tse-tse flies, each with somewhat different ecologic requirements for host and habitat. One species of trypanosome (*T. brucei*) produces a fatal cattle disease (nagana) which is so virulent, and so wide-spread, that in many parts of Africa the natives are unable to keep any domestic cattle at all (Craig and Faust, 1945). The ecologic relations between man and the other members of his ecologic communities may thus be very complicated.

Man's control of his environment

One of the outstanding characters of man is his ability to modify and control his environment. Numerous kinds of organisms besides man, however, are able to influence their own local environments. Shade-producing plants, for example, modify the local climate in their vicinity. A forest of trees affects the local temperature, air humidity, character of the soil, and other features of its habitat. Many kinds of animals, too, can exercise an influence upon their own immediate environment to make it more favorable for themselves. Burrowing forms, for example, are able in their burrows to escape many of the extremes of weather to which they would be exposed on the surface. Those animals that build nests are able partly to escape exposure to the elements during the time when they are at rest. Social forms that live in colonies modify their habitat in many ways to make it more suitable for their existence.

Man far excels all other species in his ability to control his environment. Nevertheless, the physical conditions of his habitat affect him to a considerable degree. And although he is able to improve his immediate physical environment through the use of clothing, fire, and shelter, there is a limit to the extent of his control. When he is away from his camps or his houses, he is exposed to heat and cold, rain and intense sunshine, to wind and storm and other physical hazards to his health—perhaps to his very life.

Man's place in the natural community

Primitive man is very closely dependent upon the natural communities of which he forms a part. When the food supply is adequate, and when shelter and other conditions are favorable, he may thrive. On the other hand, when food grows scarce or other conditions in his ecosystem become unfavorable, primitive man is likely to have a hard struggle to survive. Many accounts have been given of small groups or even whole tribes of primitive people being on short rations for a time or starving because of a failure in the productiveness of the natural habitat.

Civilized man has progressed far beyond any other animal in his ability to grow, and to transport, various kinds of food and other essentials for his life. By means of food storage he is able to survive short periods of adverse conditions. He can protect himself to some degree from the extremes of the physical environment, and from the attacks of most kinds of injurious organisms. A highly complex economic organization, based on the division of labor, enables him very efficiently to secure the necessities of life and many luxuries as well. Through social and political organizations, he engages in community enterprises for education, the maintenance of public order, the improvement of health, esthetic enjoyment, and for numerous other cultural purposes. This is a tremendous advance over primitive man.

At his present stage of civilization, nevertheless, man is not able entirely to prevent the periodic scarcity of food. In many parts of the world, food shortages and even famines still occur. Neither is man yet able to prevent entirely the incidence of disease. Not only do diseases of various kinds kill or injure many people annually, but certain kinds of diseases reach at times epidemic proportions. Although civilized man is able to escape much of the hardship which primitive man endures under the operation of the natural ecologic regulatory mechanisms, he is still to a considerable extent subject to the same kind of controls.

In a primitive human community, the relations of man to his animal and plant associates may be simple and direct. In a highly industrialized community, on the other hand, much of the food and other plant and animal products that man uses may be brought from distant places. The dependence of man on other species of plants and animals, however, is no less close in one case than in the other. The area covered by the industrial community may be far greater than that ranged over by a primitive hunting society, and its social organization may be tremendously more complex—but the general dependence of consumers upon producers is much the same in both.

Special features of human communities

The social, political, and economic laws that control human communities are admittedly on a level of organization different from the simpler ecologic laws that control most natural communities. Furthermore, we know as yet far too little about the laws that control human communities to be able to compare them with the laws that are effective in natural communities. Our knowledge of the precise mode of operation of the regulatory mechanisms that control natural communities is also still imperfect. Still less is known about the operation of the controlling mechanisms in those communities that are dominated by man. Nonetheless, it seems safe to assume that a human community differs from a natural community mainly in its greater complexity, and in the degree to which it is dominated and controlled by the single species, man. We can safely assume that the laws of biology, and especially those of ecology, apply at least in part to the communities of which man forms a part, even though every human community is very much more complex than any community which does not include man as a member.

It is evident, moreover, that the ecologic relations of man to other organisms and to his physical environment are vital to his welfare. Man is able to exist only as a member of some community. He may play a dominant role in that community, yet he is governed to a large extent by the same ecologic laws that control the other species of plants and animals associated with him (Hollingshead, 1940).

From the point of view of the ecologist, therefore, a human community is only a special type of community. Modern man is able to control his own environment and that of his associated species of plants and of animals to a much greater degree than can any other organism. But in their essential ecologic features, human communities do not differ from natural communities.

SELECTED REFERENCES

Burnet, Macfarlane. 1953. Natural history of infectious disease. 2d ed. Cambridge: Cambridge University Press.

Gabrielson, Ira N. 1941. Wildlife conservation. Chap. 1. New York: Macmillan Co.

Graham, Edward H. 1944. Natural principles of land use. Chaps. 7, 8, 9, 10, 14. New York: Oxford University Press.

James, Preston E. 1935. An outline of geography. Groups 4 and 5. Boston: Ginn and Co.

Man as a Social Animal

CHAPTER IV

Man is an outstanding example of a social animal. His ability to form societies gives him a great advantage in the struggle for existence, for even a small social group is far more effective in securing the necessities of life, and in defending itself against adversity, than is a single man.

Not all men, however, are equally social in their behavior. Human societies vary in size, and in complexity of organization. Some peoples live in small, partially isolated groups. Again, several millions of people may live together in a highly developed industrial country, a single closely integrated society.

The custom of certain peoples of living in small social groups may at times be related to the insufficiency of their habitat to support a dense population. Or, the cause may lie in certain basic elements of human social behavior, which are most likely inherited. Certain strains of mice are known to be more combative than other strains (Scott, 1942). Certain tribes of men are more warlike than others. The extent to which heredity controls cooperativeness and other social traits is, however, as yet unknown.

Transfer of culture

Man's ability to transfer elements of culture and information directly from individual to individual and from generation to generation, without the need to wait for the slow process of evolution of instinct, gives him an enormous advantage over other animals. Although some other animals, notably the higher apes, are able to transmit simple ideas from individual to individual, in no other species is this ability developed even nearly as high as it is in man. By gestures and speech, man can communicate to his fellows concepts of all degrees of complexity. By written and printed words, drawings, and photographs, by telegraph, telephone, radio, and television he can transmit information and ideas to his contemporaries in all parts of the world. Printed or written information may be passed on to all subsequent generations (Emerson, 1943: 113). This ability of man to transmit his culture directly from individual to individual and from generation to generation gives him a social status wholly different from that of other organisms (Thomson and Geddes, 1931: 1305).

Long period of human immaturity

The acquisition by each individual of the cultural heritage of his society, however, is a slow process. It imposes on man a long period of childhood and adolescence. Man's period of immaturity proportionally far exceeds that of any other animal (Fiske, 1899; Emerson, 1941). The average man must spend about a third of his life in acquiring the social habits and training necessary for success in his cultural environment. A professional man, to be successful, must spend an even greater portion of his life in securing added experience and knowledge.

Longevity

In compensation, to some extent, for his necessarily long period of immaturity, man is an exceptionally long-lived animal. Furthermore, the average span of man's life (though not the total span) is steadily being lengthened through the discoveries of science, and through improvements in his personal environment. This greater average span of life, however, is not an unmixed blessing; for in old age man deteriorates, first physically and later mentally.

Man reaches the maximum of physical vigor and mental capacity early in adult life. Most human abilities show a rapid growth, to attain a peak in the early twenties, after which there follows a slow but steady decline during the remaining period of life. The same types of curves are shown by the growth and decline of hand grip, vital (lung) capacity, pulse rate, visual acuity, acuity of hearing, and reaction time (Karl Pearson, 1926). Pugilists and other athletes usually pass the peak of their physical ability before the age of twenty-five. Mental performance, however, may not begin to decline as early in life as physical strength. The age of maximum mental capacity varies somewhat for various types of ability, but for most abilities, according to Wechsler (1944: 55), the age of beginning decline is in the twenties and maximum ability is seldom retained beyond the age of thirty.

As a rule, the rate of decline in man's physical and mental capacity, after its peak in early adulthood, is fortunately very slow. Older men are not so quick to learn nor so "bright" as younger men, but up to the age of forty, or perhaps much later, the deterioration in their mental ability is made up in part by their increasing store of knowledge and experience (Lehman, 1953).

Man reaches sexual and physical maturity much later in life, and lives much longer, than the chimpanzee and the gorilla, his nearest relatives among the primates. We may infer that an increase in man's longevity and a decrease in his rate of early growth have taken place in the past. Also, it is possible that a further extension of our period of immaturity and of our total life span is currently taking place. Such evolutionary changes, if indeed they are in progress, are presumably proceeding with extreme slowness. Evidence presented by Pearl (1946) indicates that the actual span of human life has not lengthened in recent centuries. Men now live longer, on the average, than they did in previous centuries, but only because of a lower mortality rate in early life. But no recent lengthening has been detected of the period of life during which man remains at full vigor.

In view of the steadily increasing complexity of our modern social and industrial life, and of the need for longer and longer training, it might be desirable for the adolescent period of man to be still further extended. Such an extension of adolescence would make desirable also a considerable lengthening of man's average span of life, perhaps to several centuries (Haldane, 1947). But even if it were possible to remodel man's physiology to such a degree, some unfavorable results would certainly ensue. Every man bears numerous scars of past accidents and diseases. The longer his span of life, the more he will be handicapped by his past history. There is the further difficulty that as man ages he grows less adaptable to the changing conditions of the environment, and more set in his way of life.

Improvements in our methods of education can certainly shorten the period of training necessary for each individual. Improvements in nutrition, hygiene, and the treatment of disease can also lengthen man's productive life. Such improvements, which are well within the realm of possibility, will perhaps make any great extension of our span of life unnecessary.

From the point of view of the ecologist, there are many advantages in a fairly rapid turnover of the population, with the
frequent production of young individuals that are adaptable to
the changing stage of evolution of human culture.

Division of labor

Division of labor, so conspicuous in human communities, helps
man to make effective use of the natural resources available in
his habitat. Many of the individuals in a human society do not
themselves gather or hunt or grow their food, but secure the
necessities of life by performing certain services for their fellows. A woman, for instance, may be provided by her husband
with food and the other essentials of life, in return for maintaining a home and caring for children. A highly complex
society offers many indirect ways of earning a living. Administrators, priests, soldiers, artisans, artists, traders, manufacturers,
miners, physicians, teachers, and others who are essential to a
well developed society are provided with food by the hunters,
fishermen, ranchers, farmers, and others who gather or grow
food. The food producers and food gatherers profit by being
provided with protection against pillage and disease, and with
tools, clothing, and other articles that make their work more
efficient and their lives more satisfying; and by the enrichment
of their mental and spiritual existence.

Not all the persons who earn a living indirectly, however,
necessarily benefit the society in return. Every society supports
a number of parasites, such as gamblers, thieves, charlatans, and
hangers-on of various kinds.

Vertebrate and invertebrate societies

Invertebrate societies have a form of organization very different from that of human societies. Among the ants, bees,
wasps, and termites, for example, the social group is a clan,

all of whose members are descended from a single pair, or at most a few pairs, of sexual individuals. Most of the members of the insect clan do not function in reproduction. Such an insect society is often divided into several castes, each with a distinct type of structure adapted for special duties. The outstanding feature of an insect society is that the clan is the biological, social, and economic unit, while the individual has little importance. An individual insect which becomes detached from his social group is only rarely permitted to join any other social group of the same species, and soon perishes miserably.

Vertebrate societies, as a rule, are far less rigid in their social organization. An individual fish, bird, or mammal which at one time is a member of a social group may, at other times, live alone successfully. The social groups of most kinds of vertebrates are open societies that will accept other individuals of the same species, though often only after a probationary period. Also, every normal vertebrate individual is at some period of his life capable of reproduction.

Individual men often leave one human social group and join another. A period of adjustment to the new group is then required. It may be brief, if no serious change of language or culture is involved; or longer, if important adjustments in habits of life must be made. That the difficulty of adjustment to a new society is not unduly great is proved by the many persons in our own time who have successfully moved from one region to another.

Individual man is not actually compelled to belong to any social group, but may for a time survive entirely alone. As a rule, however, solitary life is endured only briefly and only for some special purpose, such as exploring. The persistent hermit is usually somewhat "queer" or even mentally unbalanced. The normal man is never happy unless he is associated with others of his kind.

The members of those human tribes which secure their living by hunting or food gathering are often highly individualistic and exhibit little cooperation except within the family. A few primarily hunting and fishing societies have developed a certain amount of cooperation and community organization. Tribes which engage in agriculture usually exhibit a considerable degree of cooperation (Mead, 1937), and industrial societies require a very high degree of cooperation among their individual members.

Among the vertebrates, social organization is largely based upon intelligent behavior, rather than mostly on instinctive behavior which is the rule among the invertebrates. The individual vertebrate, accordingly, is of much greater importance biologically, and also has much more independence, than the individual member of an invertebrate society.

Because vertebrate societies are usually composed of individuals of diverse heredity, it may be assumed that their members have a greater diversity of instincts and abilities than those of an insect society, all of which are closely related in heredity and often are full brothers and sisters.

Among social insects, inherited instincts, which control behavior to a very considerable degree, are usually closely similar in all the members of a given population, though some individual variation in behavior does occur. Among the higher vertebrates, instinct is still an important basis of behavior, but intelligence plays the dominant role in the behavior pattern. In man, reason reaches a high level—though it is employed, alas, too infrequently—and offers a basis for the hope that cooperation among individuals may increase and ultimately lead to a much more satisfactory world society than exists at present.

Certain kinds of social insects are able to vary their behavior somewhat to adjust to a new situation, but in general, insects are far less adaptable than the vertebrates. The highest degree of adaptiveness in social behavior occurs in the primates, culminating in man himself (Schneirla, 1949). Human social life includes elements of social adjustment wholly lacking in other forms, for man is able to add the cultural heritage of the species to the heredity of social habit transmitted through his genes.

Altruism versus *egotism*

Man has two fundamental drives that often conflict with one another: (1) egocentric, to advance himself in competition with his fellows in his group, and (2) altruistic, to advance the interests of his social group even at the cost of toil and pain for himself—or perhaps even at the cost of his own life (Spencer, 1892; Allee, 1943). Both tendencies, we assume, have arisen by evolution, and both are necessary for the continued existence of human societies and the future progress of man to higher levels of culture. Further evolution of man toward greater social cooperation among individuals and classes is needed no less than greater physical strength, greater resistance to disease, and greater mental ability of each individual.

The conflict in man between altruism and egotism can never be completely resolved. The group is necessary for the survival of the individual, and the welfare of the individual is essential for the success of the group. A compromise must therefore be maintained between those elements that are good from the viewpoint of the society, and those that are good from the viewpoint of the individual (Pearl, 1946: 119).

In every human society, moreover, the relationships among the member individuals are constantly shifting, due to fluctuations within the community. Accordingly, if the society is to be maintained at optimum efficiency, the equilibrium between altruism and egotism in each individual must also shift from time to time.

The democratic society

The great importance of the individual within vertebrate social groups has a significant bearing on the organization of human communities. Man is a member of the order Primates, the group of vertebrates that has achieved the greatest degree of social organization. Nearly all the higher primates, including monkeys, baboons, and apes, form social groups (Carpenter, 1934). Man's social tendencies have many suggestive parallels among his subhuman relatives (Carpenter, 1942). Man's present civilization and his existing type of social organization could hardly have been derived from any ancestors other than the primates, as Clarence Day has humorously described in his book entitled *This Simian World* (1920).

Some political demagogues have asserted that the citizen's highest duty is to the state, and that the rights of the citizen are always inferior to those of the commonwealth. The implication is that there must be a supreme ruler, a ruling class, or at least a ruling body of some kind, which decides to what duties each of the common people shall be assigned. This is, of course, the kind of organization typified by absolute monarchies, oligarchies, and dictatorships, whether of the proletariat, or self appointed, or other. This was the core of the Nazi ideology, with its elite classes and favored nations. Such an ideology is contrary to man's social origin, and to his normal mode of behavior.

The democratic concept, on the other hand, is that the individual is a very important unit of every social or economic organization. The state must arbitrate and exercise control whenever the ambitions and activities of one individual or class encroach on those of another. The state also serves to integrate the activities of its citizens for their mutual welfare. Individuals will often be required to submerge their pleasures, rights, or personalities for the good of the whole society, but they will in general do this willingly, with an appreciation of the gain to themselves and to their community as a whole. The democratic organization of society has a sound basis in the past evolution of the social behavior of man. "The ability of the individual to function freely, and in increasingly complex and varied ways has had survival value and has been progressive. Development of individual dependence and loss of individual versatility have usually been degenerative. In the line leading to man, the ability to form and to manage complex social structures has certainly followed the development of ever greater individual capacities and adaptability and, socially, a growing awareness of the rights of other individuals, which is the opposite of the social subordination of individuals" (Simpson, 1941: 19).

Imperfections in human social behavior

Even the best human societies are far from perfect. All of them suffer from the incomplete coordination of the efforts of the member individuals (Gerard, 1940: 407). We can anticipate that any future improvement in our human communities will be based to a considerable extent on an increase in voluntary cooperation among men. It is not easy, however, to improve social behavior.

By the rapid evolution of his culture, man has improved his environment and his communities faster than he himself has changed to fit the world community in which he now lives. Some of the antisocial traits shown by certain persons are probably in part inherited, a residue of an earlier stage in man's evolution. These antisocial traits may be considered analogous, in the social sphere, to the vermiform appendix and other disharmonious structures still present in man's body.

If those who exhibit or carry inherited traits of antisocial behavior could be identified, their defective heredity could be eliminated by preventing their reproduction. Human traits, however, are always the combined effect of heredity and of environment; and it is seldom possible to distinguish these two factors or measure them separately.

The antisocial behavior of certain persons may be due mostly to their past exposure to poor environmental conditions. Such behavior could presumably be eliminated by improvements in culture to a point where every child and adult is given the best possible conditions for development.

Poor heredity and poor environment often work together to produce disastrous results. Parents with defective social heredity will usually provide an unfavorable home environment, and their children, consequently, are likely to grow up into misfits in their society. Parents with superior hereditary social traits, on the other hand, are likely to provide favorable homes. Children reared in such homes have the best chance both of receiving good heredity and of living in an environment favorable for their social development.

The improvement of social cooperation among men is one of the greatest needs of our time. Unfortunately, we know almost nothing about the heredity of social traits. Nor do we have much information about the effects of training and environment in modifying the basic hereditary patterns in respect to social cooperation, reliability, or integrity. In fact, no practical method is known for discriminating between the effects of heredity and those of environment in molding man's social behavior. We do not know, consequently, whether the level of social cooperativeness of the members of any human society is at present improving, remaining static, or, unhappily, deteriorating.

SELECTED REFERENCES

Allee, W. C. 1951. Cooperation among animals; with human implications. New York: Henry Schuman.

Carpenter, C. R. 1942. Societies of monkeys and apes. Biol. Symposia, 8: 177–204.

Mead, Margaret, editor. 1937. Cooperation and competition among primitive peoples. New York: McGraw-Hill Book Co.

Pearl, Raymond. 1946. Man the animal. Bloomington, Ind.: Principia Press.

Schneirla, T. C. 1949. Levels in the psychological capacities of animals. *In* Philosophy for the future, edited by R. W. Sellars. New York: Macmillan Company. Pp. 243–86.

The Dynamics of Human Populations

CHAPTER V

Compared with most other kinds of animals, man produces only a small number of offspring. Nevertheless, the potential rate of increase of the human species is so great that a high population density is rapidly produced in each inhabited area where conditions are favorable for individual survival. Too great an increase, however, may put the society concerned out of balance with its resources. When any human population has increased to the limit of the carrying capacity of its habitat, overpopulation can be prevented only by keeping birth rate and mortality rate approximately equal.

Fluctuations

The density of the human population at any given time and place is the resultant of the interacting forces of birth rate, mortality rate, and migration rate. When birth rate and immigration rate together exceed mortality and emigration, the density of the population must increase, and vice versa.

Every human society, one may presume, tends to establish a harmonious balance of its population density, its culture, and the character and resources of its habitat (Wissler, 1929: 36–38).

If such an adjustment can be reached by the society, its population density should show little fluctuation until there is a change in climate, an improvement in culture, or a conflict with some other society.

From what we know of primitive tribes, and of history, however, it seems probable that very few societies have ever actually achieved an adjustment with their habitats so efficient that their populations have remained relatively stable for any considerable length of time. The history of most peoples is rather one of slow or rapid growth in population alternating with periods of unfavorable conditions, or even disasters, that resulted in a frequently catastrophic decrease.

Although man's birth rate is very low compared to that of most other kinds of animals, it is, nevertheless, high enough in practically every human community so that the population, if not checked by mortality before the end of the reproductive period, would rapidly increase (W. S. Thompson, 1942, Chap. X). Only in a few countries is the birth rate at present so low that no increase in population is occurring (United Nations, 1949).

In most species, it is desirable that the birth rate be fairly high as a protection against possible adverse conditions. Otherwise, a population could not recover rapidly from temporary adversity such as a famine or an epidemic disease. This potentiality for rapid population growth is desirable for man also, but human birth rates often require control to avoid the evils of overpopulation.

Whenever a human population has gained access to new resources, either by opening new lands to settlement or by an increase of food productivity through the evolution of new techniques, it has increased immediately. The tremendous growth in population of North America during the past two centuries, for example, is undoubtedly due both to the bringing of new lands under cultivation, and to great improvements in agricultural, industrial, and social technology.

The actual birth rate of a population is greatly affected by its traditions in regard to marriage and child rearing. British Guiana offers an example. Most of the women of Hindu or Moslem ancestry there marry at a fairly early age, though there is no child marriage as in India. Women of Negro descent, on the contrary, often form temporary liaisons; common-law marriages are numerous, recorded marriages less frequent. The higher birth rate among persons of Hindu or Moslem ancestry is probably related at least in part to this difference in marriage customs (Taeuber, 1952).

Every individual must die. The age which a person reaches is affected by his heredity, the accidents and stresses to which he is subjected, disease, exposure to the weather, rigors of labor, and deficiencies of food. Overpopulation, with consequent shortage of food or other necessities, may be expected to raise the rate of mortality.

Serious overpopulation may develop if the mortality rate in a given population is reduced—by improved sanitary and medical services, or by other means—without a corresponding reduction in the birth rate. The overcrowding from which the populations of certain parts of the world now suffer seems to be due in part to a shift of this kind.

Migration is another cause of fluctuations in populations. Immigration serves to build up the population density of a sparsely settled area. The peopling of the United States, for example, was greatly hastened by immigration from many other countries. Over 30 million immigrants entered this country between 1820 and 1930 (W. S. Thompson, 1942: 376). As a country's population approaches its carrying capacity, further immigration becomes disadvantageous. The United States may now be approaching—or may already have reached—such a level of saturation.

Emigration from a center of overpopulation relieves population pressure. Continuous emigration permits a higher birth rate within an overpopulated region than could otherwise be supported. There is a limit, however, to the number of emigrants who can find suitable homes in foreign lands. If they cannot survive in their new homes, emigration is in effect merely a form of delayed mortality. But even if suitable home sites do exist in other countries, lack of transportation or its high cost may prevent emigration. At the estimated rate (1.41%) of population increase for 1941 in India (United Nations, 1949, Table 2), for example, the surplus of over five million individuals who were born that year beyond the number who died, could not possibly have been disposed of by emigration.

The population of the earth is at present increasing rapidly. Over the world as a whole, the rate of increase is estimated to be about 1% per year (Pearl, 1946: 87). Assuming the total world population in 1950 to have been 2.1 billions (Deevey, 1951), 21 million persons are added to this enormous number each year. The capacity of the resources of the world to continue supporting this addition may seriously be doubted.

The present period of rapid population increase is believed to have begun in the seventeenth century. In 1630, the total world population, as estimated by Pearl (1946: 90), was only 445 millions. The tremendous spurt of population growth which began then, and which still continues, has become possible by improvements in technology, transportation, political organization, and other features of culture. Many of these improvements are based on the great increase in scientific knowledge which has taken place in this period. It is fatuous to expect, however, that research and invention will forever provide new resources capable of supporting an ever increasing world population.

Population structure

The individual members of a population are not alike, but vary in sex, age, health and vigor, mental ability, physiology, and many other characters. The structure of any given population is the resultant of the proportion of each of its several components.

Part of the variability within human populations is due to differences in the combinations of hereditary factors of the several member individuals. Another part is due to environmental influences, such as the character and amount of food available to individuals in their youth, the incidence of parasites and diseases, diverse accidents, and differences in education and experience.

A feature of the population structure of our modern societies is the high proportion of immature and over-age individuals. These unproductive components are a burden on those age classes which are capable of producing goods and services for the use of the community.

A considerable proportion of immature persons is necessary in every population to provide replacements for those who every year die or retire. No important reduction in the proportion of the immature, therefore, seems desirable or possible. To the contrary, as our culture becomes more complex, the proportion of immature persons in our population is likely to increase rather than decrease, since the training period of our young people must continually be lengthened.

Nor does it seem likely that the proportion of older persons in our population will decrease in the near future. Life expectancy is steadily increasing in all the more advanced nations. Also, there is a tendency to set the age of retirement earlier and earlier. We can expect, therefore, that the proportion of old and retired persons in our population will continue to increase. The best solution to the problem of how to support these persons would seem to be to find for them occupations on a part-time basis or in light work suited to their ability, so that they may support themselves at least in part. Most old persons, if they are healthy, prefer to be active and useful, rather than be supported in idleness.

Natural regulatory mechanisms

The density of every human population, like that of every other kind of organism, is controlled by various regulatory mechanisms. Among these are such natural regulatory mechanisms as predation, famine, disease, strife, and accidents. In addition, many human societies have evolved various customs and habits that operate to prevent overpopulation.

Predatory animals now play almost no part in reducing the numbers of civilized man. In fact, this regulatory mechanism probably is of serious importance only among the most primitive human tribes.

Disease is a very important controlling mechanism in many human communities. Numerous accounts have been given of the destruction of large numbers of natives by the ravages of such a newly introduced disease as smallpox (Stern and Stern, 1945; Roe, 1951, Appendix G). Various introduced diseases greatly reduced the numbers of the early Mission Indians in Baja California (S. F. Cook, 1937). Malaria, tuberculosis, bubonic plague, cholera, yellow fever, dysentery, syphilis, and other diseases have been, and in places still are, terrible scourges.

In our modern communities, disease is being increasingly brought under control by advances in our knowledge of medicine and by the application of hygienic principles. In many parts of the world, however, there is as yet little or no modern medical service, and sanitation is poorly understood or practiced. As was pointed out by W. S. Thompson (1944: 59), sanitation must generally be a community enterprise. Modern sanitary practices can be carried through only in societies that are fairly well organized.

Disease still takes a heavy toll of human lives and seems likely to continue doing so for a long time to come. Even under the best conditions, contagious disease sometimes becomes epidemic. The world-wide influenza epidemic of 1918, for instance, took many human lives not only in backward societies but in the culturally most advanced nations. It is estimated that in that epidemic 15 million deaths due to influenza occurred in India and Pakistan alone (Davis, 1951: 33).

Famine still occurs in various parts of the world. India, for example, has had over 40 full years of famine since A.D. 650 (Wilcox, 1947: 212). Local food shortages are especially likely to result in famine in those isolated communities that have inadequate transportation facilities connecting them with the outside world. In a considerable portion of the world, famine still remains an important factor in the control of human population density (W. S. Thompson, 1944: 60–62).

A regulatory mechanism that is widespread among the vertebrates, but much less common among the invertebrates, is the habit of defending territories. It has been most studied with regard to the song birds. At the beginning of the breeding season, a male song bird which is in vigorous breeding condition selects a small area from which he attempts to drive all other males of his species. His song, his behavior, and his bright-colored plumage advertise to the other males that here a territory has been pre-empted, and that the male in possession is prepared to defend it against trespass. After a female has joined him and a nest has been built, his behavior may also serve to protect his mate and their young. Many types of territories are established by various kinds of birds and other animals, but all these territories are alike in that they are defended by a single individual or by members of a pair or a group (Dice, 1952, Chap. XI).

From the point of view of the community, this territorial habit operates to prevent the population of any species from becoming too great for the resources of the habitat. The territory seems always to include some feature essential for the success of its defenders. In the territory of most species of song birds, for example, there is likely to be a sufficient amount of suitable food both for the parents and for the young, a suitable site for the nest, and adequate protection against predators and inclement weather. The defense of the territory counteracts the tendency of every species to become overabundant. It forces surplus individuals to live in the poorer habitats, or renders them unable to breed in the region. Thus the territorial habit limits the population of a given species to the number that can thrive in each community.

The occurrence of the territorial habit among various kinds of mammals has not yet been studied thoroughly, though it is known that at least a considerable number of mammalian species share it. Domestic dogs of both sexes, for example, strongly defend their home grounds against trespass by strange dogs. Bands of howler monkeys are said to protest vocally against any encroachment on their territory by another band (Carpenter, 1934: 118).

Many primitive human tribes divide their tribal area into territories which are assigned to families or social subgroups. The area ranged over by certain Algonquin bands of eastern Canada, for instance, was divided into hereditary family hunting territories. All the males belonging to a particular family were permitted to hunt in its territory; trespass by others was occasionally punished with death (Speck, 1915).

Most modern human societies likewise divide at least part of their habitat into individual holdings for farming, trade, or residence. Such holdings are often held by a family as a group, and are handed down to children or other close relatives. This division of resources may be a factor in preventing overpopulation (Carr-Saunders, 1922: 203), because it tends to restrict the number of children to that which can be supported on the family resources.

The tendency of certain clans and tribes to defend their lands against encroachment by their neighbors also operates to prevent overpopulation, at least in simple hunting or pastoral cultures. When a territory which is under the control of a particular clan or tribe is invaded by aliens, the usual result is war.

Primitive human tribes often engage in raids upon their neighbors. We know from their fossil remains that many ancient men, for example, met violent death, and some of them are presumed to have been eaten (Weidenreich, 1939). There was constant warfare among many of the tribes of the early American Indians. But not all primitive tribes are warlike. Some of them, such as the Pueblo Indians, seem to have been generally peaceful; yet even peaceful tribes were often raided by their warlike neighbors. To this day, large numbers of men, women, and children are still being killed or maimed from time to time in wars between tribes and nations.

The mortality resulting from warfare between tribes must have had a considerable effect in keeping the densities of early human populations down. In modern societies, however, war seems to be largely ineffective as an agent of population control. The Second World War, for example, which directly or indirectly caused the death of millions of people, did not bring about any reduction in the world population. In most parts of Europe, population density was actually greater at the end of the war than at its beginning (United Nations, 1949, Table 3).

Wars reduce populations not only directly, by killing a certain number of individuals and preventing their reproduction, but also indirectly by the wastage of food and other materials, by the destruction of means of production and of transportation, and by a disruption of economic and social organization that reduces the productive capacity of the areas involved. In complex modern communities, the disruptions and epidemics resulting from war may cause more deaths than occur on the battlefield.

In the future, wars may possibly be prevented by a world organization. Lest we be too optimistic, however, we should note the view of the eminent biologist Pearl (1918) that wars are likely to continue until man has become a different kind of animal. The psychologist Burrow (1953) is of much the same opinion.

Accidents take many lives both in primitive and in highly organized societies. Here belong the human deaths caused each year by the bite of poisonous snakes, the attack of other animals, and by dangerous domestic beasts and vicious men. Accidents of other kinds also take a considerable toll; they are likely to become an increasing cause of mortality as the world becomes more highly mechanized.

Many of the natural mortality factors that operated to keep primitive populations in check are being removed by the increase of scientific knowledge and its application to human affairs, and by better economic and political organization. In spite of those natural regulatory mechanisms that are still in operation, human populations are increasing in many parts of the world. It seems certain that most of the natural controls of human populations will grow increasingly ineffective in the future. In most human populations, natural mechanisms are now far less effective than artificial regulatory mechanisms.

Artificial regulatory mechanisms

Many primitive societies have customs that operate to prevent any overpopulation beyond the resources of the habitat (Pitt-Rivers, 1927: 19). An excellent review of many such customs and their effects on human populations is given by Carr-Saunders (1922). Let us consider some of them.

Abortion seems to have been practiced widely from the earliest times on, both among primitive and among civilized peoples. The methods are often ineffective and sometimes dangerous to the women involved. In many countries, artificial abortion is at present illegal. Nevertheless, it still plays a large role in modern societies in holding down the birth rate.

Infanticide was commonly practiced by many early peoples and probably is still used by certain tribes. A child which is in any manner defective is especially likely to be removed, since it would be a burden on its parents and its social group. Under primitive conditions, a mother cannot care for more than one child at a time. When twins are born, therefore, often only one of the pair is retained. Also, if an infant is born while the mother is still caring for a slightly older child, it may not be possible to care for the newcomer. This is particularly true in nomadic tribes.

It is usually the girl babies that are disposed of. Among the Netsilik Eskimo, for example, it was the custom to kill girl babies at birth, unless they had been promised to some other family where a boy would in time need a wife. Sons can be expected to aid in supporting the parents in their old age, but a girl will marry just when she begins to be useful, and go to live with her husband's family (Rasmussen, 1931: 139–42). Discrimination against girls makes infanticide particularly effective in preventing overpopulation.

In certain primitive communities, old or sick persons who

have become a burden on their social group may be killed or abandoned (Simmons, 1945). A nomadic community in particular is handicapped by the presence of aged or ill persons. Any attempt to carry such persons along might jeopardize the survival of the whole human society. From the point of view of such a society, it is better that one rather than all should perish. Most frequently, the aged or ill are simply left behind when the band moves. Holmberg (1950: 85) has described how a desperately sick, middle-aged woman was thus abandoned in eastern Bolivia by a roving band of Siriono Indians.

Cannibalism was practiced in numerous primitive tribes but it probably was of only slight importance in regulating population density. Among the Eskimos, cannibalism seems to have been practiced only under dire necessity, and only when not all the members of a social unit could possibly survive (Rasmussen, 1931: 135). Most tribes which practiced the killing and eating of alien tribesmen, such as the native Australians (Bates, 1939), probably secured relatively few victims in any given year.

The sacrifice of human beings for religious purposes has played a large part in controlling the populations of at least a few societies. In their simpler forms, these sacrifices may involve only the killing of individuals suspected of having an evil influence, such as presumed witches. Some communities, however, have thought to please their gods by sacrificing even valuable members. At the funeral of a wealthy man or chief, his slaves, his widow, or other persons were sometimes killed. In some of the Mediterranean countries, human sacrifice seems to have been common in early times. The Jewish patriarch Abraham was willing to sacrifice even a favorite son to please his God. Although such sacrifices may often have been unfortunate for the society by removing individuals who were potential producers, they must have exercised a positive control of population density.

The extreme in human sacrifices seems to have been reached by the Aztecs. All early European visitors to Mexico were astounded by the number of people killed annually as sacrificial offerings to the gods. S. F. Cook (1946) estimates that during the last half-century of Aztec domination in Mexico 5,000 persons were lost each year in battle, and that sacrificial victims numbered 15,000 annually. The persons used by the Aztecs for sacrifice were mostly prisoners of war, but sometimes slaves were purchased for the purpose, and more rarely children of the tribe itself were offered. Wars seem often to have been waged merely to obtain prisoners for sacrifice. The losses in war, together with the number of sacrificial victims, must have had an important effect in preventing or reducing overpopulation in the regions affected.

In times past, human slavery may have been a factor in holding down the population density in certain areas. Slavery will be effective in population control only when men and women slaves are treated in such a manner that their reproductive rate is reduced, when persons of reproductive age are forced into slavery and transported out of their native regions, or when the mortality rate of slaves is higher than that of freemen. Under certain conditions, however, the labor of slaves may increase the prosperity of their masters to a point where these will increase their reproductive rate enough to compensate for any reduction of the reproductive rate among the slaves. Also, the masters may use women slaves as concubines. Some slaveholders, furthermore, may encourage their slaves to produce offspring in order to increase the number of slaves they own. Thus slavery does not always reduce the birth rate or lower the population density.

Ovulation and menstruation usually are interrupted at least

during the early months of the period when a woman is nursing an infant. In many tribes, women continue to nurse their children until these are two years of age, or even older (Carr-Saunders, 1922, Chap. 7). The exact month when ovulation begins again in a lactating mother varies no doubt greatly among individuals, and perhaps also from tribe to tribe. Insofar, however, as ovulation is inhibited by nursing, the length of the customary period of lactation will have an effect on the birth rate of the population.

Among the Fiji islanders, the mother is said (Pitt-Rivers, 1927: 129) to abstain from sexual intercourse for from twelve to thirty-six months after childbirth. The reason for the abstention is a belief that the suckling child would be injured by the act. Other native peoples have similar tabus against sexual intercourse during specific periods (Carr-Saunders, 1922: 186), and such tabus must have an appreciable effect in decreasing the birth rate.

A delay in the marriage of young women after the age of sexual maturity must reduce the birth rate of the population below its potential. Delayed marriage of men may also depress the birth rate, though less effectively. In many parts of the world, and especially among primitive tribes, young women marry soon after, or even before, puberty. In civilized societies, however, especially those in which the girls are given a long school education, marriage does not customarily take place until a number of years after puberty. Certain women may even delay marriage until they are past thirty. It is not uncommon for a professional man to postpone marriage until he is well past that age. This delay must play a considerable role in reducing the birth rate in our modern societies, though its actual effectiveness is not fully known. Not only do the women and men who marry late have fewer years in which to produce children, but their fertility also is less than that of younger persons.

Among the Nuer, a cattle-raising people of the upper Nile valley, the marriage of a son is delayed until the family owns a sufficient surplus of cattle to justify the establishment of a new household. Each son in turn must postpone marriage until the family herd has been built up to the necessary number of animals (Evans-Pritchard, 1940: 17). This custom constitutes a regulating mechanism whereby the number of marriages in each group of the Nuer is related to the number of cattle in the community. Although some children are born to unmarried mothers, the delay in the marriage of some of the sons must operate to lower the birth rate, especially during periods of cattle scarcity.

In primitive societies, practically every woman marries early in life (Carr-Saunders, 1922: 224), even though the men may not usually marry until they have reached middle age. If there are more women than marriageable men, polygyny will usually prevail. In our modern societies, on the other hand, some women never marry. This is necessarily the case in a monogamous society in which women locally outnumber men. The failure of certain men to marry will have little effect on the birth rate so long as the number of men who do marry is equal to the number of marriageable women. There can be no doubt that celibacy, both of men and women, plays a considerable role in reducing the birth rate of our modern societies.

A special form of celibacy is religious monasticism, where certain men become celibate monks and certain women celibate nuns. The effectiveness of religious celibacy in reducing the reproduction rate of human societies, however, has not been adequately measured.

Polyandry is another custom of some primitive societies that serves in part as a control of population increase. This practice, however, is effective only when the society also disposes in some way of the surplus females, usually by infanticide.

It is obvious that the only effective means to control the density of human populations that is available to modern societies is the limitation of conception. Certain civilized countries already have by this method reduced their birth rate to approximately their death rate. Unfortunately, the governments of some countries that were already overcrowded prior to the Second World War—notably Japan, Germany, and Italy—attempted by propaganda to increase their birth rates still further in order to augment their military power. In other countries, such as India and China, the feeble methods of population control sometimes practiced are wholly inadequate to keep the birth rate down, and these countries, accordingly, are overpopulated and suffer from recurrent distress.

Cooperation

In many species of organisms, competition among the individuals making up a population plays an important role in limiting population density. Strife between individual animals of the same species often results in considerable mortality. Among social animals, however, cooperation for certain objectives of the group is practiced side by side with competition within the group for individual objectives. Man, most social of all the animals, has developed a high degree of cooperation among individuals and among social subgroups.

The natural regulatory mechanisms that control human populations are frequently painful to individuals and often produce distress and disorganization in the community. Every well organized human society, therefore, tends to evolve modes of group behavior that prevent or mitigate the operation of these natural mechanisms. The habit of storing food for use during seasons of scarcity is an example of behavior that avoids the natural regulatory mechanism of starvation. Without food storage, starvation would reduce the population to a level commensurate with the food resources available at the season of greatest scarcity.

A highly organized society goes much beyond mere food storage for the control of local shortages. By a complex type of economic organization, modern society not only stores but transports food materials over considerable distances in order to supply a local population threatened with hunger.

Agricultural or industrial cultures, by cooperative effort, can support a higher density of population than competition for the natural products of the earth would allow. Cooperative efforts, therefore, lessen the danger of overpopulation to some degree. War and strife, by contrast, disrupt cooperative enterprise and lower the level of population density that the region can support.

Cooperation among men will undoubtedly in the future be raised to a much higher degree of perfection than it has reached at present. Some competition between individuals, groups, and nations will always remain; but as long as it is of a nonlethal sort, it is undoubtedly at least in part advantageous since it stimulates greater endeavor.

Birth rate and mortality rate

Primitive communities often have high birth rates, but usually high mortality rates as well. High infant and juvenile mortality is characteristic of primitive and even fairly well acculturated societies. The high mortality rates tend to balance the high birth rates in such societies.

A high birth rate, however, is not necessarily correlated with a high mortality rate, even in a primitive society. Thus, S. F. Cook (1947) has demonstrated that in an aboriginal society in which food is ample, both infant and juvenile mortality may be at a low rate. In such a society a rapid increase in the population must occur unless other checks are operative.

The mortality rate in every population is ultimately directly related to the birth rate. If the birth rate of a people is higher than its mortality rate and there is no migration, its population will increase until the full carrying capacity of its habitat is reached. As population density approaches full carrying capacity in any area, the mortality rate increases, due to starvation, disease, and other factors, until it equals the birth rate.

Planned population control

Human populations will always be controlled by regulatory mechanisms of one kind or another. If we succeed in mitigating the severity of one controlling mechanism, such as starvation, some other mechanism, such as disease, will take over. If a human population becomes too abundant for the resources of its habitat, as is the case in many sections of the world today, starvation, pestilence, strife, and other controlling mechanisms will in due time and without fail reduce it. Man's only way to avoid the painful natural mechanisms that control his numbers is voluntarily to limit the number of offspring he produces. The most desirable birth rate in any human population is that rate which is just sufficient to maintain population density at the optimum carrying capacity of its ecosystem. Unfortunately, we still lack reliable methods for estimating the optimum population density for any human ecosystem, and particularly for those modern communities where rapid changes in technology, social organization, and standard of living are taking place.

SELECTED REFERENCES

Carr-Saunders, A. M. 1922. The population problem; a study in human evolution. Oxford: Clarendon Press.

Dublin, Louis I., A. J. Lotka, and M. Spiegelman. 1949. Length of life; a study of the life table. Rev. ed. New York: Ronald Press Co.

Pearl, Raymond. 1946. Man the animal. Bloomington, Ind.: Principia Press.

Pitt-Rivers, G. H. L. 1927. The clash of cultures and the contact of races . . . London: George Routledge and Sons.

Thompson, Warren S. 1942. Population problems. New York: McGraw-Hill Book Co.

United Nations. 1949. Demographic yearbook, 1948. Lake Success, N. Y.: United Nations.

Evolution of Human Heredity

CHAPTER VI

A vast volume of scientific evidence demonstrates the fact that man has evolved from subhuman ancestors. His closest living relatives are the chimpanzee and the gorilla, though neither of these contemporary anthropoids can be an ancestor of man. Although scanty remains of a number of primitive manlike creatures have been discovered (Kroeber, 1948, Chap. III), the direct ancestors of *Homo sapiens* are still uncertain. For *Homo neanderthalensis* we have a number of records of skeletons; we also know something about his culture; but that this species of ancient man was ancestral to modern man has not been demonstrated. On the strength of the information derived from fossils, the evidence obtained from still existing primitive communities, and our knowledge of the genetics of other animals we are able, however, to offer some suggestions about certain factors that probably have affected the evolution of man.

Each individual must die, but the population of which he is a part nearly always continues to exist. Certain of his hereditary traits will be exhibited by his children, in combination with traits derived from other ancestors. Thus it is the population rather than the individual which is the major unit of evolution.

The individuals who compose each population, nevertheless, are the carriers of the heredity of the group, and important units of selection.

Each individual person, with only a few exceptions, differs in his heredity from every other person. The exceptions are those identical twins, triplets, or other identical individuals who are derived from a single fertilized ovum. Not every pair of twins or other set of individuals derived from a multiple birth, however, is identical in heredity. Fraternal twins are no more nearly alike in their heredity than any other pair of brothers or sisters. It is this variation in heredity among most of the individuals who compose a population that makes possible the evolution of the physical and mental characters of man.

Factors in the evolution of heredity

There are many factors that may affect the evolution of human heredity. Among them are mutation, recombination of hereditary factors, and outbreeding, all of which operate to increase variability in populations. By contrast, the random elimination of genes, inbreeding, assortative mating, and selection operate to decrease variability within populations.

Gene mutations and chromosomal changes   Practically all of the differences in heredity that distinguish the individuals which make up a given population are assumed to have been produced originally through gene mutation and chromosomal changes (Dobzhansky, 1951a). A gene mutation is an inherited change in one of the hypothetical hereditary units (genes) which are located in or on the chromosomes. The nucleus of each human cell contains twenty-four pairs of chromosomes. Duplications, translocations, and other changes in the chromosomes may also cause changes in heredity.

Certain kinds of mutations recur from time to time; their frequency can be calculated. The mutation which produces retinoblastoma in man, for example, is estimated to appear once in approximately 2.3 per 100,000 of those individuals who are born annually in the state of Michigan (Neel and Falls, 1951). Retinoblastoma is a malignant cancer that affects the retina of the eye of very young children, usually with fatal results. Numerous other kinds of harmful mutations occur in every human generation, producing such things as hemophilia (bleeding), hare lip and cleft palate, albinism, achrondroplastic dwarfism, certain types of idiocy, and other defects.

Mutations always occur suddenly. They may affect any part of the body. It is known that exposure to X rays, cosmic rays, certain chemicals, or severe conditions in the physical environment may produce mutations or chromosomal changes, but mutations may also occur spontaneously, without any external stimulus. Most mutations and chromosomal changes are harmful and produce abnormalities that handicap the individual. Many mutations are in fact so harmful that the affected individual dies before or soon after birth. Such a lethal mutation is thus promptly eliminated from the heredity of the population.

Mutations that produce improvement in physical or mental characters are presumed to appear from time to time, though they are not easily detected. A beneficial mutation is actually much less likely to occur than a harmful one, because most of the possible changes in so complex a structure as the vertebrate eye, for example, would cause deterioration rather than improvement in vision.

Whether a mutation is harmful, neutral, or beneficial, if the individual who carries the mutation survives, the hereditary structure of the population is to that extent altered, and the amount of genetic variability of the population thereby increased. A mutation which is recessive, however, will usually not express itself until several generations later, when two individuals who both carry the new gene happen to mate.

Recombination of genes   The hereditary units (genes) of every individual are, on the average, derived half from his father and half from his mother. Father and mother nearly always differ in a number of their genes. The child, therefore, will not be exactly like either parent, but will exhibit a combination of their characters. It also may exhibit characters of the grand-parents or more remote ancestors that do not appear in either parent, but are transmitted as recessives through the parents. The child may also show characters that are not exactly like those of any of its ancestors, but are produced by a combination of ancestral characters. Each child, furthermore, is likely to receive from his parents a set of characters which differs from that received by his brothers or sisters. No two children, then, unless they are identical twins, will be identical in their hered-ity. This recombination of hereditary factors in each genera-tion, which results from sexual reproduction, ensures that there will be a great deal of variation among the individuals who make up a population.

Random elimination of genes   Inasmuch as on the average only half the hereditary factors of each parent are transmitted, half the genes carried by each parent are not transmitted at all in the production of each child. Which genes are transmitted and which are not seems to be entirely a matter of chance. The chance of transmission or of loss can thus be computed. If a particular gene is represented only in a single individual of a population, and if this individual fails to transmit it to one of his offspring, that gene will be lost. Rare genes are thus being continually lost to all populations by the operation of chance alone (Wright, 1931). In other words, every population has a constant tendency to become more uniform through the chance loss of genes. This loss can be shown mathematically to be more rapid in very small populations than in large ones, but it occurs in populations of any size.

Inbreeding and outbreeding In every isolated human social group there occurs a certain amount of inbreeding, since mates must usually be secured from within the group. Inbreeding will be more extensive in a small group than in a large one, but some inbreeding must take place even in a large population. The more extensive the inbreeding, and the longer in time it is continued, the more uniform in heredity the population will become. Most human societies have special customs that operate to reduce the extent of inbreeding. The mating of brothers with sisters or of parents with children (incest) is nearly everywhere viewed with abhorrence. On the other hand, the mating of cousins is often encouraged in primitive societies (Kluckhohn and Griffith, 1951).

Where intermarriage between cousins or other relatives is permitted by a society, this inbreeding will cause recessive characters to be brought to light. These recessive characters thereby become exposed to the effects of selection. Recessive characters that aid survival have a tendency to become fixed in heredity. Harmful or lethal characters, on the other hand, tend to decrease in frequency, and in certain cases they may be eliminated. Many strains of domestic animals have thus been improved by inbreeding combined with rigorous selection. Inbreeding promotes uniformity of heredity not only by bringing hidden recessives to light so that they may be fixed or may be eliminated by selection; it also provides opportunity for a high rate of fixation or loss of genes.

Outbreeding, on the other hand, is permitted or encouraged by many tribes. Indeed, captured aliens, especially women and children, are often forced to become members of the tribe of their captors. This outbreeding results in an increase of variability in the heredity of the population concerned.

Size of population The number of individuals who make up any given interbreeding population has, theoretically, an important effect on the rate of random loss of genes, as well as on the possible number of new mutations to be expected in each generation. In a population consisting of only a few individuals, inbreeding will of necessity be considerable, and the random loss of genes will be high. In a very large population which is mating at random and not broken up into subgroups, there may be, on the other hand, a low rate of random gene loss. If we assume a uniform mutation rate per individual, a large population will also produce many more new mutations than a small population. Large populations, consequently, may be expected to exhibit a higher genetic variability.

Large populations, however, are often broken up into smaller subdivisions which constitute the actual breeding units. Thus, in a mountainous area a considerable degree of intermarriage is likely to occur within the subpopulation in each of the partially isolated valleys. In such a situation, outbreeding with other subpopulations may be infrequent. Even such local populations are not wholly separated, however, but do from time to time receive genes from outside. The calculations of Sewall Wright (1950) indicate that large populations which are broken in this way into smaller, partially isolated subpopulations are likely to exhibit a rapid rate of evolution of heredity in response to selection.

Assortative mating The tendency of like to mate with like, rather than with unlike, more frequently than would occur by mere chance, is called assortative mating. In those societies where the parents, or a group of elders, arrange the marriages, some general tendency toward the mating of like with like may be assumed. For example, the son of a chief would most likely be married to the daughter of another chief. Similarly, in all societies where social strata are recognized there is a tendency for bride and groom to come from the same social class. Even where the choice of mates is left to the individuals concerned, as is in part true of our own society, there is a considerable amount of mating of like with like (Burgess and Wallin, 1944). Men and women usually choose mates who are not only from their own social class, but also resemble them in stature (Pearson, 1896) and other physical features, as well as in mental ability (Penrose, 1933; Halperin, 1946).

When the selection of mates is based on their superiority in health or ability, assortative mating can be an important factor leading to the improvement of the heredity of at least part of a society. In a very small society, however, assortative mating cannot operate effectively. It can be effective only in a population sufficiently large to allow some choice of marriage partners.

By promoting marriages between those persons in the society who are best endowed with health and ability, assortative mating permits the production of still better combinations of hereditary endowment. By the same token, mating of persons of inferior ability promotes the production of very unfortunate combinations. Where selection operates to encourage the survival and reproduction of persons with superior heredity, assortative mating may be expected to have a beneficial effect, but in the absence of selection it will be expected merely to accentuate class distinctions.

Natural selection Natural selection may be assumed constantly to favor those hereditary combinations which are best adapted to the conditions of the local environment. Children born with grave defects will usually be unable to survive. Seriously harmful mutations will consequently be eliminated almost as soon as they express themselves. On the other hand, persons with superior health, vigor, and ability will be most likely to survive, and to produce offspring. Natural selection, therefore, undoubtedly is a powerful agency in all types of human communities, acting to preserve and perchance improve the level of human heredity. Any individual who is unable to adapt himself to the extremes of temperature and other physical factors in his habitat, or who is insufficiently resistant to the parasites and infectious organisms present in his community, is likely to be eliminated, while a better adapted individual may survive. Through this natural selection of individuals, the adaptation of a population to the conditions of its local environment is maintained or may be improved slightly in each generation.

If in a given population all individuals were able to survive equally well, and if mortality were completely at random, that population, because of the occurrence of mutations, would soon become filled with many kinds of inherited defects. Fortunately for the human race, many of the mutations that occur are of so extreme a character that the affected individuals die shortly after, or even before, birth. In a human community where resources are limited and life is rugged, many other defective individuals are eliminated early in life. In many primitive societies, in fact, defective children are not permitted to live. A defective individual would be a burden on his fellows and might handicap the survival of his social group. In a primitive society, the elimination of those individuals who by reason of their heredity are defective or not well fitted for life in their particular habitat will result in an evolution of the heredity toward better adaptation to the local conditions of the population. Modern societies, on the other hand, are inclined to preserve as long as possible the life of every individual, no matter how seriously he may be handicapped by various types of defects.

Natural selection no doubt plays a considerable role in adjusting human physiology and behavior to the conditions of the diverse habitats of the world (Coon, Garn, and Birdsell, 1950). Negroes, for example, are reputed to endure hot climates better than do white men. It is presumably for this reason that Negroes are employed in considerable numbers in the foundries of certain automobile factories in Detroit. A group of twenty Negro sharecroppers tested by Robinson, Dill, Wilson, and Nielson (1941) were more efficient in working in humid heat, without excess elevation of their body temperature, than a group of seven white sharecroppers. The actual physiologic mechanisms involved in the adaptation of Negroes to high temperatures, however, are largely unknown.

Some investigators also believe that Negroes are more tolerant than white men to the malaria caused by the blood parasite *Plasmodium vivax* (Boyd and Stratman-Thomas, 1933; Swellengrebel, 1940), but this cannot yet be accepted as proved.

Whether or not Negroes are more resistant than white men to the effects of heat and of tertian malaria, it is certain that no individual can long continue to live in a habitat to which he is seriously unadapted. Maladapted individuals may be eliminated by natural selection, or may be handicapped in reproduction. The population, consequently, is likely to develop in time an inherited adaptation to the conditions of the habitat.

Selection may also operate against persons who exhibit undesirable features of social behavior. That selection against antisocial individuals actually occurs in primitive societies is supported by the account given by Rasmussen (1931: 30) of the elimination of a trouble-making Eskimo. The man had a difficult and passionate temper. He had killed a fellow in a fit of temper. He had stabbed his wife several times, though not mortally. The village decided that this dangerous man must be killed. His brother, being the eldest in the family, was assigned to execute the sentence.

In modern societies, those extremely antisocial individuals who murder, rape, rob, or commit other serious crimes against society are imprisoned or, more rarely, executed or banished. The chances of their leaving offspring are consequently reduced. It may be assumed that this selection against individuals who threaten the existence of their social groups is a factor in the evolution of social cooperation in human societies.

In modern communities, adverse natural selection presumably has less importance for human evolution than in primitive ones. The lives of persons who have inherited minor defects are often preserved, and they may become valuable members of the community. Natural selection, nevertheless, still plays an important role in eliminating those who exhibit serious types of inherited defects (Holmes, 1936, Chap. XIX).

In societies of primitive man, the characters of aggressiveness, physical strength, and ability to withstand violent stress were important for survival and are assumed to have been favored by natural selection. In the greatly complex societies in which modern civilized man lives, the characters of social tolerance, mental ability, and mild disposition are desirable, and these characters likewise are presumably subject to natural selection. The changes in human heredity which undoubtedly occur as man becomes domesticated are illustrated by the difference between a wild Norway rat and his laboratory-bred relative. The wild animal is fierce, almost untamable, exhibits considerable sterility in the laboratory, and has an exceptional ability to endure stress. The laboratory animal, on the contrary, is docile and easily handled, very prolific, and reacts poorly to stress (Richter, 1952). It is not easy to compare men and rats, but it seems certain that the heredity of man must have become considerably modified as he became adapted to life in large social groups. The evolution of human heredity is probably still continuing.

Artificial selection In most human communities, artificial selection is no doubt an important agency in the evolution of heredity. Artificial selection may operate in either of two ways: by the elimination of those infants who are considered by their parents or the tribe to be unsuited for survival; and by a preferential selection of certain persons as the parents of the next generation.

In primitive tribes, those infants who at birth exhibit major defects are usually eliminated immediately, even though with special care they might be able to survive. This practice does not necessarily indicate cruelty or hardness of heart on the part of the parents. It is evidently better for a crippled or otherwise seriously handicapped child to die at once than to linger on for some time, a burden to his family and his social group. I often wonder if we, in our modern communities, are not particularly cruel when we make great efforts to preserve the lives of infants who are hopelessly crippled and will never be able to live normal lives.

The ideals of personal beauty held by a society affect the selection of mates, and in that manner may contribute to the evolution of the physical characters of the society. Thus, amongst the Hindus, social selection operates against light eye-color, among the American Negroes against dark skin color. Such social selection tends to produce uniformity in these characters which are preferred by the society (Herskovits, 1929).

There are more drastic methods that may sometimes direct the evolution of a tribe or section of a tribe toward a cultural ideal. Thus, two gentes within the Menabe tribe of the Tanala of Madagascar differ strikingly in skin color. The members of the Zafiakotry gens have a dark negroid type of skin color, while the members of the Maromena gens are "hardly darker than Mediterranean Europeans." A light-colored child born in the Zafiakotry gens is believed by his people to be destined to become a malevolent sorcerer, a leper, or a thief. Similar prejudices against dark-colored infants are reported (but not verified) in the Maromena gens (Linton, 1933: 285). Kluckhohn and Griffith (1951: 403) suggest that those infants who fail to conform in skin color to the ideals of their group are likely to be killed at birth. Linton did not, however, secure any actual evidence for such selective infanticide within the Menabe tribe.

In communities of all degrees of organization a preference for certain types of mates operates to direct the evolution of human heredity. Such a preference need not be exercised by the individual himself. It will be equally effective if the choice is made by the parents or by some other person. Nor need any knowledge of human heredity be involved in the choice.

In tribes which obtain most of their food from hunting, the best hunters often have more wives, and consequently leave more descendants, than less able ones. Amongst the Siriono Indians of eastern Bolivia, for example, good hunters and virile sex partners are preferred as husbands (Holmberg, 1950: 58). Ability in hunting is probably based in part on physical vigor, and this may be affected by age and by numerous environmental factors such as disease, infection, accidents, and inadequate nourishment in childhood. Some of the factors that make for success in hunting, however, are undoubtedly inherited. Insofar as they are inherited, the effects of social selection favoring able hunters will be to increase the frequency in the population of these hereditary factors which favor hunting ability.

There can be little doubt that preferential mating has been an important factor in raising the level of hereditary ability in most if not all human societies, and in increasing the adaptations of individuals to the conditions of their habitats.

Differential fertility   Selection can be effective in producing progressive evolution only when the favored individuals actually leave a greater number of offspring than the others. In our modern civilizations, unfortunately, many able persons leave few or no offspring, so that their valuable hereditary traits decrease rather than increase in the next generation. This has raised the fear in the minds of many that the heredity of our modern populations may be deteriorating (R. C. Cook, 1951: 6).

A voluntary limitation of procreation can take the unfortunate turn that the more prudent individuals will reduce the number of their offspring to a level below the number necessary to maintain their kind. The imprudent and socially irresponsible elements of society, on the other hand, are less likely to place a voluntary check on the number of their children. Should such a differential birth rate continue for only a few generations, the heredity of the population would deteriorate. There is a very real danger here, but we are not able to estimate its magnitude nor urgency because we have as yet no means for measuring accurately the hereditary abilities or potentialities of any individual. This topic will be discussed at greater length below in Chapter XIII.

Effects of social units

The social groups formed by man have an important influence on the evolution of his heredity. Each social group that exists for more than one generation acts as a unit of genetic evolution, because its members intermarry, while marriage between members of different social groups is less frequent.

The tribe   In primitive societies, the tribe seems to be the most important unit for the evolution of human heredity (Keith, 1947). The term tribe is here used in its anthropologic sense, to mean a simply organized population of persons, mostly related in heredity, who are potentially free to intermarry. The marriage of particular pairs of individuals, such as brothers and sisters or certain kinds of cousins, however, may be prohibited.

Every tribe is at least partially set apart from every other tribe by language, customs, religion, technology, and/or other aspects of culture. Physical barriers also may aid in isolating a tribe from its neighbors.

Each separate tribe of men, because of its isolation, may be expected to develop in time a particular assemblage of hereditary characters which differs more or less from that of any other tribe. Even tribes that have descended from the same racial stock must diverge in heredity because of the random loss of genes, the differential accumulation of mutations, and the effects of natural and artificial selection.

If neighboring tribes occupy different types of habitats, their requirements for survival may theoretically be sufficiently different so that natural selection acting on the individuals may cause a further divergence in tribal heredity. Thus, if one tribe lives on the seashore and another occupies an inland region, the difference in their modes of life could result in the evolution of certain differences in their physical characters. Among the deer-mice of the native North American genus *Peromyscus*, for example, striking adaptations of pelage color, the proportional length of tail, and the size of hind feet distinguish many of the races (Dice, 1940).

Actually, we have no undisputed instance of a divergence in heredity between any two human tribes that can be demonstrated to be adaptive. The differences between the body build of the members of certain tribes and that of their neighbors is nevertheless suggestive of the effects of natural selection. In no case, however, are we able to rule out the possibility that social selection, chance genetic drift, or differences in those environmental influences which act directly on the individuals, may have produced the tribal characters.

The selection to which each tribe is exposed is affected by the culture of the group as well as by its heredity. In fact, the type of culture of a local group may be of supreme importance in its survival. The culture of a tribe, in turn, must in part be dependent on the hereditary ability of the people. The hereditary resistance of the members to local endemic diseases, and their adaptability to the physical conditions of the habitat, must also be involved in the success of each tribe. The survival of a tribe, consequently, is dependent upon both tribal heredity and tribal culture.

The results of the trend toward an increase in genetic uniformity within each isolated tribe due to inbreeding and random loss of genes, and of the contrary trend toward increase of variability due to mutation and outbreeding, balance each other to some degree. No tribe of men seems ever to have remained isolated for a sufficient number of generations to achieve any considerable degree of uniformity in its heredity. On the contrary, all populations of men which have ever been described exhibit a considerable amount of variability.

Natural selection operating among competing tribes may be assumed to preserve in general those tribes which are best able to take care of themselves, and to eliminate those which are less effective. In this competition, the tribe is the unit of selection. It may be presumed that in a primitive state of culture natural selection among tribes has often been a powerful agency for human evolution (Keith, 1949). Reliable information about the factors which have been responsible for the elimination of particular tribes, however, is scanty and difficult of analysis.

Nation and empire A group of tribes sometimes becomes organized into a larger unit which may be called a nation. Insofar as the people composing a nation are of similar ancestry, the nation may form a unit of racial evolution. Most nations, however, are primarily political units, and only rarely are all its citizens of similar racial stock.

An empire is composed of a group of nations. Every empire, consequently, contains a greater variety of elements in its heredity than a single nation. Races with many diverse types of physical characters may be represented. Although the language of the dominant nation may be understood everywhere in the empire, various native languages will probably be spoken locally. A diversity of local cultures is characteristic of every large empire. Because of its internal diversity of race, language, and culture, an empire may be assumed to be only rarely a unit in the evolution of human heredity.

Although nations and empires seldom or perhaps never act as units in the evolution of human heredity, these political divisions may nevertheless be suspected to have important evolutionary influences. Numerous instances are recorded where a tribe or larger ethnic group has been practically exterminated or greatly reduced in numbers by wars or punitive expeditions conducted by a dominant nation or empire.

Social subgroups Social subgroups of various kinds inevitably develop within any large society. Such subgroups are sometimes based on race, sometimes on economic position, social status, religion, or other features of culture. Rulers and commoners constitute distinct classes in some tribes, and the priesthood also may form a separate class. Social strata and social subgroups are especially characteristic of nations.

Only in a few nations, such as India, have the social subgroups become transformed into rigid hereditary castes. In most nations, there is more or less frequent intermarriage among the various social classes. The social classes within each society are often complementary to one another, and only rarely in direct competition. They do not, therefore, serve as units of competition and of selection in evolution, as tribes do in primitive societies. Social subgroups, nevertheless, may be presumed to be of considerable importance in the evolution of heredity within populations.

All varieties of man are potentially able to interbreed and, so far as is known, to produce fully fertile offspring. The habit of men to live in relatively small, more or less isolated subgroups must consequently have played a considerable part in the evolution of human characters. In our modern communities, and especially in our cities, the isolation between subgroups has in part been broken down. Nevertheless, even in a city various kinds of social, economic, religious, and other subgroups occur. A modern community would be expected, therefore, to constitute a favorable environment for the rapid evolution of human characters.

Variability in heredity

An important factor in organic evolution is the variability in hereditary characters which is present in every natural population, and which affords a basis for the action of natural selection. We may conclude that the future progressive evolution of man will be aided by the continuing existence in all human communities of a high degree of diversity both of hereditary characters and of cultural elements (Simpson, 1949). We would do well, therefore, to conserve our various classes and races. A certain amount of intermarriage among classes and races is beneficial, since it produces new hereditary combinations. The absence of racial or class differences, on the other hand, would slow down evolutionary progress.

In an internationally organized world, some of the advantages of tribal competition are lost. Evolution based on tribal competition, however, is often a cruel process. It is no doubt very effective when the competing tribes differ considerably in their characters. It cannot be maintained, however, that such competition always results in the survival of the tribe with the superior heredity. Far too often, competent and peaceful tribes have been destroyed or driven out of their home region by a predatory neighbor. The advantages of internationalism may be assumed to outweigh any decrease of evolutionary tendency due to the disappearance of tribal competition. Alternate agencies that will promote the improvement of human heredity, however, need to be encouraged. The maintenance of a considerable degree of diversity in the heredity of every human population seems to be one of the factors that is of high importance as a basis of progressive evolution.

SELECTED REFERENCES

Dobzhansky, Th. 1951.
    a. Genetics and the origin of species. 3d ed., revised. New York:
       Columbia University Press.
    b. Human diversity and adaptation. Cold Spring Harbor Symposium Quant. Biol., 15: 385–400.
Holmes, Samuel J. 1936. Human genetics and its social import. New York: McGraw-Hill Book Co.
Hooton, E. A. 1946. Up from the ape. Rev. ed. Part IV. New York: Macmillan Company.
Kroeber, A. L. 1948. Anthropology: race, language, culture, psychology, prehistory. Chaps. 3, 4, 5. New York: Harcourt, Brace and Co.
Osborn, Frederick. 1951. Preface to eugenics. Rev. ed. New York: Harper and Bros.
Stern, Curt. 1949. Principles of human genetics. San Francisco: W. H. Freeman and Co.

Man's Effects on Natural Communities

CHAPTER VII

In the thousands of years since man became the dominant animal on earth, he has directly or indirectly produced profound changes in the communities of which he has been a member. Although he is a terrestrial animal, his activities have affected not only the terrestrial communities, but to a considerable extent also those of fresh-water and, to a lesser degree, of the oceans (Allee and Schmidt, 1951: 650–72).

Primitive man

Even primitive man produces important changes in the communities over which his activities extend. He gathers fruit, seeds, and other parts of plants for food, and in so doing may destroy or reduce the local populations of certain plant species. He destroys parts or all of certain other plants by gathering them for clothing, fuel, building materials, and numerous other uses. He kills various kinds of animals to secure food, clothing, and other necessities. He will, if he can, reduce the number of large predators and other kinds of animals that annoy him or his crops or herds. He often sets forest and prairie fires, and these sometimes alter the natural communities over large areas. The native Indian of northeastern North America, for instance,

had considerably modified many of the natural communities
before the coming of the white man, by clearing the forests for
village sites and cornfields, and by setting fires (G. M. Day,
1953).

Pastoral man

Early man's discovery that he could keep certain animals under
domestication constituted a great cultural achievement (Bews,
1935: 288). His domestic animals give pastoral man a source
of food and certain other essentials much more reliable than
the wild game and wild plants on which many primitive tribes
largely depend. At the same time, the herds of domestic animals
produce many changes in the natural communities of the regions inhabited by pastoral man.

Domestic animals feed more heavily on certain kinds of
plants than on others, and thereby alter the composition of
each community of which they form a part. Grazing often
greatly changes the natural communities, sometimes over extensive areas. Thus, in the Hawaii National Park, cattle grazing
destroys the forests of the native koa tree (*Acacia koa*), and
many of the smaller associated plants. The native community
is then replaced by foreign grasses (Baldwin and Fagerlund,
1943).

If a meadow or prairie is overgrazed, inedible weeds often
replace desirable forage grasses. Trampling by large domestic
herbivores may in some places compact the soil, or injure the
more delicate plants, sufficiently to cause important alterations
in the vegetation. The presence of domestic animals may also
result in the introduction or the local increase of certain predators, parasites, and other types of associates, thereby further
altering the character of the communities affected.

Some of the original animal species of a natural community
may become greatly reduced due to the changes in the habitat

produced by the activities of man and his domestic herbivores, while other species may find the new conditions favorable to their welfare, and may become exceptionally numerous. For example, in many parts of California the large ground-squirrel (*Citellus beecheyi*) occurs sparingly on natural pasture lands in locally favorable situations. But when these pastures are overbrowsed or plowed, the ground-squirrel greatly increases and may become a serious pest. If the habitat is allowed to revert to its natural state, these squirrels disappear (Linsdale, 1946).

Agricultural man

Another great cultural achievement of early man was the cultivation of plants for food, textiles, and other uses. In the process of plant cultivation, however, man often greatly changes the natural communities. By clearing fields for his crops, he destroys forests, native grasslands, and many other types of natural communities. By draining swamps, and building dams and canals for irrigation, he produces great local changes, especially in riparian communities. His agricultural operations locally extirpate, often unintentionally, many harmless or even beneficial species of plants and animals.

In his cultivated fields, man produces many new types of habitats. These attract various kinds of native and introduced species of plants and animals which, together with the cultivated crops, constitute new types of communities. Some species of insects and rodents may find an exceptionally congenial habitat in cultivated fields. They often increase enormously in numbers in such situations, and become destructive pests.

Waste

The natural resources of many parts of the world have been greatly damaged by man's wasteful exploitation (Fairfield

Osborn, 1948; Fairchild, 1952). Forests have been so completely destroyed in certain areas that the populations suffer for lack of lumber and of fuel. Serious damage to certain types of forest and marsh has been wrought by fires, which may consume not only the trees and shrubs, but even the humus in the soil. Extensive damage has been caused by improper farming and pastoral practices. In some of the southern states, for example, a one-crop system dependent on tobacco or cotton has depleted the soil, and in some places has allowed the top soil to erode (Craven, 1925).

Erosion has caused considerable areas to become largely unfit for human occupancy. Most of the fertile top soil has already been lost through erosion from more than 50 million acres of farming land in the United States. The capacity of this land to produce crops has been seriously impaired or destroyed. The soil on another 50 million acres has been seriously injured. Erosion is actively under way on still another 100 million acres (Duley, 1946: 639). In some parts of the world, fortunately, farming practices have been such that erosion has been checked and the soil enriched, so that with the passage of time the land has become more rather than less productive. This is true, for example, of considerable areas in China, Thailand, Burma, Java, and the Philippines.

Special modified communities

Man's homes and other buildings become occupied by various kinds of organisms in addition to man himself. In and around buildings may be found various cultivated plants, domestic animals, pets, pests, small predators, commensals, and parasites. Thus a special *edificarian* community is formed (Dice, 1920: 24). Of the parasites, some may attack man himself, others his cultivated crops and domestic animals. In villages, towns, and cities the edificarian community may cover extensive areas.

A ruderal (waste-land) community often springs up along the streets, roads, and trails constructed by man, in abandoned fields, and in other waste places. Various species of weeds are the conspicuous plants in such a community. Even within large cities, ruderal communities may develop on vacant lots.

Not all those special types of communities that originate in the habitats created by human activities, however, are necessarily antagonistic to human welfare. Some parts of the fire lanes, for example, which the Civilian Conservation Corps in 1934–36 cleared through forests in the state of New York, had by 1951, without further management, grown up to more or less stable types of non-forest vegetation and were still performing the functions of a fire lane (Pound and Egler, 1953).

Effects of a city

In cities with a heavy concentration of industrial activities, the natural communities are mostly destroyed or at least severely altered. Many of the native plants and animals are extirpated, and those that remain must live under conditions very different from those of their natural ecosystems. Numerous foreign species, both of plants and animals, are usually brought in. Some of these alien forms, such as the English sparrow, have been introduced intentionally. Others, such as the brown rat, are uninvited pests that follow man. The waters in the aquatic communities in an industrial region nearly always become polluted by sewage and industrial wastes. The effects of man's industrial activities often extend a great distance beyond the industrial centers due to disturbances produced by roads, railroads, secondary centers of trade, rivers, and canals.

An excellent description of the effect of a large city on the natural communities of plants and animals has been given by Fitter (1945). He shows how the communities that originally occupied the site where London, England, now stands have been progressively altered by the growth of that great city. Among the operations that have altered—or, more frequently, destroyed—the natural communities are the clearing of forests, the draining of swamps, the building of reservoirs and canals, the pollution of the waters, the production of smoke clouding the air, the construction of buildings and roads, the removal of materials for the construction of buildings, the destruction of many native plants and animals, the cultivation of domestic crops and herds, the unintentional introduction of pests, and more recently the destruction caused by war through bombing and fire.

To replace these natural communities, there has evolved within the city of London a number of new types of communities adapted to city life. Included here are the edificarian and ruderal communities and also the special communities that are formed in the parks, golf courses, recreation areas, reservoirs, and other new kinds of habitats that arise in and near every city. These new types of urban and suburban communities are made up in part of species native to the region, which here may find a habitat even more suited to them than their natural one. In some cases, the native species modify their habits when living in the city, for instance by becoming less wild than in rural communities. These urban communities also include foreign species that have been brought in by man.

Beneficial effects of human activities

Lest we give the impression that the operations of man produce only harm to nature, let us point out that the artificial communities that arise as the result of human activities are often of great scientific interest, and that some of them are beautiful. Forest plantings, and fields of grain or certain other crops, can be pleasing to the eye as well as productive. Furthermore, the animals living in a cultivated region may not be less in number than those in a wild region. Ritchie (1920: 492), for example, after a careful study of the effects of man on the animal life of Scotland, concluded that in spite of the local extirpation of certain species and the reduction in the numbers of others, the fauna had actually increased in diversity of species and in number of individuals.

In addition to domesticating certain species of plants and animals, man protects and encourages certain other forms of life that supply economic or esthetic values, and in the fields and forests that are more or less under his control, destroys or discourages species that interfere with those he is protecting or encouraging. Thus, he usually attempts to destroy weeds, and he eliminates so far as possible the large carnivores that might attack his domestic animals. On the other hand, he may encourage insectivorous birds, and certain of the smaller carnivores that prey on injurious rodents.

Esthetic value of plants and animals

Among the species of plants and animals that are protected or encouraged by man are many forms that yield only esthetic enjoyment. Trees and other plants that furnish esthetic pleasure by the beauty of their foliage, flowers, or fruit are often planted or encouraged to grow near man's habitations. Likewise, many animals are encouraged for the sake of their attractive appearance, spritely behavior, or pleasing song. Most peoples keep a considerable number of pets of various kinds. In civilized communities, many persons maintain feeding stations to attract birds, squirrels, and other kinds of wild animals. Song birds and other kinds of animals often are protected by law (Gabrielson, 1941: 169). Parks are established to provide pleasing landscapes and to protect certain kinds of plants and animals. The esthetic values of plants and animals are important for man,

and must be included in any consideration of the communities
of which he forms a part.

The need to preserve

Tremendous changes have taken place in the natural communities of the continent of North America during the few
centuries that have elapsed since its settlement by white men.
The pine forests of Michigan and adjacent states, for example,
have been almost completely lumbered off. The grasslands of
the prairies and plains have been so completely altered or destroyed by cultivation that it is now difficult to find even small
remnants suitable for scientific studies (Clements and Chaney,
1936).

Very few parts of the world remain that have not been greatly
affected by man's operations. These natural areas are mostly in
the frigid zones, in certain deserts, in rugged mountains, and
in some parts of the tropics. Most of them are areas of difficult
agriculture, or have climates unhealthful for man. The areas of
rich agricultural land in the northern hemisphere are already
occupied by man practically to the limit of their capacity, and
the same situation is rapidly being approached for the best
parts of the southern hemisphere. The population of the world
is continuing to increase at a rapid rate, and more and more
of the areas still in primitive condition are being brought under
cultivation and economic exploitation. It seems certain, therefore, that the alteration of natural communities will in future
proceed at a still more rapid rate than in the past.

We deplore the passing of any type of natural community,
and the extermination of any species of native plant or animal.
Every effort should be made to preserve a stock of every species now living in any part of the world. In every biotic province,
we should preserve an adequate sample of each natural community. These wild species and natural communities are needed

as a basis for scientific studies of ecology and evolution. They also help in the understanding of human history. In addition, these wild animals and primitive communities often have high esthetic values.

My plea for the preservation of a population of every living species of plant and animal does not imply that it is not necessary at times to kill off certain individuals. Individuals and local populations, either of animals or plants, that are harmful to man's best interests must be controlled. Likewise, many local examples of natural communities must necessarily be destroyed when forests are cut down or land cleared or drained for agricultural use. I do urge, however, that at least a few individuals of every species be preserved, and that at least a sample of every kind of natural community be saved from annihilation.

SELECTED REFERENCES

Allee, W. C., and Karl P. Schmidt. 1951. Ecological animal geography. 2d ed. Chap. 28. New York: John Wiley and Sons.
Fitter, R. S. R. 1945. London's natural history. London: Collins.
Kendeigh, S. Charles, and others. 1950–51. Nature sanctuaries in the United States and Canada: a preliminary inventory. Living Wilderness, 35: 1–45.
Osborn, Fairfield. 1948. Our plundered planet. Boston: Little, Brown and Co.
Ritchie, James. 1920. The influence of man on animal life in Scotland: a study of faunal evolution. Cambridge: Cambridge University Press.

Community Regulatory Mechanisms

CHAPTER VIII

Regulatory mechanisms are essential for the continued existence of all kinds of organisms. Such mechanisms are in operation at every level at which life exists. They keep the individual organism, the species, the society, and the community in adjustment with the conditions in their respective environments. Regulatory mechanisms of various kinds enable individual organisms and associated groups of organisms to adjust themselves to the constantly changing conditions in their habitats, so that they may continue to exist and perhaps to thrive.

We are well acquainted with many of the regulatory mechanisms in the individual organism that keep it adjusted to the frequent fluctuations in its environment (Cannon, 1939). For example, if a person drinks so much water that the water content of his body cells becomes too great for health, a regulatory mechanism goes into operation immediately to eliminate some of the surplus water, either through the kidneys or through other organs (Adolph, 1943). If the oxygen supply to the body cells becomes too low, other regulatory mechanisms at once attempt to restore the proper oxygen balance. The same holds for the carbon dioxide content of the blood, the blood sugar, the concentration of salt in the body fluids, the body temperature, and for all the many other physiological factors essential to the proper functioning of the body (Brody, 1945, Chap. 10).

The individuals of every kind of plant and animal are kept in adjustment to their particular environments through the constant operation of numerous kinds of physiologic regulatory mechanisms, many of which are similar to those that work in man. The precise mode of operation of many of these regulatory mechanisms is not yet known, although in recent years much progress has been made in their elucidation. The important point is that every organism depends on regulatory mechanisms for its continued existence. The possession of such mechanisms enables many kinds of plants and of animals to adjust themselves to a considerable range of external conditions, and often to survive even violent fluctuations in their habitats.

In natural communities

In every natural community, regulatory mechanisms of various kinds operate also to keep the associated member species of plants and animals in balance with one another and with the resources of their habitat. Among the most important of such regulatory mechanisms may be mentioned the feeding of herbivores, the activities of predators, destruction caused by parasites and disease, competition between individuals and between species, dispersal of individuals, seasonal migration, dormancy, social behavior, and the services rendered by certain species to their associates. By the action of these mechanisms, a tolerable balance is maintained constantly between those species in the community which are producers of food and those which are consumers. The community thus is kept in adjustment with the resources of its habitat (Dice, 1952, Chap. 14).

Through the action of one or more regulatory mechanisms, each species that has become overly abundant will in time be reduced in numbers to a level at which it no longer can disorganize its community. Contrariwise, a species that for any reason has become greatly reduced will usually enjoy some relief from its predators and other controlling mechanisms, so that it may again be able to increase.

In spite of the operation of the usual regulatory mechanisms, severe disturbances do sometimes occur in natural communities. For example, the introduction of a foreign species of plant or animal for which natural controlling mechanisms are not present may produce a serious alteration in the composition of the community. An unusually wet, or dry, season may allow one or more of the regular members of the community to increase unduly at the expense of its associates.

Any species that increases so rapidly in number that its usual regulatory mechanisms cannot control it effectively creates an epidemic, or plague. Such an outbreak often runs its course until all the food available to the species has been consumed. If the pest species is a parasite, disease organism, or herbivorous insect, it may greatly reduce its host species. Once its host has been so reduced in number, the pest species can no longer thrive. The outbreak will ultimately be brought under control, but only after certain of the member species of the community may have been severely altered in abundance.

Any single ecologic regulatory mechanism may produce oscillations, of lesser or greater magnitude, in the communities in which it operates. No biologic mechanism can be perfect. Nearly always, a considerable degree of change in the community must occur before the regulatory mechanism begins to operate. By the time it is working at maximum efficiency, the community may have suffered considerable change.

Presumably, the greatest degree of stability in any given community will be achieved when numerous regulatory mechanisms of diverse types are available for community control. Highly organized communities, composed of many complexly interrelated species and provided with many diverse kinds of regulatory mechanisms, should therefore be in theory more stable than simpler communities in which the regulatory mechanisms are few. Little actual information, however, has been published about the relative stability of different kinds of communities in nature.

In modified communities

When a natural community is altered by man's interference, or when an artificial community is developed, the natural regulating mechanisms are interfered with and may no longer be able to control the community. There is, consequently, a considerable difference in stability between natural and modified communities.

Modern man dominates so completely most of the communities in which he operates that their natural controls can no longer be depended upon to regulate the interrelations between the various member organisms. Man himself must then artificially provide community controls in order to avoid being left without food, shelter, and the other necessities of life. If, for example, he has killed off the predators that prey upon herbivorous rodents, he must now wage campaigns against the rodents or they will ravage his crops. If he has inadvertently destroyed the birds or other organisms that check the increase of an insect pest, he must himself keep that insect pest under control or suffer the consequences.

Although modern man has greatly modified many habitats, and utterly destroyed numerous kinds of natural communities, he has not been able to establish complete control over any type of ecosystem. In his cultivated fields, he may destroy countless numbers of weeds and of noxious insects, yet many will remain to compete with or to attack his crops. Predaceous animals still exist in many regions in spite of all efforts to eradicate them. Parasites and disease organisms frequently attack man's cultivated crops and his domestic animals. Many diseases, parasites, and small irritating pest animals even attack man himself.

The number and variety of small wild animals living in some of the habitats that are of importance to man may be very great. On certain pastures in New York state, for example, the total weight of the various kinds of invertebrates may exceed the total weight of the domestic animals in the same communities. On some of these pastures the grasshoppers, cutworms, and white grubs eat almost as much of the forage as does the domestic stock (Wolcott, 1937). The activities of these uninvited guests thus often seriously affect man's welfare.

Not all the small organisms that live in association with man, however, are harmful. Many species are beneficial to man either directly or indirectly. A predator that kills the rodents which attack man's crops is to that extent beneficial. The birds and spiders that prey on harmful insects are also indirectly beneficial to man, and so are the parasites that attack harmful insects or destructive rodents.

Only seldom are the activities of any given species of plant or animal in a particular community either wholly beneficial or wholly harmful to man's welfare. Thus, a predator that preys to some extent on man's domestic animals may at the same time be an important factor in preventing injurious rodents from destroying the cultivated crops or native forage plants. Valuable game animals, such as deer, are sometimes destructive to certain cultivated crops. The burrows made by the badger in capturing injurious rodents may be a hazard to horses and horsemen. In some places, the function of the pocket-gopher in soil enrichment may increase forage production sufficiently to compensate for the damage done to vegetation (Horn and Fitch, 1942: 129). Elsewhere, this species may be a destructive pest.

Certain species are of particular value to a community because they serve to regulate the numbers of one or more of the other members. A parasite that attacks a leaf-eating insect, for instance, may prevent that insect from defoliating an important forest tree. Many predators are valuable members of their communities because of the control they exercise over herbivores. The relationships among the several members of a community, moreover, are often extremely complex. Any evaluation of the ecologic position of a given species in a given community must take into consideration all the relations of that species to each of its associates. Due weight must be given to the beneficial services it performs directly or indirectly, as well as to the damage it causes.

To control some plant and animal pests, it is often possible to utilize certain existing biological agencies as regulatory mechanisms (Allan, 1942; Graham, 1944: 198). Rodent pests can often be controlled in part by their native predators, such as hawks, owls, skunks, and snakes. On wild lands the native predators, if protected against needless killing by man and provided with proper shelter and nesting sites, may be able to keep the rodents at a harmless level. Insect pests may be controlled to some degree by encouraging their enemies, among which are the insectivorous birds. However, birds alone seem never able to control an insect outbreak once it has started, though they probably are important in preventing injurious insect species from reaching the pest level (Gabrielson, 1941: 168).

Species that are useful as biological controlling agents are sometimes introduced from other regions. An inadvertently introduced pest may thus sometimes be controlled by the intentional introduction of its natural enemies. In Australia, for example, several introduced insects have brought the previously introduced prickly-pear cactus largely under control (Sweetman, 1936: 365–76; Dodd, 1940). Prickly pears of several species were introduced into Australia by the early colonists. These plants soon got out of control and became most serious pests. By 1920, they had infested an estimated 60 million acres of the continent. Plowing and other mechanical means of control were entirely ineffective, as were plant poisons. Several kinds of cactus-eating insects were then experimentally introduced. Of these insects, a moth of the species *Cactoblastis cactorum* and several species of cochineal insects of the genus *Dactylopius* proved to be especially effective. Although these insects have not exterminated the cactus, and cannot be expected to do so, they have in most parts of Australia brought the pest under control.

A word of caution is needed here. Before a foreign species is introduced into any community, a careful study should be made of the ecology of the situation and of the probable results of the proposed introduction. Otherwise more harm than good may result (Sweetman, 1936). The mongoose, for instance, was introduced into some of the West Indian Islands to control the introduced rats, which were causing damage in the sugar-cane fields. The mongoose did control the rats to some degree, but also killed most of the native ground-nesting birds and became as great a pest as the rats (Gabrielson, 1941: 177).

The ideal arrangement in all those communities with which man is concerned would be to develop artificial mechanisms that would automatically regulate the relations among the various associated species so as to achieve with little effort to man the results he desires. This ideal, unfortunately, seems impossible of complete realization. In most artificial and seminatural communities, the farmer or forester is compelled to exert much effort and often to incur considerable expense to prevent weeds, insects, rodents, and diseases from destroying the crops. Still, much assistance in controlling these artificial communities is given by various biologic regulatory mechanisms, some natural, others introduced by man. Diligent search, it is certain, can discover other valuable community regulatory mechanisms, and apply them to man's advantage.

Productivity and stability

The most efficient agricultural community, from man's point of view, is one that is well regulated and stable and at the same time highly productive of food and other materials and services for man. Stability and productivity, however, can seldom be secured simultaneously. A natural climax community, such as an Illinoian prairie field, for example, is relatively stable because it has, over a long period of time, developed many regulatory mechanisms. Such a prairie, however, will be only moderately productive of the things that civilized man requires. If the prairie sod is broken and the land planted to agricultural crops, on the other hand, it may be far more productive of food and of the other things that man uses, but it will no longer be a stable community. To maintain the land in productive crops requires frequent resowing of the desired plants, periodic cultivation to reduce competition from weeds, constant protection against the attacks of animal pests and various kinds of parasites and diseases, and the periodic addition of fertilizer to maintain the soil in fertile condition.

A working compromise between stability and productivity may often be established in any given community over which man is exercising control. Intelligent management practices, for example, may often considerably improve the productivity of pasture lands with only slight changes in the community. It is important not to overgraze the forage plants, but to encourage these food-producing species in their competition with weeds. Any great increase in productivity, however, such as would accompany the replacement of a prairie by a cornfield, is almost certain to result in instability. The cornfield can be made pro-

ductive only at the expenditure of considerable effort to prevent natural succession from re-establishing the climax grassy
prairie.

It seems unlikely that a cornfield can ever be made into a
fully stable, self-perpetuating community that is also highly
productive of food. Nevertheless, the development of disease-
resisting strains of corn, the introduction of parasites and other
organisms that may aid in the control of insect pests, and other
kinds of management practices, can to some degree improve
the amount of self-regulation of the cornfield. The effort needed
to maintain the cornfield in production, accordingly, can be to
that extent reduced.

Similarly, the productivity of forests may be increased by
such forestry practices as the prevention of fire, the encourage-
ment of natural reproduction, the planting of highly productive
and disease-resistant species or strains, and the maintenance, so
far as possible, of the natural regulatory mechanisms of the
community.

In the past, man's efforts to control those communities in
which he is interested have in part been directed toward allevi-
ating merely the local disturbances of the ecologic balance. If
a fox steals a chicken, for example, the farmer often will attempt
to kill all the foxes in the area. But foxes may be important in
controlling the rodents that damage pastures and cultivated
crops. By killing off foxes and similar predators, the farmer may
alter or destroy some of the regulatory mechanisms that were
actually aiding him in the production of his crops.

It may be hoped that a more complete knowledge of ecologic
interrelations and a broader viewpoint may in the future enable
man to preserve, so far as possible, those natural regulatory
mechanisms which are useful in his modified communities. In
well-settled situations, for instance, it may sometimes be necessary to destroy certain of the native large and small predators.

Before these predators are destroyed, however, some other means for controlling rodents and other pests should be devised.

The balance of nature

The adjustment in numbers which exists among the several species of plants, herbivores, carnivores, parasites, and other members of a natural community is sometimes spoken of as the balance of nature. This balance is, however, not a fixed relationship but rather a dynamic equilibrium. A community has no fixed center of gravity around which the population densities of its component plant and animal species fluctuate. The numerical relationships among the several species which make up any given community are constantly changing. In a favorable year, when an abundance of plant food is produced, a community may be able to support larger populations of both herbivores and carnivores than in unfavorable years, but the numbers of herbivores and of carnivores never increase together precisely in step.

The physical conditions of every habitat fluctuate constantly because of changes from season to season and from year to year. The member species of every community respond to these fluctuations in various ways. A change in the habitat that permits one species to increase in abundance may cause another to decrease. The population density of every member species also undergoes constant changes due to reproduction, mortality, emigration, and immigration. Although the general cycle of population turnover for any given species is usually similar from year to year, its population density will rarely remain constant over any long period of time. The ecologic balance among the member species of a natural community is thus constantly shifting.

Notwithstanding these constant fluctuations in ecologic balance which are characteristic of every natural community, most communities are relatively stable. Only rarely do the natural regulatory mechanisms fail so completely that a community becomes seriously altered, except where man has interfered. It is evident, for example, that such a complex community as a hardwood forest, in which the individual trees may be several hundred years of age, must have persisted without serious alteration for a long period of time. Ecologic regulatory mechanisms of various kinds actually are effective in maintaining a considerable degree of stability in most natural communities, so that these communities continue to exist in spite of constant fluctuations in the conditions of their habitats. The dynamic balance which is maintained within every natural community by the operation of its various internal regulatory mechanisms is one of the most significant features of community organization.

SELECTED REFERENCES

Brody, Samuel. 1945. Bioenergetics and growth. Chap. 10. New York: Reinhold Publishing Corp.
Cannon, Walter B. 1939. The wisdom of the body. New York: W. W. Norton and Co.
Dice, Lee R. 1952. Natural communities. Chap. 14. Ann Arbor: University of Michigan Press.

Regulatory Mechanisms in
Human Communities

CHAPTER IX

Many of the same types of ecologic regulatory mechanisms are
in operation in communities dominated by man and in natural
communities, although in human communities their effectiveness may be lessened by human activities. Some of the most
effective regulatory mechanisms that control the populations of
man himself, however, are inherent in human culture and have
no parallel in natural communities.

Natural regulatory mechanisms

Among the regulatory mechanisms that are important in natural
communities, and more or less effective also in human communities, are starvation, predation, diseases and parasites, migration, and competition. In communities where man exercises
only slight control, they may operate very much as in a completely natural community. In a highly organized human community, on the contrary, certain of them may be only slightly
effective.

Starvation Starvation has been largely eliminated from many
modern communities as a mechanism for the control of human
populations, though food shortages and famines still occur from

time to time in certain primitive communities and overpopulated parts of the world. Food supply, nevertheless, is an important regulating factor in all the communities that man dominates. The amount of forage which grows per year, for example, controls the number of domestic animals that can be grazed on pasture lands or kept in feeding yards. Where human food is abundant and cheap, human populations tend to increase up to the limit of carrying capacity. Whenever a population has increased to that limit, its food supply becomes a regulatory mechanism which prevents further increase in population density.

Predation Predation by large carnivores is of negligible importance in the control of modern human populations. It is, however, of great importance to many human communities in the control of injurious rodents, insects, and other animals. If it were not for the control exercised by predaceous insects, spiders, birds, and mammals, many of man's crops would be devastated by the attacks of small or large herbivores, and man himself would suffer more than he does now from the attacks of biting insects of numerous kinds.

Predaceous species may also be harmful to man by preying upon his domestic animals or upon wild food or game species. In some areas a heavy toll of domestic fowls, for instance, is taken by hawks, owls, skunks, foxes, coyotes, and other predators. Even large domestic animals such as cattle and horses may be killed by wolves and cougars. Although the losses from predation can usually be controlled by special herding or fencing methods, the extra expense involved may be beyond the resources of the farmers concerned. In most areas, consequently, man tends to eliminate the large and medium-sized natural predators, with the result that these species have been removed or made largely ineffective as regulatory mechanisms in many communities that man controls.

Diseases and parasites   Diseases and parasites are important regulatory factors in human communities. Diverse kinds of diseases attack the crops on which man is dependent for his livelihood. Parasites and diseases attack domestic animals or even man himself. Sometimes damage to a particular crop can be avoided by growing only disease-resistant strains. Special methods of culture, sprays, or other treatments are effective in the control of many types of disease-producing organisms. On the other side, there are the attacks of disease on those organisms that are harmful to man's crops, domestic animals, or man himself. In spite of the progress that has been made in recent years in combating disease in crop species and in other members of human communities, diseases and parasites still are important regulatory mechanisms in all types of human communities.

Migration   Migration is a natural regulatory mechanism which operates to equalize the opportunities in neighboring communities (Hawley, 1950: 327, 332). In seminatural communities, migration may be an effective regulatory mechanism for many of the animal species associated with man. Certain species regularly perform daily or seasonal migrations. Other species may from time to time spread out from a center of overpopulation to more thinly populated areas.

Where men are free to move from one community to another, many will migrate from a community in which the conditions of life are hard, to one in which conditions are more promising. Many of the early settlers of North America, for example, came here because the opportunities for successful living appeared to them brighter in this country than in their homelands.

Migration between communities, however, is not always possible. Barriers of race, language, religion, politics, or special regulations may prevent the entry of immigrants into a community. Persons who might wish to emigrate may be held back by family ties, a lack of the necessary resources, or by force. The effectiveness of migration as a regulatory mechanism for human populations thus varies from community to community and from time to time.

Competition Competition among individual organisms for a resource in limited supply operates as a powerful controlling mechanism both in natural and in human ecosystems. When the supply is ample for all demands, there will of course be no competition for it.

The density of many populations of plants and of animals is controlled by competition for sunlight, food, nesting sites, and other essentials. Competition is particularly effective as a regulatory mechanism in natural populations. When the population density is high, competition among the individuals will operate to reduce it. On the other hand, when population density is low there may be little or no competition among the individuals, and the population will be free to increase. In human populations, likewise, competition is a most important regulatory mechanism, although within organized societies its effects are frequently mitigated by cooperation among the individuals.

Even severe competition does not always result immediately in the elimination of a considerable part of the population. The individuals may be able to adjust their activities so that all of them survive, though less successfully so than when no competition exists. In populations of plants and animals under heavy competition, for example, many of the young may survive though they be stunted in growth. More frequently, many of the individuals may starve or be killed as a result of the competition, and even those that survive may become stunted and unhealthy (Allee, 1951: 16). If subjected to shortage of food and to other unfavorable conditions, most kinds of fishes, for example, fail to grow as rapidly and as large as their potential would permit (Carbine, 1945). In human societies, severe competition for the necessities of life usually produces a lowered standard of living for most or all the people, and may lead to famine, disease, or other unfortunate consequences.

In those human societies in which there is a high degree of social cooperation, the rigor of intragroup competition may be considerably less than in a non-cooperative society. When food is scanty, for instance, most human societies divide the supply more or less equally among the people. The greater the degree of cooperation in such a society, the more likely it is that all the individuals will suffer, and possibly be stunted, in times of scarcity. The greater average stature of the children of Japanese immigrants reared in Hawaii than of their parents, for example, is assumed to indicate a less favorable environment in the homeland than in Hawaii (Shapiro, 1939). The children of Mexican immigrants to the United States also are on the average taller than the children of Mexicans who have not emigrated, and also differ in other measurements (Goldstein, 1943). The same can be observed in Mexicans who have lived in the United States during several years of their growing period and then have returned to Mexico (Lasker, 1952).

Special regulatory mechanisms

Human communities are controlled by numerous special mechanisms, in addition to the regulatory mechanisms that are effective in maintaining the ecologic balance in natural communities. Special regulatory mechanisms that seem to be highly important in human communities are public opinion, punishments and rewards, wealth, taxation, the law of supply and demand, and social cooperation. These special mechanisms affect the human individuals. They may also indirectly affect all the other species of the community.

Public opinion   Public opinion is a powerful regulatory mechanism which operates by approving such individual behavior as is in accord with the folkways of the group, and disapproving unorthodox behavior. The human animal is highly social; the approbation of his group affords him satisfaction, disapproval gives him pain. Consequently, the individual person is likely to conform his behavior to that expected by his group. The degree of disapprobation by the group becomes the stronger, the greater the departure of the individual from the course of behavior expected of him (Sumner, 1940). Public opinion is thus an exceptionally effective social regulatory mechanism.

Religious beliefs often profoundly influence public opinion about certain types of behavior. The success of any human society, therefore, may be related to the effectiveness of the automatic community controls provided by its prevailing religious beliefs. The rapid spread and success of Mohammedanism in the Middle East, for example, was probably in part due to its rules of personal behavior which fitted the habitat, and its institutions which were adapted to the people (Coon, 1951: 342–43).

Punishment   In addition to the punishment of social disapproval, a serious breach of accepted public behavior is likely to have more serious consequences for the person concerned. He may be injured, killed, ostracized, imprisoned, or banished. In those societies that have written laws, certain acts are classed as misdemeanors, others as crimes. Both misdemeanors and crimes carry prescribed punishments. The probability of being apprehended and punished has a tendency to deter most persons from committing those acts that are seriously disapproved by their society.

When a person who is potentially dangerous to the functioning of a society is imprisoned, the society profits by his removal. Imprisonment of a dangerous person may serve as a regulatory mechanism not only through punishment, but even more importantly through the temporary or permanent removal of a potential menace to the society.

Rewards As regulatory mechanisms, also, we must class bonuses or other special rewards for acts believed to benefit the society. For example, bounties are paid for the destruction of injurious animals. Special payments have recently been made in the United States to farmers who follow approved practices for the conservation and improvement of their soil. Medals, citations, presents, grants of land, and payments in cash are other means to induce the type of behavior that at the time meets the approval of the people. Remission of a certain proportion of his annual income taxes to a man who is supporting a wife or children may thus be considered a reward for meritorious behavior.

Wealth Wealth is a regulatory mechanism which operates to prevent certain of the more violent fluctuations in the economic welfare of a human community. In natural communities, many organisms store food or other essentials against periods of scarcity, and thereby lessen the natural fluctuations in the community. Human communities, likewise, practice the storage of foods and other essentials. It operates to even out the seasonal and annual fluctuations in the productiveness of the habitat. Such stored materials are wealth. In human communities, wealth can take other forms, such as money, bank deposits, bonds, stock certificates, or notes.

Instead of being stored, the surplus of any useful material which an individual may happen to possess or be able to produce may be used for exchange with his neighbors or with outsiders. The habit of producing a surplus of a certain item or items, and of exchanging it for other desired materials, results in a division of labor. The development of a system of regular exchanges serves to integrate the several parts of the community and to promote community efficiency. Exchange may also contribute to the integration of a group of local communities into a larger economic unit.

A system of exchanges, however, will not by itself provide community stability. A breakdown of any part of such a system may seriously cripple the whole. Furthermore, certain individuals may by profitable exchanges accumulate large holdings of money or related items of wealth, while other members of the society remain poor. Such a division of a society into rich and poor is likely to contribute to community disorganization.

Taxation   Taxation is often considered primarily a device for raising money for the operation of government. Actually, taxation nearly always involves certain elements of regulation. High taxes are often imposed on those activities which are to be restricted but not entirely prohibited. High import taxes may be placed on certain foreign goods which compete with those of domestic manufacture. Partial or complete relief from taxes, on the other hand, may be given to religious and educational institutions because they perform activities that are to be encouraged.

Supply and demand   The economic law of supply and demand is a regulatory mechanism of great importance in human communities. As such, it is closely related to the similar mechanism of competition which is so effective in natural communities. This law, however, has so many special applications to man that it will here be considered as a special regulatory mechanism peculiar to human communities.

Under free competition, the price of any article of commerce that becomes scarce will tend to rise to a level at which the potential purchasers are no longer eager to buy. The price will ultimately come into an equilibrium which is adjusted to the available supply of the commodity, and to the demand for it. If the supply of an article increases, its price will fall until a new level of price equilibrium is reached. Numerous examples of the operation of the law of supply and demand as a regulatory mechanism are given in textbooks on economics, such as that by Boulding (1946).

When the operation of the law of supply and demand is interfered with by rationing or artificial price fixing, inequalities may arise and black markets flourish. Competition in wages and in materials is essential to community stability (Lippmann, 1937). The unsatisfactory results of attempts to control the prices of materials and wages in the United States during the Second World War seems to demonstrate the impossibility of planning an economy that will operate by edict, or of achieving in this way a proper balance among all the parts of a complex community.

Uncontrolled competition, however, can and often does result in many economic and social ills. Individuals, firms, or cartels may secure a monopoly of certain commodities or services, and make exorbitant profits at the expense of the public. Competitors may be driven out of business by price wars, gangsterism, or other unfair methods. Alliances of grafting politicians with businessmen and labor leaders have been only too frequent in the past and, alas, still continue. Monopoly of any commodity or service destroys the value of the law of supply and demand as a regulatory mechanism for the community.

In all economically complex communities it has thus been necessary to place certain restrictions on competition. In the United States, for example, many kinds of monopolies are prohibited. Where a monopoly is permitted, such as for telephone service, rates to be charged and other conditions of operation are sometimes regulated by a commission responsible to the public.

Unfortunately, governments often yield to the demands of politically potent pressure groups and permit or even compel certain other kinds of limitation on free competition (Griffin,

1949: 310). Thus, collective bargaining by labor unions results in a monopoly for certain kinds of labor. The so-called "fair-trade" laws limit competitive pricing for certain manufactured articles. Such limitations on competition are not necessarily all harmful, and some of them may be beneficial to the community as a whole; nevertheless, in the field of their application the effectiveness of competition as a community regulatory mechanism is destroyed, and only rarely is provision made for any other compensatory mechanism to take its place.

Some social reformers have gone so far as to assume that any kind of competition within or between human communities is harmful. A few political doctrines that are popular at the present time teach that if competition among the individuals in a human society could be abolished, a state of economic and social bliss would ensue. This view, for example, seems to be the basic philosophy of communism.

The competition that occurs among those species of plants and animals, including man, which together compose a primitive human community, is not necessarily unfavorable to the community or the competing species themselves. Competition among organs and cells of an individual organism may serve as an integrating force, because the several parts of the organism are dependent upon one another. The tendency of each part of every organism to expand leads that part to produce at the maximum rate needed for the welfare of the whole organism. Should any part of an organism expand too greatly, so that the welfare of the whole organism suffers, that part automatically injures itself. Other controlling mechanisms, in addition to competition, may therefore be needed to keep all the parts of the organism in balance (Holmes, 1948b: 26). Still, in an organized unit composed of several parts competition is a very important regulatory mechanism.

It may be doubted that political controls, exercised either

by a dictatorship or by a bureaucracy, can ever fully take the place of the law of supply and demand as a regulatory mechanism in human communities. The interrelations among the innumerable parts of a modern human community are so complex and change so rapidly that it is inconceivable that any ruler or bureau, no matter how wise or how well-intentioned, could, even with an army of assistants, maintain such a community very long in a state of health.

The law of supply and demand, nevertheless, is only one of the several regulatory mechanisms that control human communities and by itself will not maintain stability under all conditions. In order to prevent the recurrence of cycles of booms and depressions in a modern industrial community, other regulatory mechanisms also are needed (Boulding, 1945).

Cooperation Some of the most important regulatory mechanisms in human societies involve, in one way or another, cooperation among the members. Through cooperative efforts, every society achieves objectives which otherwise would be unattainable. As communities increase in complexity, higher and higher degrees of social cooperation become necessary for successful existence.

In a society composed of a single family, a large amount of cooperation is always in evidence. Although some of it is enforced by parental authority, most of it is given voluntarily. In a small society composed of several families, a number of men or women may operate temporarily as an organized unit for hunting, fishing, herding, cultivating, house building, religious practices, or feast preparation. Such a group may appoint one or more of its members as leaders, but control and discipline usually are exercised by group opinion. In a large society there may be a highly complex organization, but this also is based on cooperation among the various elements of which the society is composed.

A society cannot achieve its highest efficiency unless all, or nearly all, its members work together in harmony. A thief, arsonist, murderer, dog-poisoner, disease carrier, bully, or insane person can seriously disrupt the operations of an otherwise efficient social unit. Certain of the cooperative efforts of most human societies are, therefore, directed toward the maintenance of internal order. Other important cooperative efforts are directed toward securing protection against encroachment or warlike raids from neighboring communities.

Every phase of social life in a human community is, in fact, affected by controls that are imposed through cooperative effort. In the field of public health, to take one example, certain community-sponsored activities involve the building and maintenance of sanitary water systems, sewage systems, hospitals and clinics, the employment of public health officers, the training of physicians and nurses, and the care of the mentally ill. There may be quarantine of infectious diseases, compulsory vaccination, sanitary regulations, inspection of markets, food and drug laws, and other types of controls. Where these controls are to be successful in achieving their objectives, they must have the support or at least tolerance of the people.

Cooperation among the members of a human society often is organized under various types of institutions. These institutions range from the very informal to the highly organized. Certain institutions operate to promote desirable activities. Others, such as the police, operate in part to inhibit activities that are deemed harmful to the community.

Among the institutions that exist in every large human community are those concerned with internal security, military affairs, public health, religion, education, agriculture, business, transportation, communication, natural resources, individual welfare, and entertainment and recreation. Each of these types of institutions requires the services of a group of men who devote either a part or the whole of their time to the affairs of their particular organization. Each institution also accumulates property and has other vested interests in the community. A military organization, for example, is made up of officers and men of various ranks and of diverse special training. It owns weapons and ammunition, and probably also armories and forts. Its power may become so great that it absorbs an undue proportion of the available resources, so that in the end the community suffers. The same may happen with religious or business institutions. If the community is to survive, it must develop means for controlling the excesses of each of its parts while preserving the benefits which these parts provide. In other words, there must be cooperation among all elements of the human society.

The steady growth of cooperation among the citizens of our own country, and of the world as a whole, is one of the most encouraging features of the times. New volunteer groups are frequently being organized to work toward civic improvements of various kinds, to support research in particular fields, to alleviate suffering, or to promote other desirable objectives. Cooperative enterprises also are organized to manufacture, market, or buy certain commodities, to supply insurance to members, to furnish music, art, or lectures, or to provide other community benefits.

The success of many community-sponsored or local cooperative enterprises, however, does not necessarily imply that all types of business should be operated under public ownership either now or in the immediate future. Certain essential services, such as water supply, sewage disposal, and fire protection, are successfully provided, it is true, through municipal ownership and operation. Many of these successful publicly-owned enterprises are managed by boards, commissions, or departments that are responsible to the public but not under the direct influence of party politics. A separation of economic administration from political administration seems often to be desirable (Fairchild, 1952).

On the other hand, numerous experiments in public ownership or operation of such things as banks, housing, railroads, power plants, and manufacturing have ended unsatisfactorily. Politics, bureaucratic inefficiency, or graft may prevent the best functioning of such institutions. At the present stage of evolution of economic and political organization, private enterprise seems able to provide certain services more efficiently than government. Notwithstanding the high importance of social cooperation for the success of every human community, still other types of regulatory mechanisms are likely to be needed for a long time to come.

One of the major features of Marxist doctrine is its emphasis on competition among the social and economic classes. This competition among the classes is to be encouraged and increased until in the end the working class gains supreme power. From the ecologic point of view which I have here presented, however, competition is by no means the most important feature of human communities. On the contrary, cooperation among the classes is essential if any community is to remain in a state of health. Only by cooperation and by mutual tolerance and respect among its economic and social classes can a community achieve the highest success.

The democratic process as a regulatory mechanism The essence of the democratic process is that it is a kind of regulatory mechanism whereby all groups, classes, and individuals are accorded a voice in making the rules that govern the society of which they form a part. When community administration is truly democratic, any group that is suffering from an inequity in the distribution of the resources of the commonwealth or any other kind of inequality, or from any natural calamity, can bring its needs to the attention of its fellows. As the needs of any individual or group for assistance becomes greater, its importunities for succor are likely to become more vociferous and to command more immediate and more adequate relief. To the extent, therefore, to which the presumed greatness of a need affects the amount of attention given to it by the society, the democratic process is a regulatory mechanism.

The unity of biological systems of all ranks has been achieved in ways that are essentially democratic. In the individual organism, for example, the cells and organs cooperate on a general basis of equality, the objective being the success of the whole organism. There is no such thing as a dictator, or even a bureaucracy. The brain has no dominant position among the organs. It only carries out its particular functions, some of which involve coordination among certain other organs. But the other organs in their turn exercise a certain amount of control over the operations of the brain. For example, the brain is affected by the supply of oxygen, nutritive materials, and hormones carried by the circulatory system.

At a higher level of integration, the natural ecologic community also operates as an essentially democratic system. Certain species of green plants capture the energy from sunlight and through photosynthesis produce food substances out of relatively simple chemical compounds. Herbivores feed on the plants and transform the foods thus obtained into animal tissues. Carnivores in turn feed upon the herbivores. Various important services, in addition to the furnishing of food, are exchanged among the member species of such a community (Dice, 1952). However, no one species ever completely controls the operations of a natural community. Rather, the several species which together compose the community form a cooperating system.

In animal societies of all kinds, likewise, no particular individual ever holds a ruling position. The queen of a bee hive, for example, is merely an egg factory with no control over her offspring. It is true that in a band of mammals or birds some individuals may bully their companions because of their strength or aggressiveness. Also, some individuals may assume temporary responsibility for giving a warning of the approach of a dangerous predator. But even so they lack any general authority over the other members of their social group.

Most primitive societies of men also seem to be organized on a generally democratic basis. A certain individual in the tribe may be given a special responsibility, such as to serve as a medicine man or as a leader of a hunting or war party. In general, however, these persons are obeyed only in so far as they are able to provide effective leadership. Even the position of chief of a tribe is often more honorary than authoritative.

There can be no doubt that organization is essential to survival and success, in human societies just as in any biotic system. But there is no dictator in any biologic system other than a human society. I am in complete agreement with Pearl (1946: 128) that no man, or group of men, should ever be given more than a minimum of power over the souls, bodies, or lives of fellow men. Neither aristocrats, ecclesiastics, politicians, bankers, manufacturers, labor leaders, nor the proletariat can be trusted with power. Neither should any race, nation, economic or social class, or political group be permitted to hold more than its necessary minimum of authority, or to absorb more than its proper share of the world's goods.

This does not mean that the world's goods should be distributed equally among all living human individuals, or be given according to the needs of the individual irrespective of his value to society. On the contrary, the improvement of human societies through further evolution seems to require that those elements in the population which are of most value should be encouraged, while those which are harmful or unessential to the society should be discouraged.

It must be admitted that true democratic processes are not always employed even in a presumably democratic country, such as the United States. Pressure groups, special interests, and pork-barrel politicians often are able to secure for themselves or their constituents an unfair proportion of the available resources. As a biologist I am unable to suggest how the legislative and administrative functions of our government can be made more truly democratic. I can state, nevertheless, without fear of successful contradiction, that the more completely the political and economic administration of a country can be made to function through the operation of automatic regulatory mechanisms, the more efficient it will be.

Ideal regulatory mechanisms

For the most satisfactory functioning of the political and economic systems of the world it will be necessary to perfect still further those regulatory mechanisms that now exist in our cultures, and to devise many new ones for the control of each human community. Cannon (1941) has pointed out that the regulatory mechanisms in our existing societies give only imperfect control of economic processes, with the result that violent fluctuations from boom to depression occur quite frequently.

A good regulatory mechanism must be automatic in its action, prompt in its response, uniformly dependable in application, not easily subject to change according to legislative or bureaucratic whims, smooth and effective in operation by increasing or decreasing its control in proportion to the need for it, and economical in that it should itself consume as little as possible of the resources of the ecosystem.

When a controlling mechanism yields benefits mostly for a particular class in the community, this class often is charged with the cost of maintaining the control. Thus, the cost of maintaining a highway patrol may be met, at least in part, from fees charged for licenses to drive automobiles and trucks. The Social Security program of old-age benefits is financed by taxes on the workers who expect to benefit, and on their employers. Such a distribution of the costs of a controlling mechanism has the advantage that those who are bearing the cost are likely to be concerned that their investment is economically managed and that the mechanism itself achieves its objectives. If the class to be benefited were always required to pay at least part of the cost of the program, much less political pressure would be exerted to secure certain types of government support.

Many kinds of public institutions, however, are of such value to the whole community that their cost cannot properly be charged to any one particular class. The cost of maintaining schools, for example, cannot properly be charged to the students or their parents alone. Many other types of public institutions serve all the people, and consequently should be supported and managed by the community as a whole.

Certain activities are of patent value to the whole community, but at the same time may be of particular importance to one or more of its classes. Thus, the grazing of live stock in the national forests is of great economic significance to those who range their stock there. Indeed, certain stockmen have attempted to obtain permanent rights to graze their stock on these public lands. Yet, if the forest values are to be maintained, the Forest Service, which manages the forests for the interests of the whole public, must be free to make decisions concerning carrying capacity and the proper seasons for grazing. Some of these forest values concern timber growing, watershed protection, and recreation. The interests of the stockmen must be considered, of course, but no one class should ever be given special rights at the expense of the other classes in the community. It is not easy, however, to devise controlling mechanisms that are practical and at the same time fair to all the classes and special interests that are involved in a complex human community.

Our knowledge of the regulatory mechanisms that operate in modern communities is woefully inadequate. The operation of supply and demand as a regulatory mechanism has received much attention from economists, but far less information is available about the effectiveness of other possible types of controls. Studies should be made of all the types of mechanisms which in any way regulate human communities, in order to discover their effectiveness under various conditions of habitat, heredity, and culture. These regulatory mechanisms will then need to be improved so that they will effectively control our existing human communities. Man has the great advantage over all other animals that he is able to discover through research the laws that govern the operation of the world, and to use this knowledge to plan for his future.

One of the important problems now before man is to develop mechanisms for controlling population density that will replace the natural regulatory mechanisms of predation, famine, disease, and war. If man can adjust his numbers to the resources of his habitat, without the necessity of killing in some way the surplus individuals, he will have made a great stride forward. The practice of birth control, unfortunately, may operate to reduce disproportionately the numbers of children produced by the more intelligent and more prudent members of society.

Many other regulatory mechanisms besides birth control are needed if modern human communities are to function smoothly. The economic law of supply and demand has often failed to prevent surpluses and scarcities, especially when the control of an important commodity has fallen under the domination of some person or "trust," and many of the attempts at a planned economy through government control have also failed.

According to the hypothesis here advanced, a main function of government is to discover and organize appropriate regulatory mechanisms for the control of the political unit concerned. Every government should continually scrutinize the operation of the mechanisms it has set up. Further, it should constantly attempt to improve its regulatory mechanisms, and to this end it should support appropriate research institutes. But it may strongly be doubted that any individual or government bureau can itself effectively fix the details of rates, prices, allotments, rations, subsidies, quotas, or similar items of everyday economic life.

Our concept of the function of government is very different from that of most past writers on the subject. The evils of government dictatorship must be avoided as well as those of *laissez faire*. The police state is highly objectionable, no matter what person or class is in control, and irrespective of the degree of altruism the rulers may exhibit.

It should be possible for government to provide over-all planning without regimentation (Mannheim, 1950: 29). Leadership is needed to encourage each special group in the community to develop plans for promoting its own interests in a way that will not hamper the activities of related groups, and will not lay a financial burden on the commonwealth.

Governments often have a tendency to smother innovations by the people (Malin, 1947: 325), and thus to retard evolution. Most social planning, too, seems to aim at freezing the presumably most desirable existing cultural values (Kroeber, 1946: 384). A special effort must be made, therefore, to provide means for testing new suggestions and inventions, and for incorporating those that are useful into the body of existing government machinery. At the same time, due caution must be used in accepting new suggestions just for the sake of change, without adequate testing.

Stability in human communities

To maintain their stability, human communities have evolved many types of regulatory mechanisms, some of which have been described in the preceding paragraphs. The pages of history are replete with examples of the attempts of particular societies to devise new and more effective mechanisms to control their internal organization. Many of these attempts have resulted in failure. But every continuing society has of necessity developed more or less effective mechanisms for community control under the special conditions of its existence.

Stability is one of the most desirable features of any community. In the individual organism and in the community, stability seems actually to be more important than economy. Cannon (1939: 317) has pointed out that the individual organism, to maintain its homeostasis (state of balance), will throw away not only water and salts, but even sugar if necessary. Human communities faced with a crisis such as famine, war, or other catastrophe, may likewise uneconomically consume or discard many valuable materials in the attempt to maintain their stability.

Among complex human communities, those which are controlled by many diverse regulatory mechanisms may be presumed to be the most stable. This should be true because in simple communities, relatively fewer ecologic regulatory mechanisms are necessary than in larger and more complex communities. The greater the number of regulatory mechanisms in a community, the less the likelihood that any fluctuation in community composition reaches a serious amplitude before being brought under control.

We should expect, then, that the most stable human communities would be composed of many diverse types of plants and animals, some of them domesticated, and that the human population would be composed of many specialized types including workers, administrators, and thinkers, but no unproductive classes. The members of the well-adjusted human community, furthermore, will be complexly cooperative in numerous ways. The regulatory mechanisms will be many and various, so that a crop failure in one locality, an epidemic of disease, or any other type of catastrophe will be compensated for without serious alteration in the community.

Safety factors   Every organism, to maintain itself, must possess a high factor of safety in each of its more essential parts. It has been pointed out by Meltzer (1907) that the more important organs of the human body carry rather high factors of safety. Thus, the bones have a resistance to crushing far above any internal stress that is ever likely to be encountered. Most land vertebrates have two kidneys and two lungs, where one would suffice for all ordinary uses. Likewise, the testes and ovaries produce many more germ cells than can possibly achieve fertilization. Many other mechanisms in the body are duplicated, for example, the parallel sets of digestive ferments. Furthermore, many of the organs of the body have the ability to effect self-repair, the nerve cells being the one conspicuous exception.

Many factors of safety are operative in human communities. The storage of food and other supplies against future need is a good example. Supplies that do not rapidly deteriorate can be stockpiled to provide a reserve against emergencies. A good transportation system is another factor of safety against local emergencies, because supplies which suddenly become needed in one area can be brought in from some neighboring community or even from a distance.

Another type of factor of safety is the provision of alternate facilities for accomplishing a desired result. If the wheat crop is short in one year, for example, other cereals, potatoes, or similar foods which happen to be in ample supply may be partially sub-

stituted in the diet for wheat. It is always better to have two factories that both manufacture an essential commodity, rather
than to depend on a single large factory which might be dis-
abled by a fire or other disaster. When telephone and telegraph
lines are destroyed by storm or flood, the alternate use of radio
has often proved extremely useful. In a war emergency with its
increased demand for labor, the reserve labor of women, children, and over-age men has often prevented a severe labor shortage. These and many other types of factors of safety are operative in a complex human community and contribute to
community stability.

For those essential services in a community that are in danger
of being interrupted from time to time, it would be the part of
wisdom always to have reserve sources of supply. If the national
supply of natural rubber, for example, can be cut off because of
a war, then at least a few synthetic rubber factories should be
kept in readiness at all times on a standby basis. Some standby
factories may in times of peace produce nonessential but useful
commodities whose temporary lack during an emergency will
not be serious to the welfare of the community.

Probably no nation in the history of the world has been more
prompt in the alleviation of distress among its citizens than the
United States. We have been able to extend prompt relief because of our excellent transportation systems and because
of our highly developed organization for the distribution of
food and supplies. Above all, however, we have been able to
extend help to local communities in distress because in the country as a whole there has always been a sufficient surplus of food
and other materials to allow us to give a share to our neighbors
without seriously depriving ourselves.

Hard times inevitably come to every human community. A
crop failure due to unfavorable weather or to a disease outbreak
may bring widespread distress. Disruption of the ordinary ma-

chinery of food distribution by war or by industrial strife may also bring hardship to many persons. Such disturbances can never be entirely prevented. It is possible, however, to prepare against certain kinds of emergencies by carrying reserve facilities and reserve supplies. Not every contingency can be prepared for, but provision should be made for at least the more frequently recurring types of disaster and distress.

The population density that a region can support at a specified level of culture is not the maximum that can be maintained under the average conditions of the environment, but rather that density which can be carried successfully through a series of adverse harvests or other kinds of disaster. No people can live in security if all its resources are being currently consumed. Some reserve of supplies should be built up during periods of plenty, to be used during periods of adversity. A little fat is desirable for a society as well as for an individual, to serve as a factor of safety. A slight excess of productive capacity and of transportation is also necessary if distress is to be avoided during emergencies. For these reasons, a slight underpopulation will always be preferable to complete saturation.

Supply of leaders   All men, including leaders in politics, industry, medicine, law, engineering, science, art, and other essential fields in a human society, must ultimately die. If the society is to continue to function and perhaps to advance, its leaders must continually be replaced by younger men. Every society, therefore, must have suitable means for selecting and training a steady supply of leaders (Cannon, 1941: 9).

The rapid progress made in the past half-century in technology and science has undoubtedly been due largely to the very considerable number of exceptionally competent and experienced men who have occupied positions of leadership in their communities. It is the good fortune of mankind that, through a happy combination of democracy and available surplus resources, these persons were given the opportunity to demonstrate their abilities, and that they were supported by their societies.

The potential leaders in any given field of endeavor, however, always constitute a very small proportion of the total population. The discovery of young men with capabilities for leadership, and their adequate education, are thus essential for the continuing welfare of every society.

A serious difficulty here is that we have no reliable criterion for the recognition of superior ability. Nor do we make adequate provision for the education of promising students beyond high school. In fact, tuition and living expenses are so high at most colleges and universities that as a rule only well-to-do families can give their children an advanced education. As a result, many competent young men and women are denied the opportunity to develop their abilities fully. The giving of tuition scholarships to the more able college students, and especially to graduate students, might aid in increasing the supply of trained persons in our societies. Other devices to increase the supply of such persons should be sought.

Preservation of the independence of the individual

In the human communities that possess strong regulatory mechanisms, there is always the danger that the initiative and independence of the individual will be too greatly curtailed. Any system which imposes rigid limitations on occupations, for example, must ultimately hinder the advance of human welfare. In a very simple human society, few restraints to individual action may be required, though it may be doubted that any society is so lacking in artificial controls that the behavior of its individual members is completely uninhibited.

Individual freedom must of necessity be curtailed to a considerable degree in societies that have a complex organization. Not

only is the behavior of each individual affected by the training
he has received in his youth, and by the approval or disapproval
of his associates, but rules and laws set many definite limits to
his activities. Customs and laws are essential for the orderly
maintenance of a complex society. It is possible, however, for
customs and laws to become so rigid that they handicap the evolution of heredity and of culture.

Improvement in culture within the confines of an existing
community will be possible only if the individuals are permitted
to try out types of behavior which are new to their community.
Also, individual human beings work most effectively if they are
given a considerable degree of freedom in their activities. A
complex community, however, must insist on general conformity to its customs and laws if it is to function smoothly. It may
be assumed, then, that the most stable and at the same time
most progressive kind of human community will be one in which
there exists a large variety of effective community regulatory
mechanisms, a high degree of social cooperation, and at the
same time the maximum possible freedom of behavior for the
individual citizens.

SELECTED REFERENCES

Boulding, Kenneth. 1945. The economics of peace. New York: Prentice-
    Hall.
Boulding, Kenneth. 1948. Economic analysis. New York: Harper and Bros.
Cannon, Walter B. 1941. The body physiologic and the body politic.
    Science, 93: 1–10.
Griffin, Clare E. 1949. Enterprise in a free society. Chicago: Richard D.
    Irwin.

Hawley, Amos H. 1950. Human ecology; a theory of community structure. Chap. 9. New York: Ronald Press Co.
Lippmann, Walter. 1937. An inquiry into the principles of the good society. Boston: Little, Brown and Co.
Mannheim, Karl. 1950. Freedom, power, and democratic planning. New York: Oxford University Press.
Pearl, Raymond. 1946. Man the animal. Lecture I. Bloomington, Indiana: Principia Press.

Limits of Human Population Density

CHAPTER X

The number of human beings who can be supported on a given unit of land area varies tremendously from place to place, depending upon the character of the climate, physiography, and soil; upon the kinds of organisms which are associated with man; upon the available resources; upon the state of culture of the people; and upon their standard of living. For every region there must be a maximum density of population that can be supported at any given level of culture and standard of living. Many authors (Malthus, 1826; Keller, 1915; East, 1923; W. S. Thompson, 1944; Pearson and Harper, 1945; and others) have pointed out these relationships. The fundamental laws that govern human populations are the same as those for other organisms (Pearl, 1937: 51).

It should be emphasized, however, that human societies vary in their standard of living, and this seriously affects the density of population that each society can tolerate. Human communities also vary in culture, and consequently in the efficiency with which they utilize the resources of their habitats. Overpopulation and underpopulation, therefore, must always be relative terms only (E. F. Penrose, 1934: 49). No estimate of the maximum limit of density for any human population can have meaning unless the limiting factors of resources, technology, and standard of living are also specified.

An area may have too sparse a population for the most efficient utilization of its resources. At the present time, however, only a few parts of the world appear to be seriously underpopulated. Many regions, on the contrary, have such dense populations that the inhabitants are unable to achieve a comfortable standard of living. An increase of population is nevertheless taking place in many parts of the world, and this increase is very rapid in many sections that are backward in their economic development. In some regions, such as parts of India and of China, famine is always imminent, and even a partial crop failure may result in widespread suffering among the people. Because the population of the world is rapidly increasing it seems certain that overpopulation will be a serious problem for many years to come.

Overpopulation may bring many ills to man, including malnutrition or even starvation, unsatisfactory housing, low standard of living, inadequate education, lack of control of contagious disease, over-work, heavy mortality rate, industrial and social unrest, war between nations, and stagnation or perhaps deterioration in culture. Not all of these ills, however, appear necessarily in every overpopulated area. It has been pointed out by Hsu (1953: 289), for instance, that although many parts of China are evidently overpopulated, the Chinese people have shown little tendency to attack their neighbors. On the other hand, overpopulation in Italy was at least used as a pretext for waging aggressive war.

Overpopulation will ultimately be reduced by various regulatory mechanisms, but at a terrible price in human misery. If the recurrent disasters of famine, war, internal unrest, and other ills which sometimes are related to overpopulation are to be averted, the birth rate of every country must be adjusted to the population it can support. Some countries already have adjusted their birth rates to approximately a maintenance level, but in many other countries, even in some already overpopulated ones, the population is still increasing.

The present world population

Certain areas of the world are very inhospitable to man and can support only sparse populations. In the more productive areas, on the other hand, the people often live densely crowded together. Pearl (1939: 266) estimated that in 1930 an average of less than ten persons per square mile was living on 57 per cent of the land area of the world. The average density in 1930 for the whole land surface of the globe, including desert, glacier, and cultivated land, was 40.9 individuals per square mile (*op. cit.*: 252). In twenty countries, on the other hand, the population density averaged more than 125 per square mile, and in Belgium it was 705 (*op. cit.*: 272).

In some areas dominated by desert, mountain, or snow and ice, the human population is extremely scanty. Semi-arid areas also have sparse populations. In 1940, for example, one or more counties in nine states of the United States had population densities below 1.0 person per square mile. One county in South Dakota had an average population density of only 0.1 person per square mile. In the United States as a whole, the population density averaged 44.2 persons per square mile (U. S. Bureau of Census, 1942).

From the calculations of Deevey (1951), the total number of human beings on earth in 1951 may be taken to be 2.1×10^9 (2.1 billion) individuals. Assuming a mean longevity of 25 years, the rate of reproduction is about 84,000,000 persons per year. The average mean weight per person may be taken to be 60.55 kg. The total weight of all persons living on the earth in 1951 thus amounted to 1.27 $\times$ 10 ^{11} kilograms (279,400,000,000 lbs.); 5.09 $\times$ 10 ^{9} kg. represented the annual reproduction and growth. Of this amount, 35.7 per cent is organic material. The annual production of human protoplasm, therefore, may be estimated to be 1.8 $\times$ 10 ^{9} kg. (3,960,000,000 lbs.). This rate of production presumably exceeds that of any other species of organism.

Over the world as a whole, the rate of population increase in the recent past was estimated by Pearl in 1939 (p. 255) to be about 1 per cent per year. At that rate the world population would double in about 70 years. In numerous countries (*op. cit.*: 276), the populations are growing at annual rates of 2, 3, 4, or even more than 5 per cent per year.

One part of the world that at the present time is much too densely populated for its resources is the island of Puerto Rico. This island was estimated in 1946 to have a population of 618 persons per square mile, or about two persons for each acre of arable land (R. C. Cook, 1947). In the same year, the average population of the continental United States was only 47 persons per square mile. The average standard of living on Puerto Rico is deplorably low. Many of its people live under conditions of abject poverty. Of those aged 10 years or above in 1949, 31.5 per cent were illiterate (Coombs and Davis, 1950). Unfortunately, the population of Puerto Rico is still growing. In 1949, the crude birth rate was 39.0 and the crude death rate only 10.8 per 1000 inhabitants, with the result that the population was increasing at a rapid rate. Furthermore, there is no evidence of a decline in the birth rate (Coombs and Davis, 1950).

Factors in population density

The actual density of population that any region can support may be assumed to be controlled by the interaction of the heredity of the people, their type of culture, their standard of living, and the resources available in their habitat. These several factors are very complexly interrelated and cannot be considered separately.

The role that heredity plays in controlling human population densities is largely unknown. It is possible that certain stocks of men are naturally more fertile than others. Variability in fertility is obvious among strains of domestic animals. Inbreeding often decreases fertility in laboratory animals. There is a strong suspicion that inbreeding in man also may decrease fertility. Most human populations, however, seem naturally to be highly fertile. It may consequently be doubted that heredity usually plays any direct role in controlling human population density.

The relationship between population density, state of culture, and standard of living has been summarized by Sumner and Keller (1927, Vol. 1: 46) in a law which states that the density of population in any given region varies directly with the state of culture and inversely with the standard of living. The density of population that a given amount of available resources can support at a given standard of living, for instance, will be greater for a high than for a low level of technology. A population that has a simple type of technology, or a poor economic organization, may be unable to utilize its natural resources efficiently. In a given area, a dense population, if well organized socially and economically, may have a considerably higher standard of living than a sparse population that has a more primitive organization. On the other hand, for any given state of culture and any given resources, the standard of living will be lower the greater the density of population, down to the population density at which competition is no longer a factor.

In the Kalahari desert of Africa, for instance, it is estimated that with the there prevailing hunting and food-gathering type of culture only one family of Bushmen on the average can be supported on each 40 to 200 square miles (Havemeyer,

1929: 9). In a more productive area in Canada, the hunting area of one group of Algonquian Indians was estimated by Hallowell (1949) to average 55.6 square miles per person; of another group, 6.2 square miles. For comparison, it is estimated that under a nomadic pastoral type of culture 100 to 200 acres of land will support one person, while on rich land with skillful farming one to two acres will suffice (Semple, 1911: 61).

When the culture of a given region is improved so that more efficient use is made of the resources of the ecosystem, the maximum density of population that can be supported in that area can often be increased. It cannot be expected, however, that improvements in agricultural, industrial, economic, and social techniques will forever continue to allow increases in the density of every human population. In fact, in a region that has only meager resources, such as a desert, the culture may be unable to advance beyond a very simple type, and the population must thus always remain sparse.

Increases in technical knowledge and improvements in the social organization that allow a more effective use of natural resources will allow an increase in the standard of living and/or in the density of population that can be supported (Fairchild, 1939: 70 ff.). Populations, however, often increase rapidly when the economic situation permits, while technological improvements usually come more slowly. Furthermore, a practical limit must ultimately be reached beyond which improvements in the utilization of the natural resources of any region will yield only decreasing results. The law of diminishing returns must in time become effective here as elsewhere.

Food is one of the most essential elements for human life, as it is for the life of all organisms. The quantity of food available to a society has thus a powerful effect in controlling its density of population. Any society which has a surplus of food has a tendency to increase its population (R. C. Cook, 1947). Unless war, disease, or other regulatory mechanisms intervene, the population density will ultimately reach a level at which the food supply is just enough to feed all the people. A community which is in such a state of food balance may suffer disastrous starvation in consequence of any serious temporary reduction in the food supply, such as might be caused by a partial crop failure.

The maximum carrying capacity for human population of any region is thus largely fixed by the productivity of human food in the area. Certain industrial countries, however, are able to support populations larger than their own food resources permit by importing foods and other materials from abroad. It is probable that many of the countries that are now exporting foods and raw materials will in time build up their own populations and industries to levels where they will no longer have a surplus for export (Vogt, 1946). The exchange of manufactured goods for food and raw materials, nevertheless, will undoubtedly continue to allow dense industrial populations to thrive in certain regions.

For a given state of technological knowledge and of economic and political organization, the resources of a given area may be used to support either a relatively dense population at a low standard of living, or a somewhat less dense population at a higher standard of living. The increase during the present century of population density in India and China, for example, has probably been accompanied by a lowering of the standard of living in those countries (Baker, 1928: 356). Freedom from want can be achieved only by a proper balance between the resources of the habitat, the existing state of culture, and the population density. Even then, freedom from want must always be a relative term, varying with each change in the standard of living.

The food productivity of the earth could perhaps support

three billion persons on the Asiatic standard of living. This is a considerably greater number than the present estimated world population of 2.1 billions. But at the United States standard of living, the present food productivity of the globe could support fewer than a billion persons (Pearson and Harper, 1945: 69). The standard of living of the continents other than North America, therefore, can be raised only by great increases in their productiveness, or by drastic reductions in their populations. Even if a considerable amount of food were to be exported from America, with a resulting decrease in our own standard of living, and presented as a gift to the people of the overpopulated parts of Europe and Asia, little more than very temporary relief would likely be gained (W. S. Thompson, 1949). The only effect to be expected from such food shipments is that the populations of those overcrowded areas, due to their high reproductive rate, will increase still further, thereby aggravating rather than solving the problem.

If it were possible to divert to the production of food and of other useful commodities the efforts and resources now devoted to preparations for war, the estimates of total world population that could be supported in comfort might be much increased. Unfortunately, there seems no likelihood that war among nations will soon be abolished.

One element in standard of living that sometimes is overlooked is the space needed for each individual and for each family. It is true that man is a social animal and likes to live in the near vicinity of his neighbors. Most individuals, nevertheless, resent too close a contact with other persons and prefer to have homes of their own to which they may at times retire. Human populations can endure heavy crowding for a short time, but they do not then thrive best. Under crowded conditions, disease spreads easily, family life is disturbed, and individual independence and happiness are threatened.

Optimum population density

As has already been pointed out, a population can be too sparse to develop or maintain a culture capable of making effective use of the resources of its habitat. On the other hand, overpopulation may result in a deplorably low standard of living and adversely affect the culture. For a given locality and for a given type of culture, accordingly, there may be presumed to be an upper as well as a lower limit of effective population density (Wissler, 1929: 39).

The optimum density of population is that density at which a society in a given state of culture is able to utilize the resources of its habitat most efficiently (Carr-Saunders, 1922: 201; Fairchild, 1939: 88). The optimum density of population necessarily varies with the state of culture and with the amount and kind of available resources. The optimum density is also affected by the amount and kind of foreign trade, and by the internal and external restrictions on trade imposed by the governments concerned (Gottlieb, 1949). Any area that has a population density less than the optimum may be said to be underpopulated, while any area that has more than the optimum density is overpopulated.

In the past it has been too fatuously assumed by some that an increase of population is always desirable. But in each area there must ultimately come a time when an increase of population can lead only to a lowering of the standard of living of the population. Should the excess of population become very great, widespread distress must occur at every period of crop deficiency.

In using the term "optimum density of population" we must not expect such an optimum to have sharp limits. In part, the optimum density will also be dependent upon our point of view.

The ecclesiastic, for example, might wish the population to increase so that there will be more souls to be saved. The real-estate booster may desire a dense population so that he can make more sales. The military man, if short-sighted, may wish for more cannon fodder. The local politician may desire more votes which he can control. But the statesman may be apprehensive of the results of overcrowding. The conservationist, fearful of wasteful exploitation, may desire a sparse rather than a dense population. The boundaries to the optimum of population density will thus always be rather vague. The optimum density itself must fluctuate from year to year depending upon annual variations in the productivity of the habitat.

Few estimates have been made of the optimum population density for any country. Whelpton, Eldridge, and Siegel (1947: 64), however, are of the opinion that the optimum population density for the United States is at least several million less than its present population of more than 150 million. At our present stage of culture and technology, according to this estimate, our population is already too large. With a smaller population we could have a higher standard of living. If this be true, then our population can be supported at our present high standard of living only because we are exploiting our nonrenewable natural resources such as petroleum, coal, and iron, and are over-utilizing such renewable resources as lumber. Many demographers, however, would not agree that the present population of the United States is above the optimum density.

Possible increase in resources

The resources available to man can be increased in many ways. An increase in resources occurs, for example, whenever a new deposit of a useful mineral is discovered. Technological advances, also, have in the recent past greatly increased the re-

sources available to many modern communities. Improvements
in the distribution of materials have resulted in bringing a
greater amount and variety of commodities to consumers.

Development and conservation of natural resources   Many of
the natural resources of the world are at present being utilized
to only a fraction of their full capacity (Sinnott, 1945). By the
better development of the known resources, the discovery of
new resources, and the conservation of those resources that are
now being overused or wasted, the world can be made a better
place for human life.

At present, we actually waste many valuable resources. Sewage is an example of a valuable resource that frequently is
wasted. In parts of Asia, especially in China, human excrement
is generally used as fertilizer (Pearson and Harper, 1945),
though this practice permits the spread of many kinds of diseases. In North America, however, sewage is not only generally
discarded, but often poured into streams or lakes, where it pol-
l .es the waters, destroys the natural aquatic organisms, and
endangers the health of the people who live nearby. Adequate
methods are available for treating sewage in disposal plants and
rendering it wholly safe for use as fertilizer (Winslow, 1952,
Chap. 4). Most cities, unfortunately, continue to pour their
sewage into some convenient stream where most of its potential
value is wasted.

The ruinous exploitation of natural resources must be carefully guarded against. There is a special need for conservation
of the soil. All human cultures are based ultimately on the productivity of the soil. Measures for the conservation and proper
utilization of the soil are thus of paramount importance to the
future of the human race, as has been ably pointed out by H. H.
Bennett (1939), Graham (1944), and many others.

The earth is said, by Mather (1944), to contain an adequate
supply of coal, petroleum, iron, and other minerals to support a

human population of any size that is likely to be attained in the near future. Other scientists, however, dispute this assertion. In any event, these nonrenewable resources must not be too rapidly depleted if the world is in future to have a supply of raw materials sufficient to support an industrial civilization. Forests, grazing lands, and natural stocks of fish and wild animals supply many materials of immediate use to man. These biotic resources, also, need to be utilized conservatively and wisely, so that they may continue to supply man's needs to the maximum possible extent.

Technological advances Space does not permit me to dwell here on the many improvements in man's material welfare which can be expected from the invention of new mechanical and biological devices and processes (Brown, 1954). I would point out, however, that many possible sources of power for man's use still remain undeveloped. Great potential sources of waterpower in many parts of the world are unharnessed. No effective means has yet been devised for making use of the energy in the ocean tides. The tremendous power present in the winds of the earth is still largely unused. The invention of practical means for storing and transporting power efficiently might enable man better to utilize these and other potential sources of energy. We await also the invention of effective devices for converting directly into power some part of the solar energy that falls every day upon the earth (Daniels, 1949).

Improvements in the domestic varieties of plants and animals have in the recent past greatly increased the resources available to man. Further increases in the productivity of man's crops and herds can confidently be expected to result from a continuation of research and controlled breeding. According to an estimate by Baker (1928), agricultural production in the United States seems likely to keep pace with the increase in population until the total population reaches about 200 millions.

Improvements in the distribution of resources   Many of the earth's resources occur in areas of sparse population. Other resources cannot be effectively utilized until they are combined with resources that occur in distant areas. Thus, iron ore and coal must be brought together before steel can be manufactured. Many of the commodities which are used in modern communities are transported from distant regions. Improvements in facilities for transporting and distributing materials can consequently increase greatly the resources available to every human community.

The social and economic organization of a society also affects its population density. If the society is divided into wealthy and very poor classes, as is true in many parts of the world today, the usual mechanisms that control population density may be hampered in their operation. In a "share-cropper" system, for example, where most of the work is performed by human labor, a large family may be an economic advantage. The system that keeps the standard of living low for the very poor class keeps fertility in that class high. An equitable distribution of wealth and opportunity for education among the several social classes is therefore essential for the orderly control of population density.

Relation of energy to population density

The ultimate maximum limit of population that can be supported by any ecosystem is determined basically by the amount of energy available in it in the form of food or power (O. P. Pearson, 1948; Brown, 1954, Chap. 5). Food and power are to some degree interchangeable, though not completely so.

Food that is eaten by man or other animals produces energy; animals require energy for the muscular work they perform, for reproductive activities, digestion, breathing, circulation of blood, excretion of urea and other wastes, and for numerous additional kinds of physiologic activities which are necessary just to keep alive (Brody, 1945). In their daily lives, all animals require a certain amount of energy which they must obtain from their food. It is proper, then, to evaluate foods in terms of the energy they can supply. However, foods also contain many elements essential for life whose value cannot be expressed wholly in terms of energy. The lack of a particular vitamin in the diet of an animal, for instance, may prevent it from operating efficiently, or lead to its death.

Wood, coal, petroleum, and other organic materials are utilized by man for the production of heat and power. Many of the materials elaborated by green plants can by proper industrial processes be oxidized (burned), thus producing heat. This heat can then be used in steam engines to produce power. Some food materials produced by plants, especially the carbohydrates such as sugar and starch, may also be used to produce substances such as gas or alcohol, which can be used directly in special types of engines to supply power.

Conversely, power may be used to aid in the production, by mechanical means, of food and other necessities for the life of man. Much mechanical power is thus consumed in the growing of modern farm crops. Mechanical power may also be employed for the processing or transportation of food, activities which might otherwise require the consumption of a certain quantity of food by man or his domestic animals to furnish the necessary muscular power. The direct manufacture of food from inorganic materials through the use of power, on the other hand, is not yet practical.

Plants and animals also use a small amount of energy that is obtained from other sources than their food. The wind distributes the pollen, seeds, and spores of plants; it also serves to disperse certain kinds of animals or their disseminules. Water currents in lakes, streams, and oceans distribute whole plants and animals and also the reproductive units of certain of these organisms. The total amount of energy utilized by organisms in these ways, however, is very small.

A more important direct use of energy is the absorption by plants and animals of part of the solar energy that falls upon them, or is obtained indirectly through transfer from the surrounding air, water, or soil. By such direct or indirect absorption of heat, the body temperatures of organisms often are raised appreciably and their life processes thereby accelerated. Energy obtained in this way enables warm-blooded vertebrates to conserve that part of their food which otherwise would have to be oxidized in order to maintain a proper level of body temperature.

Man utilizes energy in many ways. He expends energy for his metabolic processes and for the maintenance of his body temperature. In addition, even primitive man utilizes the power supplied by his dogs and other domestic animals for assistance in hunting, for help in transporting his goods, and for other services. Modern industrial man utilizes power in agriculture, in transportation, in industry, in comfortable living, in war, and in many other phases of his complicated life.

A part of the energy that modern man utilizes is obtained directly from the sun through the absorption of radiant energy to warm his own body or that of his domestic organisms. A part is obtained more indirectly through the use of winds and water currents to supply power for various purposes such as sailing boats or running hydroelectric plants. Still another part of the energy used by man is obtained from the burning of coal and petroleum, materials derived from plants and animals that lived in past ages. The energy that drives the human body is derived from the sun indirectly through the plants, and still more indirectly through food chains that involve animals also.

All the energy that is obtained by man from winds or water

currents, or from substances elaborated by plants through photosynthesis, came primarily from the sun, just as does the small amount of radiant energy that man uses directly. It may, therefore, be said that at the present time the radiant heat and light from the sun, past and present, is the source of all the energy that allows man and other living beings to exist on earth. This energy also furnishes all the power that drives man's industrial machinery.

Should man ever learn to harness the ocean tides and utilize their energy, this tidal energy would provide a source of power that is not dependent on radiant energy from the sun. Atomic energy, also, if it can be applied to constructive rather than destructive uses, is not derived from the sun at all, though the process is presumably similar to that which produces the energy of the sun.

Of the radiant energy from the sun that falls upon the earth, only a very small fraction is utilized by organisms or in any other way that aids man. Riley (1944: 134) estimated that only 0.18 ± 0.12 per cent of the solar energy that falls on the earth is fixed by plants. Most of the radiant heat that comes to the earth from the sun is reflected or otherwise dissipated, so that it is wasted as far as the earth is concerned. It seems unlikely that all this radiant heat can ever be captured for man's use, though it is not impossible that at least a part of it may in future be utilized as a direct source of power.

It is possible that our chemists will in time learn how to synthesize foodstuffs directly from inorganic materials, using the energy from the sun directly or indirectly but without the use of plants. That day, however, seems far off. It appears unlikely that any engine or method will be invented in the near future which will transform the radiant energy from the sun into food and other materials essential for human existence so cheaply as does the chlorophyll of green plants. Consequently, it seems

probable that man must for a long time and perhaps forever remain dependent to a considerable degree on the plants and animals that live in association with him.

The efficiency of chlorophyll for producing food and other
desirable materials can undoubtedly be increased. Our agricultural experiment stations and plant breeders are continually improving the yield in food that an acre of farm land can produce.
Yet there must ultimately be a practical limit to the productiveness of crops on a given area under any given climate. Unless
new sources of power are discovered, there must then be an ultimate limit to the productivity of the earth.

The density of human population that can be supported on a
given area has, as we have seen, a general relationship to the
state of culture, which in turn is to a considerable degree dependent upon the amount of utilizable energy in the habitat.
The amount of energy consumed per individual in a human
community may thus be used as a rough measure of its level of
culture. In a state of culture, for instance, which includes only
hunting, fishing, and the gathering of natural plant foods, almost the only energy available to man is that which he produces by his own muscular exertions. With the use of the energy
produced by domestic animals, a much more complex type of
culture can be developed and a more dense population supported. Part of the reason the dense human population now
living in the most highly industrialized parts of the world can
be supported is that our modern culture is able to utilize the
energy stored in coal and petroleum (White, 1943).

The energy obtained from coal, petroleum, water power, and
to a lesser degree from wind power, is extremely important to
man's present industrial culture (Hubbert, 1949). These sources
of power aid in the growing of crops, in transportation, and in
the processing of foods. Furthermore, they make it unnecessary
to utilize current plant products for most of our annual power

requirements. Nevertheless, the maximum limit of human population in the world seems likely to be fixed, for a long time to come, by the maximum productivity of green plants. As the resources of coal and oil stored in the earth become exhausted, we shall have to utilize a greater proportion of the productivity of green plants to supply power for our industrial operations; we must then decrease to that extent the amount of food available for human consumption.

The population of the United States is at present increasing fairly rapidly, and the same is true of most other parts of the world. With the improvements in technology that may confidently be expected in the immediate future, the standard of living of our citizens will undoubtedly rise for at least a few decades, even while the population density is increasing. No man can predict just how soon the interrelations among the factors of available resources, improvements in technology, and increasing density of population will begin to produce a leveling off or perhaps decline in our standard of living. It is fatuous, however, to assume that technological advances can be depended upon to permit the present rate of population increase to continue indefinitely without serious danger to human welfare.

Many parts of the land areas of the globe are arid, frigid, or have other unfavorable features that make them undesirable habitats for man. Most of the more productive lands are already fully populated (Bowman, 1937). The capacity of the earth to support an expanding population must ultimately reach its limit. No one, however, can estimate what the limit of human population density now is for any given region, or what it will be ten years hence.

It seems certain that the world population will increase during the next hundred years, though at increasingly slower rates as time goes on. Certain parts of the world, however, will probably not show any population increase at all, and in some areas there may be a decrease in population density in the immediate future. Eventually a balance must be established between population density, resources, and standard of living.

SELECTED REFERENCES

Brown, Harrison. 1954. The challenge of man's future . . . New York: Viking Press.
Carr-Saunders, A. M. 1922. The population problem; a study in human evolution. Oxford: Clarendon Press.
Hatt, Paul K., editor. 1952. World population and future resources. New York: American Book Co.
Osborn, Fairfield. 1948. Our plundered planet. Boston: Little, Brown and Co.
Pearl, Raymond. 1939. The natural history of population. New York: Oxford University Press.
Pearson, Frank A., and Floyd A. Harper. 1945. The world's hunger. Ithaca: Cornell University Press.
Sears, Paul B. 1935. Deserts on the march. Norman: University of Oklahoma Press.
Sumner, William G., and A. G. Keller. 1927. The science of society. Vol. 1. New Haven: Yale University Press.
Thompson, Warren S. 1942. Population problems. 3d ed. New York: McGraw-Hill Book Co.
Thompson, Warren S. 1944. Plenty of people. Lancaster, Pa.: The Jacques Cattell Press.
Vogt, William. 1948. Road to survival. New York: William Sloane Associates.
Whelpton, P. K., Hope T. Eldridge, and J. S. Siegel. 1947. Forecasts of the population of the United States, 1945–1975. Washington: Census Bureau, U.S. Department of Commerce.
White, Leslie A. 1947. Evolutionary states, progress, and the evaluation of cultures. Southwestern Journal of Anthropology, 3: 165–92.

The Human Society
and Its Habitat and Resources

Every society is directly dependent upon the character of its local environment, and upon the resources available in it. Every human population must adjust itself to its habitat if it is to continue to exist (James, 1935; Huntington, 1951). By a modification of its culture, by evolutionary changes in its heredity, and by control of its population density, each human society ultimately does adjust itself so that it at least tolerates the conditions under which it lives. Along a marine coast, for instance, where fish and other sea animals abound, the human economy is usually based largely on the food that is so easily secured from the sea (Ransom, 1946), and may be very little dependent upon domestic animals or plants. An inland society, on the other hand, often develops a pastoral or agricultural culture.

The regions of the world vary greatly in their capacity to support human societies. In a rich and fertile valley, for example, a large population may thrive; through efficient organization and division of labor, a complex agricultural and industrial civilization may evolve. Mountainous areas, on the other hand, are likely to be poor producers of food and the other essentials of life, and consequently can support only a relatively sparse population. Furthermore, the rugged topography of a mountainous area enforces local isolation. A wholly different type of culture must therefore develop in mountains than on lowlands (Semple, 1911: Chaps. 15–16; Thomson and Geddes, 1931: 1396; James, 1935: 307–44).

Adaptation to a given local environment may be achieved by man in three possible ways: by individual physiological adjustments; by an adaptive change in human heredity; and by the modification of the culture of the social group concerned. Each of these three methods of adjustment to the environment may be presumed to be represented in varying degrees in every human community, and indeed in every individual.

Individual adaptability

Each individual man, as was pointed out in Chapter II, has a considerable ability to adjust to his personal environment. He can endure and even thrive under conditions of extreme heat, cold, moisture, or drought. He can tolerate persistent winds, extreme sunlight, or constantly cloudy skies. He can live on cold and rainy ocean shores, in hot deserts, or high in the mountains. The ability of the individual man to become adjusted to various types of climate aids him greatly in becoming acclimated to diverse kinds of local environments. Adaptability is itself an adaptation of very great importance to man (Dobzhansky and Montagu, 1947).

Hereditary adaptations

Human populations undoubtedly also have the power to adjust to the characters of their habitats by adaptive changes in their heredity. The evolution of a hereditary human adaptation, however, must be at best a slow process, requiring probably tens or even hundreds of generations, and often affecting the population of a considerable part of a continent. Unless a population lives under the same general climate for hundreds or perhaps thousands of years, it would not be expected to evolve hereditary characters especially adapted to that type of habitat. From what we now know about the rate of evolution in mammals, we would, therefore, not expect small or temporary populations of men to become adjusted to their local environments by changes in their heredity.

Human Races In recent years, much nonsense has been written about human races, ranging from the crude doctrines of Nordic or Aryan superiority to the denial that races exist at all. The excesses of the Nazi regime, which were based in part on an assumed German racial superiority, did much to bring the concept of race into disrepute.

Races do exist among men as well as among other kinds of animals. By race I here mean any population in which the members exhibit an average difference from the members of other populations of the same species in one or more inherited characters. Race is thus a statistical as well as a genetical concept. It must be pointed out, however, that not all biologists and anthropologists would accept this simple definition of race.

Certain members of a given population may not exhibit the characters typical of their race, though some of their relatives may be typical. Such variability is to be expected of characters which are transmitted according to Mendel's laws of inheritance.

Racial characters among animals are known to be often adaptive in relation to the environment. Thus, in the genus *Peromyscus,* a group of small North American rodents, the color of the pelage is generally correlated with the color of the surface soil on which the animals live. On dark-colored lava rock, the animals are usually dark in color, while on pale-colored rock or sand they are pale (Dice and Blossom, 1937). In many other genera of North American birds and mammals, moderately dark-colored forms live on the dark soils of the eastern deciduous forests, pale forms on the pale soils of the western arid plains and deserts, and very dark forms in the humid forests of the Pacific northwest coast.

Certain of the characters of human races may likewise be adaptations to particular features of their habitats. Thus, the dark skin colors that are characteristic of most African peoples may be related to the intense sunlight of many parts of that continent. The dark pigment in the skin protects the body from an excess of ultraviolet light, and perhaps from other harmful forms of radiant energy. Most persons' skins have some ability to tan when exposed to intense sunlight, thus protecting the underlying tissues, but in the dark-skinned races this ability is especially high. The pale skin colors of the peoples of northwestern Europe may be adapted to the prevailingly cloudy skies of that region. The general lack of dark pigment in the skins of these peoples permits such ultraviolet light as may be present to penetrate the skin and aid in the formation of vitamin D, the antirachitic factor, and perhaps to produce other beneficial results (Coon, Garn, and Birdsell, 1950). The actual adaptive value of human pigmentation under natural conditions, however, is still largely unknown.

Not all racial characters, either in men or in other animals, are necessarily adaptive. Any population that is isolated for a number of generations will theoretically be expected to develop unique characters through the random processes of mutation and genetic drift.

Adaptations of culture

Through local modifications in his culture, man has become able to exist in many highly diverse types of habitat. In a cold climate, for instance, he usually wears heavy clothing and lives in a heated dwelling. In a hot climate, on the other hand, he wears only light clothing or none at all, and usually uses fire only for cooking. By storing food he can exist in regions where at certain seasons the supply of food is scanty.

Important adaptive elements of a human culture may include such things as the kinds of foods used, the means by which food is obtained or grown and then distributed, the use made of forests, minerals, soils, and other natural resources, the density and distribution of the human population, and the relations of the human society to the other animals and plants that make up the regional community.

Not all elements of culture, however, are necessarily adaptive. Thus, certain valuable foods, useful tools, or desirable items of clothing may be under a tabu for a given sex or age group, or at particular seasons (Herskovits, 1952: 83, 271). In the United States, for instance, the meat of horses is rarely eaten by man, though in certain other countries it is considered excellent food. A tribe may set other handicaps to its own success. Thus, it may adopt a tabu against hunting or other necessary operations on a certain day of the week or the year.

A group of people who possess a common culture may be called a cultural group. A nation may be composed of several cultural groups. On the other hand, a given culture may be common to several nations, as is illustrated by the generally similar culture of Canada and the United States.

Care must be taken not to confuse cultural group with race. Racial characters are inherited, while culture is acquired by each individual during his lifetime. It is true that race and culture are often closely related (Fairchild, 1947). Different races, however, may share essentially the same culture, as, for example, negroes and whites do in the United States. On the other hand, subdivisions of the same race in different areas may possess very different cultures. The culture of the corn-growing Mayan Indians, for example, is very different from that of the hunting Indians of the Canadian north woods.

By modifications in his culture, man has been able to adjust himself to very diverse climates, often without any great change in his heredity. Peoples of similar heredity and common origin, therefore, sometimes have very different cultures. Likewise, peoples of very diverse ancestry and of widely different heredity may have similar types of culture. Modifications of culture can arise quickly, while modifications in the heredity of a stock theoretically evolve only slowly, except in populations composed of very few members.

The elements of which every culture is composed may conveniently be classified under three divisions (White, 1949a: 364): (1) The technological aspect of a culture is concerned with those instruments and operations by which individual men obtain their necessities and luxuries, such as food, shelter, dress, instruments, ornaments, and similar items. (2) The sociological aspect of culture includes those customs and institutions that control the interrelations among individuals. Families, clubs, economic groups, churches, and political parties are examples of institutions that help to organize social behavior. (3) The third aspect of culture, the ideological, is concerned with ideas, beliefs, and knowledge, whether spoken or written. Folklore, religion, common knowledge, science, and philosophy are examples of systems of ideas that affect culture.

We shall here be concerned mostly with the material elements of culture. Although the social, religious, and artistic elements of culture also exhibit many important ecologic relationships, these are in general more indirect and more difficult of precise evaluation than are the elements of material culture (Herskovits, 1952: 73).

Every culture must be tolerably adapted to the conditions of its habitat if the people who practice it are to survive. This does not imply, however, that similar environments necessarily produce similar types of human behavior. The hypothesis, for example, that a desert or grassland habitat tends to produce co-operation among the inhabitants is not tenable (Malin, 1947: 162). Adaptation to a given type of environment may in different societies be achieved in diverse ways.

The environmental factors that may affect the material culture of a people may be listed as: (1) the physical factors, including climate, physiography, and soil, and (2) the biotic factors.

Adjustment to physical factors Among the physical factors of the habitat, climate is usually more powerful in controlling the culture of the human population than either physiography or soil. Climate, in fact, pervades almost every feature of culture and controls the use of dress, shelters, and habitations, the modes of transporting materials and persons, and many other human operations and customs.

A very different type of culture is needed in a desert, for example, than in a well-watered region. Similar pastoral types of culture based upon the grazing of domestic stock have been evolved in widely separated arid regions (Semple, 1911: 509). Because the growth of the grass on which the domestic animals feed is dependent in considerable part on irregular rains, the dwellers in deserts must mostly be nomads. Only in the scattered oases can there exist a more sedentary type of culture.

Another example of the influence of climatic conditions on the character of human culture is furnished by the failure of the pueblo type of agriculture to extend into the Artemisian biotic province (Great Basin area) of western North America. The pueblo culture is based mostly on the growing of maize and certain other cultivated food plants. Maize requires for its growth either summer rains or artificial irrigation. In the Navahonian biotic province (Dice, 1943: 39) of Arizona, Utah, Colorado, and New Mexico, where the pueblo culture is best developed, summer rains are of regular occurrence and maize thrives. In the adjacent Artemisian biotic province of the Great Basin, however, summer rains are generally lacking, and streams that might furnish water for irrigation are few. Maize, accordingly, does not thrive in that province. Due to the lack of summer rains to the westward, the pueblo culture has been unable to spread from the Navahonian into the Artemisian province (Kroeber, 1939: 46).

The Nuer, a tribe of the upper Nile, are dependent for their livelihood upon the products of their cattle and other domestic animals, supplemented in season by fish and by millet and other cultivated crops. They are largely limited to these food resources by the alternate seasonal flooding and drying-out of the land. Their culture is well adapted to the available foods and to these seasonal changes in the habitat (Evans-Pritchard, 1940).

The considerable influence that physiography has on culture is evident when we contrast the dress, crops, habitations, means of transportation, and customs of lowland peoples with those of mountaineers. Stratification of culture into altitudinal belts and the restriction of most human activities to favorable spots are characteristic of mountainous areas (James, 1935: 322–50).

Every textbook of geography gives many illustrations of relationships between physiography and human cultures. The history of every people has been greatly influenced by the distribution of sea and land, mountains, valleys, rivers, and seaports. Oceans and valleys often supply highways for communication within or between nations, while mountains and deserts often are serious barriers. The inland waterways of North America, for example, were of great service in the early development of the United States (Semple and Jones, 1933).

The character of the soil has its most important effect on human culture through its control of the kinds of natural plant foods, wild life, forests, cultivated crops, and domestic animals which can be produced in each region. A high type of culture is most likely to develop in a region that has a fertile soil. Soil exercises a lesser influence on culture through its relation to the construction of dwellings, trails, roads, and canals. Clay, for example, is used in many regions to make bricks for building houses and other structures. Sandy soil, while it may provide good drainage, may be a hindrance to the building of roads. Easily worked soils of sand, silt, or loams are more conducive to the evolution of primitive types of agriculture than are gravel or clay.

Every people utilizes at least a few mineral resources. Common examples of such use among primitive folk are salt, stone implements, building materials, and stones and gems for personal adornment. At a higher level of technology, certain kinds of metals may be worked into tools. In our modern industrial world many kinds of minerals are used. Our high standard of living is due especially to our utilization of coal and petroleum as sources of energy.

Adjustment to biotic factors   Among the biotic factors of the habitat that influence culture, vegetation is probably the most important. The kinds of plants that can exist in any region, however, are to a considerable degree determined by the climate and soil. The plants in their turn largely control the occurrence of the animals. There is, accordingly, a close correlation between the biotic and the physical factors of the environment.

Plants furnish many items of food, clothing, building supplies, and other materials needed by every human society. Animals, too, furnish many useful materials. Domestic animals give especially valuable materials and services to man. The local predators, pests, parasites, weeds, and diseases are still other biotic factors to which each culture must be adapted.

The food resources of the habitat constitute one of the most important biotic agencies for molding the human culture of any given area. From a study of the relations of the human population of Fiji to the plants and animals of the island, for example, Laura Thompson (1949b) has concluded that the customs of the Fijians are adjusted to conserve and to make very effective use of their natural food resources.

The gathering, growing, protection, and distribution of food often requires cooperation among individuals, and consequently compels some degree of social organization (Richards, 1932). A very large share of our modern industrial organization is, in fact, directed toward the growing, processing, and distribution of food.

The importance of food for the culture of the American Indians has been emphasized by Wissler (1938a: 1–25), who has divided the New World into a number of food areas, each characterized by the presence of a particular food resource and forming the basis for a particular culture. Wissler's classification of food areas is necessarily oversimplified, but there can be no doubt that the types of human food which occur naturally in a given region, or which can be produced there by agricultural techniques, are extremely important factors in the evolution of culture. When a specific type of food is the basis for a culture, that culture tends to spread to the limits of the area where that food is found or can be grown (Wissler, 1924).

The amount of food available to a given human society often shows much seasonal and annual variability. Numerous methods of food storage have been evolved by various cultural groups to tide them over periods of food shortage. Game animals and fish, for example, may be stored in dried or frozen state. The Hopi of Arizona were in the habit of storing sufficient maize to carry them over two or more years of deficient harvests (Thompson and Joseph, 1944). This habit, among others, enabled the Hopi to succeed in a very inhospitable desert environment. On the other hand, many tribes of North American Indians were very improvident. They gorged themselves when food was plenty, and went hungry when food was scanty. Thus, the Yuman Indians and related tribes, living in the Colorado Valley area of Arizona and Baja California, stored only small quantities of food. They were very generous in giving away food so long as they had any left. When hungry, they would eat even their seed corn (Costetter and Bell, 1951).

Human communities often exhibit remarkable local adaptations to the available foods. W. H. Adolph (1944), for example, has noted that in China each local community has worked out a diet whose protein mixture, based on the agricultural products available in that particular region, is of high biological value. In those parts of middle North America where wild rice grew in abundance, the native Indians had developed many special customs for harvesting and utilizing this food resource (Jenks, 1900).

Many other resources of the habitat, besides food, may influence the cultures of peoples. The materials available for the making of clothing, for example, have a great influence on the actual use of clothing, and on the type manufactured. Hunting peoples may use the skins of animals for clothing. Pastoral peoples may wear the skins of their domestic animals or develop methods for weaving the hair of these animals into clothing. Some tribes weave cloth from fibers obtained from wild plants. Agricultural peoples often weave the fibers of certain domestic plants, such as flax and cotton, into cloth which they may make into garments.

The bison of North America furnishes an excellent example of the influence of a particular natural resource on culture. At the time of the coming of the white man the bison was widely distributed over the continent, but was most characteristic of the Great Plains. There it occurred in immense numbers, and many special features of culture relating to the bison had been evolved by the various tribes of Plains Indians (Roe, 1951). The flesh of the bison was an important item of food. Its skin was used for clothing, bedding, tipi covers, and other purposes. Certain of the tribes had developed elaborate rituals and customs in connection with the hunting of the bison (Gilmore, 1932). The culture of every tribe in the Plains region used this valuable natural resource as fully as possible.

Enrichment of culture through imports   The inhabitants of a given region often obtain valuable materials from adjacent regions, in addition to the natural resources present in their own. Such materials are sometimes secured by expeditions sent out for that purpose. The young men of the Hopi tribe, for example, in the early days went on long expeditions to the Grand Canyon to get salt and pigments (Thompson and Joseph, 1944). Likewise, certain Eskimos travel at times to forested regions to get wood for building sleds and kayaks (Weyer, 1932: 160).

Even primitive societies secure many materials by trade with their neighbors (Herskovits, 1952, Chap. IX). In our modern civilization, the amount of trade between regions is enormous. Important elements in our own culture, for example, are dependent upon the receipt from foreign lands of tea, coffee, spice, rubber, hemp, silk, and many other items of exchange. Imports obtained through trade greatly expand the resources available to a society.

Cultural climax

The material culture of the people of any given region may be assumed to have a tendency to evolve toward the type best suited to the physical and biotic features of the habitat, and best fitted to make efficient use of the natural resources of the area (Wissler, 1929). The culture of every human population, therefore, has a tendency to progress toward a cultural climax

(Kroeber, 1939). According to this point of view, a cultural climax is the limit up to which the culture of a human population of given heredity may evolve in response to the physical and biotic conditions and to the natural resources of a particular area.

The building materials available in a region, for example, largely determine the kind of living quarters constructed by the people. In a forested region, where there is plenty of wood, the people are likely to construct fairly permanent homes of wood. If trees of a size suitable for building are absent or scanty, dwellings must be constructed of other building materials such as stone, clay bricks, brush, animal skins, or bricks of sod.

Similarly, the materials available for the making of tools influence the kinds of tools that are made and used. Flint knives and arrowheads obviously require that flint be available. Likewise, a culture based in any way on copper tools can develop only if copper is available in its area, or is obtainable by trade. Our modern complex civilizations are possible only because modern man is able to draw on the whole world for raw materials.

In each geographic region, therefore, the material culture of the human inhabitants has a tendency to evolve towards a climax adapted to the conditions of climate and of physiography, to man's plant and animal associates, and to the available natural resources. Along the North American shores of the Arctic Ocean, for example, the Eskimos have developed a culture adapted to a frigid climate, to the absence of trees, and to the availability of numerous kinds of fish and other animals (Nansen, 1893; Jenness, 1922; Weyer, 1932; Forde, 1934). Marine animals, including especially seals, whales, and fishes, are the most important natural resource of the habitat. They furnish food for man and his dogs, oil fuel for cooking and for the heating of dwellings, skins for clothing, and bones for tools. The capture of the marine animals on which the Eskimo culture is largely based requires highly specialized tools and techniques, which have been evolved as the result of long experience. The houses of the Eskimos, their clothing, and their modes of travel, all are well adapted to the conditions of their environment and to the materials available to them. Even the winter snow is put to use in the construction of snow houses, and for travel by sleds.

The Indian tribes in the forested parts of the interior of northern North America have a culture very different from that of the Eskimos who live adjacent to them. These Indians have wood available for fuel, for the construction of their dwellings, and for making tools. They hunt mostly terrestrial animals, though they also catch fresh-water fish. Consequently, the culture of the Indians is very different from that of the Eskimos, even though the two types of people live in closely adjacent areas. The cultural climax of these northern Indians must evidently be very different from that of the Eskimo.

Cultural climax is somewhat analogous to ecologic climax, but there are several important differences. The ecologic climax is the most stable community of plants and animals that can exist in a particular region inhabited by a given assemblage of wild species. It is the climax type toward which all the ecologic communities of a region tend to develop through ecologic succession. Thus, beginning with a bog lake in southern Michigan, the trend of succession proceeds from open water through sedge mat, sphagnum, leather-leaf, shrub, tamarack and other stages, leading ultimately to beech-maple forest, the climatic climax of the region. Similarly, ecologic succession starting in the same region would pass from bare sand or from bare rock through various stages, but in southern Michigan it would always lead toward the same type of beech-maple forest climax. The ecologic climax community is composed of a considerable number of species of plants and animals, among which several species are often of almost equal importance.

Cultural climax differs from ecologic climax in that it is concerned principally with the one species, man. The cultural climax of a human society, furthermore, can be approached or attained without any actual change in the composition of the human population, and theoretically without any change in its heredity. The succession of communities leading toward an ecologic climax, on the other hand, usually involves considerable changes in the aggregation of species that compose each successive stage. The concept of cultural climax, therefore, has only a distant analogy to ecologic climax.

Each climatic region inhabited by man must of necessity ultimately produce a distinctive human culture. This is true because each climatic region is usually characterized by distinctive types of topography, soil, fauna and flora, and cultivated crops (Dice, 1943). The resources of each region for the production of human food, building materials, and materials for the manufacture of clothing and other necessities are to a large degree controlled by the climate. As has been pointed out earlier, customs and social institutions must be adjusted to the climate as well as to the physiography, the soil, and the presence of dangerous wild beasts, infectious diseases, and noxious insects—many of these features being in turn controlled by the climate. The material culture of the people of each climatic region, therefore, must differ at least to a slight degree from that of every other region.

The heredity of a people undoubtedly has some influence on the character of its cultural climax. The climax which is possible for a tribe many of whose members are dull-witted, for instance, must be very different from that of a tribe which contains many highly intelligent individuals.

Variations in hereditary ability occur in every tribe, and the more intelligent and inventive individuals in any group may doubtless considerably influence the evolution of the tribal culture. The type of culture exhibited by any given social group, however, probably reflects the average level of ability of the individuals rather than the ability of the best endowed persons. The ideas of any individual who is very far in advance of his group are often not accepted, and the individual himself may be suppressed, banished, or killed.

The conditions in each ecosystem of which man forms a part mold the characters of the human population and its culture, even while the activities of man modify the characters of the habitat to a greater or lesser degree. Thus, as Thomson and Geddes (1931: 1307) point out, the Dutch have to a very considerable degree made Holland what it is, but Holland has at the same time modified and selected the Dutch people so that they fit surpassingly well into this particular lowland environment. Likewise, the Swiss and Switzerland are to a considerable degree adjusted to one another. The nomadic type of life of desert folk, in the opinion of Huntington (1907: 11), produces not only certain types of human behavior and customs, but is also reflected in the moral qualities of the people. Moral qualities, however, are difficult of precise measurement, and the evidence that they are related to climate and type of habitat is not convincing.

The intimate ties between human social groups and their habitats have long been appreciated by anthropologists and geographers. Many social scientists, unfortunately, have been slow to recognize the dependence of man on the characters of his local environments. In recent years, however, sociologists in particular have become increasingly concerned with regional studies in which ecologic relations are emphasized (Barnes, 1948b: 677–94; H. W. Odum, 1951: 355–60).

Each human society develops a plausible philosophy of the universe and of the relation of the individual person to his habitat. This philosophy is expressed by many symbols and controls much of the daily routine of the individuals. The customs of every human society include items which deal with their beliefs and general philosophy of life, besides those items which directly adapt the society to existence within the physical and biotic factors of its local environment. It does not matter that the philosophies of many societies are, from our point of view, based on false premises, and may be fanciful or illogical. Even though many persons in a society may recognize that the accepted philosophy of their society contains defects, their behavior will be largely controlled by it.

As an example of the role that philosophy and its symbols may play in the life of a society let us consider the Hopi of northern Arizona, whom we have previously mentioned. These Indians live in relatively small pueblos and subsist principally on corn (maize) and other agricultural crops. The social organization of each Hopi pueblo constitutes a balanced whole in which each sex serves an indispensable part (Laura Thompson, 1950a). However, the habitat is arid and subject to prolonged droughts. It is not surprising, therefore, that certain Hopi beliefs and customs center around supernatural means for initiating the annual rains.

Every culture has a tendency to evolve toward an integrated whole, with its several elements adjusted to each other (Murdock, 1934: ix) as well as to the conditions of its habitat. A culture is not just an accidental assemblage of customs, modes of behavior, and beliefs, it must also be tolerably consistent within itself. No enduring culture could possibly be composed solely of a chance aggregation of diverse and unrelated customs and beliefs. The more perfectly the several elements of a culture operate together and the more efficiently the resources of the habitat are utilized, the more closely that culture approaches a climax (Laura Thompson, 1950b).

Not all the elements of a culture, however, are necessarily adaptive. On the contrary, numerous elements of every culture may be presumed to be neither advantageous nor seriously harmful to the existence of the folk. Moreover, a custom which is to some degree harmful may theoretically persist, at least for a time, if it is counterbalanced by the presence of beneficial elements. The great majority of the elements in every culture, nevertheless, if they are not actually adaptive, must at least be not seriously harmful to the society. Otherwise, the society could not long continue to exist.

The several elements of any given culture may not be wholly consistent with one another. Unresolved conflicts between opposing precepts, and between precept and practice, are frequent in every culture. The more essential material features of each culture, however, must be adapted at least tolerably to the conditions and resources of the habitat. The beliefs and practices of the people then usually rationalize these material elements of the culture in some more or less coherent way. In other words, the whole culture is sufficiently well integrated to make sense to the people concerned, though not necessarily to strangers.

In the process of cultural evolution, it must often happen that at any given time certain elements of any given culture are out of adjustment with others (Linton, 1938: 247). Over the period when one major type of industry, for example, is being supplanted or supplemented by another type, many inconsistencies and conflicts are certain to exist in the customs of the society. Although each culture has a tendency to become an integrated whole, only a culture which has stagnated will be likely to approach complete integration.

Certain cultures are exceptionally well integrated, while others are more loosely coordinated. A tribe that has recently migrated to a new habitat where the resources are different from those to which its culture was adapted, for instance, is for a time likely to have an uncoordinated culture. Similarly, a tribe that has by diffusion acquired a new feature of technology or behavior will likely require some time to assimilate this into its pattern of culture. The complete integration of culture may consequently be assumed to be an ideal which is constantly approached, but rarely reached.

The culture which any given people exhibits at a particular time often falls far short of being fully adapted to the conditions of the habitat. Certain resources fail to be fully utilized, others may be wastefully exploited. James (1935: 354), for example, points out that the rice culture that is of such high perfection in certain Oriental regions fails to utilize some kinds of arable land which are adapted to the growth of crops other than rice. The culture of a given society may in many ways fail to be fully adapted to the climate and the resources of its region.

The culture of the Eskimos, referred to earlier in this chapter, is by no means perfectly adapted to the arctic habitat, and is in fact now in process of rapid modification. The addition of steel tools secured from white traders, for example, has greatly improved the efficiency of many operations of this people. Nevertheless, Eskimo culture, even before contact with modern civilization, was at least sufficiently well adapted to the inhospitable arctic habitat to enable the people to survive.

That culture is not wholly produced or directed by the environment, however, is proved by the fact that two or more tribes with differing cultures may sometimes live in the same region at the same time. Thus, the Hopi and the Navaho tribes both live at present in northeastern Arizona. The Hopi are a sedentary, agricultural people who succeed in raising crops under very difficult conditions. The Navaho have a pastoral type of culture, based mostly on their herds of sheep and other domestic animals (Dixon, 1928: 28–29; Lowie, 1929: 50). The simultaneous presence of two such diverse cultures in the same general region illustrates the wide adaptability of cultures. It further demonstrates the weakness of the concept of cultural climax.

The best cultures that exist today or have existed in the past do not closely approach perfect adaptation to their habitats. New inventions for the better utilization of the local natural resources, the extension of facilities for the interchange of materials with other regions, the increasing stabilization of its political organization, and improvements in human heredity can greatly improve every existing culture. Cultural climax, then, is an ideal which can never be fully realized anywhere.

Limits to man's adaptability

Each people thinks that its own is the best possible culture. Every people consequently attempts to introduce its special culture into every region into which it penetrates. European dress has thus been carried into many climates to which it is not well suited. Too often, moreover, the attempt to replace the culture of a native people with a foreign culture unsuited to the environment leads to a less, rather than more, effective utilization of the natural resources of the region. The decline in the population of many native tribes, and the extinction of certain others, is considered by Pitt-Rivers (1927) to be at least in part due to the imposition of alien cultures unadapted to the conditions of their habitats.

Many of the colonies of Europeans now living in the tropics are said to be highly infertile and to continue to exist largely because of the frequent addition of new European immigrants. Evidence is presented by Price (1939), however, which shows that at least a few colonies of white settlers have persisted in the tropics or subtropics for a number of generations. The general failure of the white races to establish permanent colonies in the tropics may be due as much to their attempt to continue there their temperate-zone culture, as to any lack of adaptability of their heredity to tropical conditions.

Inherited human characters that are superior in one type of habitat may be inferior in some other environment. If the natives of a certain tribe, for example, should have an inherited resistance to an endemic disease, they may be better fitted for life in their habitat than foreigners with much superior mental ability but without the necessary disease resistance. Perhaps this native tribe might ultimately develop a combination of heredity that would produce both high disease resistance and high mental ability—but this would not be possible if unwise policies of administration or of acculturization had led to the elimination or deterioration of the native stock.

The more advanced types of cultures are less directly dependent on the local natural environment than are more primitive cultures. Through the use of special clothing, of devices for heating and for cooling habitations, and of means of storing and transporting food, a society that has a highly developed culture may be able to live in unfavorable local situations and to survive unproductive seasons which would be disastrous to a primitive tribe.

There is a limit, nevertheless, to the degree to which man can modify his heredity and his culture in order to adjust to the more severe types of habitats on the earth. At the present time, for instance, man is not able to thrive in numbers in the arctics, nor in the most extreme deserts. Certain humid tropical climates also are unfavorable for his health. Further evolution is undoubtedly possible in the direction of making the physiology of man better adjusted to these more extreme types of habitats. The adjustment of culture to climate and other features of the environment could also be improved in most regions. But we cannot expect that man will ever achieve fully satisfactory adaptation to the more extreme types of habitats that exist on the earth.

SELECTED REFERENCES

Coon, C. S., S. M. Garn, and J. B. Birdsell. 1950. Races; a study of the problems of race formation in man. Springfield, Ill.: Charles G. Thomas.
Evans-Pritchard, E. E. 1940. The Nuer . . . Oxford: Clarendon Press.
Forde, C. Daryll. 1934. Habitat, economy, and society . . . London: Methuen and Co.
Gillin, John P. 1948. The ways of men: an introduction to anthropology. Part II. New York: Appleton-Century-Crofts.
Herskovits, Melville J. 1952. Economic anthropology . . . New York: Alfred A. Knopf.
Huntington, Ellsworth. 1951. Principles of human geography. 6th ed. New York: John Wiley and Sons.
James, Preston E. 1935. An outline of geography. Boston: Ginn and Co.
Kroeber, Alfred L. 1939. Cultural and natural areas of North America. University of California Publ. Amer. Arch. Ethnol., 38: 1–242.
Richards, Audrey I. 1932. Hunger and work in a savage tribe . . . London: George Routledge and Sons.
Semple, Ellen C. 1911. Influences of geographic environment . . . New York: Henry Holt and Co.

Steward, Julian H. 1938. Basin-Plateau aboriginal sociopolitical groups. Bull. U.S. Bur. Amer. Ethnol., no. 120.

Thomas, Franklin. 1940. The role of anthropogeography in contemporary social theory. *In* Contemporary social theory, edited by H. E. Barnes, H. Becker, and F. B. Becker. New York: D. Appleton-Century Co. Pp. 143–211.

Thompson, Laura, and Alice Joseph. 1944. The Hopi way. Chicago: University of Chicago Press.

Weyer, Edward M., Jr. 1932. The Eskimos . . . New Haven: Yale University Press.

Wissler, Clark. 1938b. Man and culture. New York: Thomas Y. Crowell Co.

Evolution of Human Communities

CHAPTER XII

Communities, just as species and other biologic units, are subject to change. In the biologic history of the earth, very simple organisms are assumed to have been the first to appear. Through evolution, an early diversification into food producers, herbivores, carnivores, parasites, and other ecologic types must have occurred, and these diverse kinds of organisms must have become associated to form natural communities of at least simple kinds. As geologic time progressed, these communities may be presumed to have evolved into more and more complex associations of species, leading up to those complicated natural communities which exist today. A modern hardwood-forest community, for example, is composed not only of numerous species of trees and many types of shrubs and herbs, but also of almost innumerable kinds of viruses, bacteria, algae, and fungi, hundreds of kinds of insects and other invertebrates, and a considerable diversity of vertebrates. These species exhibit many adaptations to one another, and it is evident that the community as a whole has developed through a long course of evolution (Dice, 1952).

The possibilities for evolution in a system composed of a number of species of plants and animals seem practically unlimited (Lotka, 1948). The combinations possible in a given physiochemical system are limited, but no such limitations exist in the world of organisms so long as conditions favorable to life persist. During the course of geologic time, an enormous number of diverse forms have been evolved by organisms, yet these actual types by no means exhaust the possible variations of body form and structure of which plants and animals are capable. The aggregation of diverse kinds of organisms to form communities opens a realm of possibilities for symbiotic combinations in which, given time, almost anything can happen. At least no factor is now evident that is likely to limit community evolution.

With the coming of man and his increasing dominance over nature, a new sequence of evolutionary changes has been initiated in many of the communities of the world. The evolution of human communities, just as the evolution of natural communities, is not always an orderly process. Nevertheless, every human community that now exists must have evolved from some previously existing kind of community. Furthermore, every human community that now exists may be presumed to be subject to still further change.

Evolution is not synonymous with progress. In the animal world, for instance, the nervous systems of certain parasites have degenerated during the course of evolution while their reproductive systems have become greatly enlarged. In a human community, it is often difficult or impossible to decide whether a particular change is progressive or retrogressive, beneficial or harmful. Thus it is simplest to consider that any permanent change in a community constitutes evolution.

Change

Evolution in a human community may occur through the addition of a new species of plant or animal, the loss of a member species, an evolutionary change in the hereditary characters of an associated non-human species, a change in the heredity of the human population, or a modification in the culture of the human society.

Addition of a new species of plant or animal   Any change in the assemblage of plants and animals that are associated with man to form a human community may be considered to constitute evolution. Many of the plants and animals that occur in a particular human community, however, are of such minor ecologic importance that their addition or subtraction would have hardly any noticeable effect on the operations of the community. On the other hand, the addition to a human community of a new species of food plant, food animal, harmful pest, or disease-producing organism may have far-reaching consequences.

A spectacular change in a human community often results from the introduction of a new food plant. The human population must, of course, acquire new customs in order to grow and to use successfully a newly introduced food species. Old customs, however, are often slow to change, and the new source of food may be accepted only reluctantly. Thus, the potato, which became well known to botanists shortly after the discovery of America, did not come into wide use in most of Europe until the nineteenth century (Aiton, 1951: 122).

The acquirement by a community of new domestic animals also may profoundly modify its customs and activities. Great changes must have taken place in the customs of the Navaho Indians, for example, following the introduction of sheep, goat, and horse from Spanish sources. They now use wool for weaving their blankets, and mutton is a staple article of food. Though the Navahos are not nomads, the horse has greatly increased their mobility (Kluckhohn and Leighton, 1948).

When a human society has accepted a new food plant or animal it may neglect earlier food sources, with the result that customs associated with the displaced foods may be modified or lost. Because of the increase in the total amount of available food, furthermore, the human population may increase, and this increase may lead to a change in the organization of the society, and in its relation to neighbors.

Not every species that may be introduced into a human community, however, is beneficial. Introduced weeds, parasites, or disease organisms may cause serious damage. A new weed, for example, that competes with one or more native food plants may seriously affect the welfare of a human community.

Control of harmful associated species   When the pioneers first settled the forests and fields of North America, their crops and domestic animals were attacked by many kinds of disease organisms, and had to compete with many native and introduced plant and animal pests. The settlers themselves were often attacked by malaria and other diseases. In our modern communities, many of these diseases and pests have now been extirpated or brought under control. Man now thrives in many regions which formerly were notoriously unhealthful. In order to maintain his health, modern man has adopted customs that promote sanitation, and has built elaborate water-supply and sewage-disposal systems. By the control of wild animals, of plant and animal pests, and of many types of disease-producing organisms, the human communities that now occupy North America have become greatly different from their more primitive antecedent stages.

Evolutionary changes in associated species   A change in a human community may also be produced through a modification in the relationship to man of some plant or animal member of the community, and without involving either gain or loss of any existing species. The two most important ways in which such a modification can occur are through the domestication of a wild species, or through an improvement in the heredity of some domestic plant or animal.

Most of our more important kinds of food plants and domestic animals were acquired by man centuries ago. The ancestors of many of our domestic plants and animals are actually unknown. Thus we know very little about the effects on a primitive community of the first domestication of a new species. Judging, however, from the effects on the customs and success of many existing communities produced by the introduction of a valuable new kind of food plant or domestic animal, we must assume that the domestication of any important wild species must have produced revolutionary changes in the human community concerned.

The heredity of a domestic variety of plant or animal can often be improved by breeding and selection. The science of genetics has produced such a marvel as hybrid corn, greatly increasing the yield of this important food crop. Even without a knowledge of genetics, however, man has been able in the course of time to raise considerably the productivity of his cultivated crops. He has also been able to increase the fertility, resistance to disease, tractability, size, and efficiency of many species of domestic animals. A rise in the productivity or usefulness of any domestic species of plant or animal will, of course, increase the resources available to human society, and will inevitably result in at least some evolution in the characters of the human community.

It should be emphasized that every strain of domestic plant or animal, to be successful, must be adapted to the particular local ecosystem where it is to be raised. A variety that succeeds exceptionally well in one type of climate may be a failure in a different region. Or, a variety that is resistant to the diseases common in one biotic province may be seriously injured by a disease or pest that is prevalent in some other province. The course of community evolution is thus likely to vary from area to area.

Change in human heredity Any change in the heredity of the human population of an area may be assumed to produce at least a slight alteration of the characters of the human community concerned. Such a change might result from the acquirement of a new gene, either by mutation or by introgression from neighboring people; or from the loss of a gene, either by adverse selection or by random elimination. A third possibility for evolution in heredity would be a change in the proportions of gene combinations represented phenotypically by the individuals. Hybrid vigor, resulting from racial crossing, is a fourth factor that might promote community evolution.

Changes in the heredity of a human population are usually assumed to occur only slowly, often requiring many generations before any important evolution takes place in the characters of the population. Evolution in heredity, however, can in theory occur rapidly whenever a character is exposed to strong selection. Selection for inherited resistance to a particular disease, for example, could under favorable conditions result in a considerable change in heredity within a few generations, with a resultant improvement in the success of the human community concerned.

It may be assumed that the evolution of every complex society depends in considerable part on the possession of a high level of ability by at least some of the people, and of certain necessary special abilities by others. Natural ability can be used profitably even in a nonliterate society, and many individuals in such societies do, in fact, exhibit high ability. It is possible, moreover, that some of the less capable members of a modern society have much less natural ability than the more able members of certain nonliterate societies. Still, a high average level of inherited ability is probably more necessary in a complex than in a simple society.

The degree of hereditary inventiveness of a people, for example, will have a considerable effect on their culture. An inventive people will constantly evolve new methods for the more effective use of the resources of their habitat, and invent new and better methods for living with the climate and the physiography of their country. Inventive peoples, consequently, may be expected to have cultures that are better adapted to their ecosystems than people who are stereotyped in their thinking and behavior.

Not all the individuals in a population, of course, will ever measure up fully to the cultural level of the community of which they are a part. Because of defective heredity, lack of proper training, or unfortunate experiences some individuals are likely to be antisocial, and to lower the general culture of their social group. Other individuals, fortunately, will be above the average in heredity and cultural level. These others, presumably, play a considerable role in the further improvement of the culture of their community. The actual existence of persons of ability in "primitive" societies is demonstrated by those numerous American Indians who have made good records in our universities.

The types of human heredity that are needed for the success of a highly complex industrial culture may be assumed to be considerably different from those needed in a simpler type of community. In our modern culture, with its emphasis on division of labor, many diverse types of special abilities are needed by the people. The complex machines in our factories reflect the high mechanical competence of the engineers who design them and the mechanics who operate them. Our professional men, such as physicians, dentists, lawyers, artists, and teachers, must have many diverse special aptitudes, besides high general ability and a long course of specialized training. Farming, also, has become a highly skilled profession. The diversity of special aptitudes needed in our society is an important feature of modern social organization.

In certain families and tribes, the individuals seem able to work together in social harmony, while other social groups are continually involved in disputes or even violent quarrels. Although we have no dependable information about the heredity of social cooperativeness, this trait may be assumed to be at least in part inherited and consequently subject to selection. A certain degree of individualism is desirable in every society, but its extreme development would make community organization impossible. The evolution of some degree of altruism and social tolerance among the associated citizens would seem essential for the development of any complex type of human community.

The most important factor of all for continued improvement in the heredity of a community is probably a rise in the general level of hereditary ability of the people. But in a community with a complex culture, an increase is also needed in the proportion of persons who inherit certain special abilities. Constant improvement in the hereditary ability of the people, coupled with an increase in its diversification for special types of hereditary ability, therefore, is presumably necessary if the level of the culture of a highly organized society is to continue to rise over any long period of time.

Advance in culture The most important way in which evolution in human communities takes place is undoubtedly change in human culture. The most conspicuous result of the addition or loss of an associated species of plant or animal, or of a change in the heredity of an associated species or even of man himself, is the change which occurs in the culture of the human society concerned.

Advance in culture may be conveniently, though roughly, classified as being due to (1) the addition of a new cultural element, either by invention or by cultural diffusion, or (2) selection among the cultural elements available.

Every invention or adoption of a new tool, a new technological method, or a new custom must necessarily change to some degree the culture of the social group, and consequently must constitute a step in the evolution of the community. Even the modification of a previously existing cultural element must result in at least a slight change.

The acquirement, by diffusion, of cultural elements from neighboring societies is an especially important factor in the evolution of cultures (Dixon, 1928: Chap. 3). Throughout its history, every human society receives cultural elements from its neighbors. Cultural diffusion may be assumed to take place with special rapidity between those societies which frequently exchange trade goods, or which have the practice of capturing wives, children, or slaves (Boas, 1924).

In the diffusion of elements of culture from one society to another, selection plays a very important role (Herskovits and Herskovits, 1947). The conditions in a particular region may not be well suited to certain elements of the cultures of the neighboring peoples. A plains-inhabiting people, for example, would not be likely to adopt customs suited only to life in a forested region. New items of culture which are acquired by diffusion are furthermore generally modified to fit the prevailing modes of behavior of the receiving group (McDougall, 1920: 157).

A good example of the diffusion of a new group of cultural elements, and of their effect in modifying a culture, is afforded by the acquisition of the horse by the Indians of the North American plains (Wissler, 1914). Each tribe, as it acquired the horse, modified its culture within a very brief period in order to utilize this valuable domestic animal. In part, the previous customs by which dogs were used as baggage carriers were adapted to the new species. The new techniques required to feed, breed, and ride the horse were either acquired, in part from Spanish sources, or invented. The Indians became more nomadic because of their increased mobility. Certain of their previous cultural traits, such as the use of pottery, basketry, agriculture, and fixed houses were modified or lost. Thus the culture of every tribe of Plains Indians was greatly changed in a short period of time through the acquirement of the horse.

Division of labor is a conspicuous feature in the organization of every complex individual and of every complex community. In a highly developed individual organism, for example, the several organs of the body are usually highly specialized for their particular functions. Because of this division of labor among its organs, the organism is liberated sufficiently to devote part of its energy to more complicated activities such as thinking and social behavior (Cannon, 1939: 303).

In a complex natural community, certain species specialize as producers of food, some as controlling mechanisms; others pollinate flowers, transport seeds, or perform similar special services for their associates. In a highly developed human community, division of labor among numerous kinds of wild and domesticated plants and animals and among various kinds of specialized human workers allows the resources of the habitat to be utilized more efficiently than would be possible otherwise.

One of the most common ways in which evolution occurs in human communities is through an increase in specialization for particular types of labor. Even in the most primitive societies there is some division of labor, because women and children perform duties different from those of adult men; however, the classes of labor are few. In a modern industrial society, on the contrary, the fields of specialization are almost innumerable, and each individual is often tightly restricted to a narrow type of work. As communities undergo progressive evolution, further and further subdivision of labor takes place, nearly always with a concomitant increase in efficiency. In our modern, highly organized human communities, the rapidity of evolution in the direction of increasing division of labor is very striking.

Not every change in the culture of a community means an increased adaptation to the conditions of the habitat, or a more effective use of the available resources. A change in the type of design drawn on a clay pot, for example, may not make the pot any more useful, however much it may increase its esthetic value. Nonadaptive changes in culture are especially likely to occur in connection with religion and with art.

Changes in fashion furnish many examples of nonadaptive changes in culture. The dresses which women wear, for instance, vary in style from time to time, often for no apparent reason. Kroeber (1919) measured certain of the proportions of the evening dresses illustrated in fashion magazines over a number of years. The measurements showed temporarily consistent trends, ups and downs, of fashion. These fluctuations of fashion are not random. Nor are fashions created or directed solely by any one individual; they are responses to complex and largely unknown cultural forces.

Many other features of culture may also be subject to unadaptive shifts of fashion. Certain of the food prejudices of every society seem to be irrational, though most customs relating to food have a sound biological basis. The most unadaptive cultural items seem often to be related to religion. Almost every conceivable type of unadaptive behavior, including destruction of valuable property, self-punishment, self-starvation, use of drugs, prostitution, suicide, and murder, has been practiced by some religious group. Still, most of the material elements of every culture must be adapted to the conditions of the habitat and its resources. The folkways of each people are basically adaptive (Sumner, 1940).

Evolution

Many factors are concerned with directing the course of evolution of human communities. Certain of these factors have been discussed in Chapter XI and need here only be mentioned. Certain other factors that may affect community evolution, however, deserve further elaboration.

The physical habitat That the factors of the physical habitat have a powerful influence on the evolution of human communities has already been pointed out. Climate has an especially potent effect on the evolution of culture. Every person must adjust his behavior to the weather. Clothing, type of habitation, and time of human daily activity must always be adjusted to the local climate. Every culture also must adapt itself to the physiography of its region, whether it be mountains, plains, or seashore.

A change in the climate of a given region may be expected to result ultimately in a change in the culture of the inhabitants. Such a change in climate might either stimulate evolution in the culture of the residents, or result in their replacement by immigrants with a culture better adapted to the changed conditions. Thus, following the retreat of the glaciers in northern Europe, the tundra culture, which presumably existed in front of the ice, was in time replaced by a culture adapted to the forests of various types which succeeded the tundra (Kroeber, 1948: 388). Evolution of culture in response to climatic change must necessarily be extremely slow, since climatic change itself is slow.

The total area in any region of a habitat of a given type suited for human existence probably also affects the rate of evolution of the local human communities. A large area of favorable and fairly uniform habitat would be expected to stimulate the evolution of a particular kind of human community adapted to it.

On the other hand, a small area or one containing a great diversity of habitat types would be unlikely to permit the evolution of a unique kind of human community.

Associated plants and animals   The plants and animals, native and introduced, of each region also control the evolution of many features of local culture. Man is dependent upon his plant and animal associates. His customs must consequently be adapted to utilize these associated species effectively, or at least to tolerate them. The suitability of the local kinds of plants and animals for domestication, for example, has undoubtedly had much to do with the trend of cultural evolution of primitive peoples. The folklore and religious beliefs of many primitive peoples, too, are richly colored by the habits and characteristics of the local species of animals.

Prevalent local parasites and diseases also limit and control the evolution of human communities. Certain societies have evolved customs that enable the individuals to escape particular kinds of infection. The Chinese habit of drinking tea, for example, enables them to avoid infection by the injurious organisms that abound in the unsanitary waters of most of their streams, but are killed by boiling. Certain other populations have developed a physiologic immunity to particular disease organisms. Thus, most Europeans have developed a high natural immunity to measles, which is often highly fatal when introduced into tribes which lack this immunity. Nevertheless, certain parts of the world are still largely unpopulated because of the prevalence of one or more disease organisms to which no human society has yet become resistant.

Available local resources   The natural resources available in a given region control the cultural evolution of the local human population to a large extent. Natural food of either plant or animal origin, materials suitable for making clothing and for constructing buildings, pastures for domestic animals, soils adapted for cultivated crops, water supplies, fuels, minerals, and all other types of local resources affect, and in considerable part direct, the evolution of the material elements of culture. The quantities of the various kinds of available resources, moreover, determine the density of population that can exist in the region, and thereby set a limit to the degree of complexity that can evolve in each local human community.

The mineral resources available to a human society are of very great importance in the evolution of its culture. A deposit of flint suitable for making arrowheads and other tools, for example, is a resource of high importance for the evolution of stone implements. Likewise, the availability in England of coal and iron had much to do with the development in that country of an industrial culture (Lovering, 1949).

A high type of community may be able to develop under special conditions even though it may lack certain of the resources which elsewhere are a requisite for cultural evolution. A number of desert societies, for example, have reached high levels of culture in spite of the lack of metal tools (Steward, 1949). Such tools are usually necessary for the development of a high state of agriculture and its associated type of culture. In arid climates, however, the soils are often sandy and consequently can be worked with other than metal tools. Furthermore, the grasses and other weeds are more easily controlled in arid climates than in areas with heavy precipitation.

Certain of the resources in a given region may fail to be utilized by the human society. Thus, the Indians of North America were unable to utilize the petroleum, iron, and most of the other minerals buried in the earth beneath them. Their culture, therefore, largely ignored these materials. A resource that is utilized only slightly or not at all will have little or no effect on the evolution of culture. Whenever a new resource is discovered, or its use is expanded or made more efficient, we should expect a longer or shorter period of rapid evolution in the culture of the people concerned.

Imported materials   Materials imported from adjacent or from distant regions may form the basis of significant features in the culture of a human society, as has already been pointed out. Such materials may be secured by means of trade, capture in war, or the exploitation of subject peoples.

Whenever a new article becomes available to a people through trade, the local culture may expand to make use of it. This is true whether the new trade material is a useful item of food, a raw material for industry, or only an item of adornment, such as jewels, or a stimulant to the sense of taste, such as spices.

Resources captured from other peoples have sometimes served to improve for a time the culture and standard of living of a predatory human society. Gold and silver taken from the American Indians thus served to promote the culture of Spain. Many warlike tribes and nations have profited by plundering their neighbors. The labor of slaves captured in war has often played a large role in the construction of public works, and also has served to improve the standard of living of private slave owners. Certain empires still draw a considerable part of their wealth from their colonies.

As a rule, only certain classes in the conquering society are enriched by the capture of treasure. The nobility serving as military officers and the priesthood usually profit most. Very rarely is captured treasure used to improve the condition of the common people. On the contrary, success in war often leads to heavier demands upon the common people for military service in attempts at further conquests.

Size of population   The total size of the population which makes up a society must play an important role in the evolution of its culture. A very small society will not be able to develop a complex culture based on a diversity of skilled trades. Only a very populous society can afford a culture such as ours, which is based on a high degree of specialization of labor. A group of independent small societies will generally have a much simpler type of culture than a single large society (Kroeber, 1948: 273). Evolution of culture does occur, of course, in small societies, but it follows a different process from that in a large and populous society.

A culture based on hunting and fishing alone can never attain a very high level, because the bands into which the population is divided must always be small. For the Chippewa Indians of the Lake Superior region, for example, a band of 25 to 75 persons is estimated to be about the maximum that any local area could support (Kinietz, 1947: 16). Where fish or game are especially abundant and in dependable supply, somewhat larger societies can be maintained. Even so, it is evident that no great complexity of organization will be possible in such small social groups, and that their culture must accordingly remain on a primitive level.

Surplus of resources An important relationship exists undoubtedly between the rate of evolution of culture and the presence of a surplus of the necessities of life available to all, or to an important part, of the population. Improvement in a culture may result when certain individuals are encouraged to devote themselves to occupations that are to some degree artistic, scientific, or inventive, rather than being forced to produce merely the essentials of life (Boas, 1920: 316). No rapid advances in art or science can be expected in a population all of whose members are continually engaged in securing the bare necessities of life.

According to this hypothesis, a culture will usually improve whenever a surplus of the necessities of life is available to the people. Such a surplus may be acquired by the expansion into a previously not fully utilized habitat, the discovery of a new technical process that makes more of the necessities of life available, or an improvement in the organization of the society which renders the distribution of food and other materials more efficient. A reduction in population density without a corresponding reduction in resources can have the same effect as an increase in resources. Thus, Boulding (1945) points out that the Black Death of the fourteenth century in Europe was followed by a sudden great increase in the rate of economic progress.

The rapid growth in culture now in progress in North America may in considerable part be due to the fact that the population in most parts of the continent has not yet reached a density at which it utilizes all the resources of the habitat for mere subsistence. It thus has a surplus available to support a certain number of teachers, physicians, scientists, inventors, engineers, musicians, artists, and other creative workers who do not directly produce food or other materials needed for maintaining human life, but who are largely responsible for the prosperity and the advancement in culture of our nation.

In support of this hypothesis, it may be pointed out that at least some of the civilizations of the past originated in areas where the production of food had recently been increased due to the development of new agricultural methods or industrial technologies. In Mesopotamia and Egypt, for example, the first application of irrigation to the growing of cultivated crops must for a time have made a plentiful supply of food available to the peoples of those areas. The Maya, Aztec, and Inca civilizations of the New World also arose in areas of intensive agriculture. The recent tremendous advances in the culture of the United States has certainly been aided greatly by the increase of food supply made possible by improvements in agricultural technology.

Another important use of a surplus of resources is the export of part of it for trade with neighboring communities. In exchange, the community receives commodities that it lacks or has in short supply. Its standard of living may thereby be improved and new industries may be developed.

Many things obviously may interfere with this direct relationship between cultural evolution and a surplus of resources. A military society may flourish for a time and evolve a fairly high culture by living on materials produced by subjugated peoples. A military or aristocratic caste may flourish temporarily at the expense of the other classes in a society. On the other hand, war often leads to the destruction of so much of the natural resources of an area that all become impoverished. Likewise, a priestly, military, or aristocratic ruling caste may waste many of the resources of an ecosystem without improving the culture of the people to any great degree. Again, a high level of culture may be continued for some time with little change even after improvements in the culture have ceased.

A surplus of resources, alas, is not always used to improve a people's standard of culture. When we examine our own culture we will note that much of the leisure time of our citizens is wasted, or even devoted to debauchery. Relatively only a few devote their spare time to invention, science, art, or civic betterment. It is to our credit, however, that our society is giving increasing support to scientific and artistic efforts. It is also to our credit that a considerable number of our men and women devote part of their spare time to community affairs.

In an aristocracy, only a very small proportion of the "leisure" class seem as a rule to devote themselves to serious cultural improvement. A few individuals may become outstanding scientists, artists, or political leaders, but many waste their time in personal pleasure. I do not object to personal pleasure, but I do consider any life wasted that does not contribute in some manner, and at least to a slight degree, to the improvement of the welfare of society.

In the past, the construction of monuments, temples, cathe-

drals, and other extravagant edifices has often for a time consumed all or most of the surplus resources of a particular society.
While the building of imposing structures may be assumed to
produce an expansion in one or more phases of the artistic elements of the culture, the general welfare of the people may not
be promoted. We must not assume that the peoples of the past
who have left archeological wonders lived in an age of plenty,
and that rapid evolution in all elements of culture was then in
progress. Even today we find local communities where people
with a relatively low standard of living are being persuaded or
compelled to deny themselves many comforts and even necessities in order to contribute to the building of an expensive
church or other public structure.

The tendency of cultures to evolve most rapidly in regions
where there is a surplus of resources must thus be considered a
general trend only. No direct relationship between the amount
of surplus and the rate of cultural evolution can possibly exist.
Numerous factors, operating differently in each particular region, will affect the trend and rate of evolution of a local culture.
It is by no means assured that any improvement at all of culture
will take place in every region where there is a surplus of resources.

Capital Every human society uses tools, clothing, and at least
simple habitations in the day-to-day operations of living, and of
producing the materials needed by its culture. The better organized societies also use permanent buildings and numerous
kinds of special equipment. Such objects constitute capital. A
society that lacks proper equipment cannot make full use of the
natural resources of its habitat. An important relation exists between optimum population density and capital (Bowen, 1937).
The building up of capital may consequently be an important
factor in the evolution of a culture.

Under the heading of capital must be included breeding

stocks of domestic animals and the seeds of cultivated plants, for these carry potentialities for production. An improved strain of domestic animal or plant which is more productive than those strains man possessed previously is a tremendous gain for a society. The hereditary qualities of the domestic animals and plants of pastoral and agricultural man, therefore, should properly be considered to be important items of capital. Superior hereditary qualities in the members of a human population are from this point of view also to be treated as capital.

The technology, social institutions, and science of a human society are its most valuable items of capital, even though they are not material possessions. The "know-how" to make tools, to construct buildings, factories, and highways, and to remodel social organizations is infinitely more valuable than these items themselves. Natural and social sciences are the most valuable of all items of capital, because through knowledge and research, improvements can be made in all features of the human ecosystems.

Any society that has a surplus of resources can use them in various ways. It can employ the surplus to raise its standard of living. It can store certain surplus supplies as a reserve against future hard times. It can build more and better tools to increase the productivity of the habitat. Or it can expand the population. When a surplus is applied to improve permanently the productivity of the habitat or to provide facilities for increasing the standards of living, the capital of the society is increased and its culture may be improved.

An increase in population is, from this point of view, also an investment in capital, so long as overpopulation does not result. It costs a considerable amount to rear an individual to productive age. Having reached that age, the individual presumably becomes an asset to the society by his productivity (Bowen, 1937).

Reserves   Reserves of food, fuel, and other materials are necessary for every stable society to carry its population over periods of scarcity. Such reserves constitute wealth. Wealth of this kind has a relationship to capital, even though such reserves are themselves not always utilized in production. The amount of reserves that any given society should maintain against periods of scarcity will depend upon the amount of variability in the seasonal and annual productivity of the habitat.

The possession of capital and wealth is by no means restricted to human societies. The burrows, runways, and nests of certain animals are as much capital as the more elaborate structures of man. It is interesting to note that among animals other than man, the heaviest investment in capital is found among the social insects, some of whose homes represent large investments in labor and often also in materials.

Wealth in the form of reserve food also is accumulated by many kinds of animals for the purpose of surviving unfavorable seasons or years. Reserve food may be stored within the body of an animal in the form of fat or other chemical compounds; herbivores also store it frequently more or less in its natural form, as seeds, nuts, fruits, bulbs, tubers, roots, or hay. Certain wasps store paralyzed insects or spiders as food for their larvae. Carnivores also store food. A bear may store the remainder of a carcass which he is unable to consume at one feeding.

Although capital and wealth are thus of importance to many animals, man far exceeds them all in his use of special equipment and in his accumulation of reserves. He is consequently far more dependent upon capital and wealth for survival and success than is any other species.

History of the human society   The history of every human society must evidently have an important effect on the evolution of its culture. Tradition plays a large part in the behavior of the society. This is illustrated by the persistence with which peoples who migrate to other climatic regions carry with them customs that are inappropriate to the new locality. For example, coats often are worn by white men in hot climates and also in hot weather in summer in many parts of the Temperate Zone, in spite of the discomfort they cause. Numerous other elements in the cultures of societies exist because of their place in the cultural history of the people, rather than because of their adaptation to the local habitat.

The thinking of any group of persons is controlled to a greater degree than we usually realize by the customs of the society to which they belong. The limitations on originality of thought in our own society is forcefully illustrated every time some new and radical idea is proposed. An outstanding example in the last century was the opposition to Charles Darwin's proposal of the theory of organic evolution through natural selection. Customs and modes of thought are the contemporary manifestation of the history of the society, and they cannot easily be circumvented or changed.

Even when an invention of value has been made by one member of a society it may not always be adopted by the group. Most societies resist changes in their customs (Spicer, 1952). History is replete with examples of inventions and valuable new ideas that have for a time failed of adoption (Dixon, 1928, Chap. 2). Many a brilliant idea has been squelched and the inventor exiled or killed because his suggestion did not conform with the current beliefs and customs of his people.

It is to the advantage of every society to be conservative to a considerable degree and not to change its customs rapidly. A sudden change in customs may result in anarchy. Many suggested innovations are no better than the old ways of doing things and some changes could prove disastrous to the society. On the other hand, evolutionary progress is retarded when a society clings too stubbornly to its old customs and refuses to try out desirable new inventions.

The various aspects of culture vary greatly in their rate of change. Religion, art, or language, for example, may change very little in spite of a great change in the technology of the society. Thus, the negroes of parts of the New World still retain many features of their ancestral African magic, music, and other nonmaterial elements of culture, even though they have greatly changed their food, clothing, and other elements of technology (Herskovits, 1948: 615). In the United States, also, improvements in technology are usually accepted with eagerness, while the people are conservative in religious, social, and economic concepts. In certain other lands, on the contrary, the peoples have been converted to a new religion and have greatly changed their social and political life while at the same time they have tenaciously retained their old technologies (Herskovits, 1952: 80–82).

The type of organization which a human society exhibits at any given time has much to do with the rate at which progressive evolution can occur in the community. A society in which there is a stratification into overprivileged classes, such as nobility, aristocrats, or theocrats, and into underprivileged classes, such as the common people, serfs, or slaves, is certain to be conservative. The privileged classes in such a society will be in general satisfied with their lot and will be fearful that any change may mean a loss or decrease of their special privileges. The underprivileged classes will usually have little power and, consequently, will be able to do little toward securing reforms that might improve their lot.

A democracy, on the contrary, may be expected to be more receptive to innovations that may mean an improvement of the community. Although complete democracy seems never yet to have existed in any very complex human society, still, a democracy is, of the various types of political organization, undoubtedly the most favorable to progressive community evolution.

Heredity of the population The hereditary level of ability in the human population must have a considerable effect on the trend and rate of its evolution. No community can have a culture which is above the capabilities of its people. This is true in spite of the certainty that no human society has yet approached even closely the limits of its hereditary capacity.

We know far too little about the mode of heredity of most human traits to be able to say very much about the relation of human heredity to community evolution. It is generally admitted, however, that many of the physical characters of man are inherited. Insofar, therefore, as large or small stature, pale or dark skin color, straight or curly hair, and other similar traits are important for survival in a particular region, the possession of these characters may affect the type of community which evolves.

A tribe whose members are susceptible to a serious prevalent disease would of necessity either perish or evolve customs which would enable most of the individuals to escape infection. If, to use another hypothetical example, the individuals of a particular race of men should inherit a tendency to be injured by bright sunlight, those affected would have to adjust their habits so as to be most active at a time of day when the sunlight is not at its full strength.

The heredity of most peoples, however, is probably adequate for the development of a complex culture. Accordingly, it may be doubted that heredity has been as important as other factors in directing the evolution of most human societies.

The evolution of human heredity in relation to community affairs has been discussed at some length in Chapter VI. It is necessary, however, to consider here the possible effects on community evolution of hybridization between races of men.

In the course of history, alien immigrants have frequently been absorbed into local human populations. The suggestion is sometimes made that the offspring of human racial crosses of this kind may be superior to their parents both in vigor and in ability. Thus Angel (1945; 1946) suggests that the mixed racial ancestry of the ancient Athenian Greeks may have been in part responsible for their becoming a great people. The vigor of the North American white population has similarly been ascribed to their hybrid origin.

It is true that racial crossing might produce hybrid vigor among the descendants (Snell, 1951). The hybrids produced by crossing diverse strains of plants or animals are in certain cases superior in their characters to either of the parent stocks (Gowen, 1952). Hybrid corn is a dramatic illustration of this phenomenon. Should the effects of hybrid vigor last for a number of generations, a considerable amount of community evolution might result.

In man, however, it is difficult to distinguish the results of hybrid vigor from other effects, such as those that might be produced by an improvement in the diet. In any case, the benefits of hybrid vigor would not be expected to continue for many generations after a racial cross has occurred. The white subraces which are the ancestors of the present white North American stock were themselves of hybrid origin, and it is not certain that their further hybridization, which has taken place on this continent, has actually resulted in any increase of vigor. No actual proof has been given that hybrid vigor due to racial crossing has influenced the evolution of any human community, although some such effect of a temporary nature may have occurred in certain situations.

In addition to its possible effect of hybrid vigor, racial crossing should usually produce a considerable amount of variability in the characters of the subsequent generations of the mixed population. The characters of the crossed races will be recombined in their offspring in many diverse ways. Many of the descendants will be no better and no worse than either parent stock. A few, however, may combine the worst features, and a few may exhibit combinations of the best qualities, of the parent races. Should selection be effective, so that the superior individuals become the leaders of their people or produce more offspring than persons of mediocre or inferior ability, then the chances for rapid improvement in culture and in heredity would be excellent. Actually, we know so little about the heredity of human traits that we are unable to estimate what effects racial crossing may actually have had on the evolution of any particular community.

Neighboring human communities   The evolution of a particular human community is likely to be considerably influenced by the characters of its neighboring communities. Unless there are very strong barriers between them, they are almost certain to interchange materials through trade; new cultural elements will be acquired by diffusion; and new genes will be received through intermarriage. Competition between neighboring communities also may greatly affect the rate and trend of community evolution. Certain of these effects of neighboring communities will be treated in more detail in Chapter XIV.

Degree of isolation   The degree of isolation of a society from its neighbors must have a considerable effect on the uniqueness of its culture. Isolation will especially affect the rate of acquirement of cultural elements by diffusion (Dixon, 1928: 272). A society wholly isolated from its neighbors for any considerable time must be expected to evolve a distinctive type of culture. On the other hand, a society that has many contacts with its neighbors will from time to time receive new elements of culture from them by exchange. Such a society is also likely to be in strong competition with its neighbors. The society with many contacts must consequently be expected to have a more rapid evolution of culture than an isolated society; and its culture must be expected to be less distinctive.

If the evolution of culture follows the same rules as are believed to control the evolution of heredity, the rate of cultural evolution should be most rapid in a large population that is finely divided internally into subpopulations among which there is only partial isolation (Wright, 1950). On the other hand, complete isolation between the subgroups of a human society may be assumed often to result in the fixation of cultural as well as of hereditary characters, in combinations that are not always adaptive. According to this hypothesis, the rapid evolution of culture that has recently occurred in North America is probably in part the result of the subdivision of our society into numerous relatively small and only incompletely isolated economic and social subgroups.

Differences in language often serve to isolate human societies even more effectively than physical barriers. Rivers, seas, and mountains are seldom impassable, but a difference in language between adjacent societies makes the interchange of goods or ideas very difficult. Cultural interchange, nevertheless, does take place between societies of radically different languages. Nearly always, a few individuals will be able to understand both languages, and they will make the transfer of culture possible.

Competition among communities Competition among adjacent communities undoubtedly has many important effects on community evolution. It may sometimes stimulate the evolution of culture. Should competition for land or other resources result in the expansion of one community at the expense of a neighbor, then the victorious community may be able to improve its culture or expand its population, while the losing community may be eliminated, driven from the region, compressed, or absorbed in whole or in part by the victors. It may be assumed that sometimes, though by no means always, the victorious community will be more fitted for survival under local conditions than the vanquished. There is thus a natural selection among communities which is analogous to the natural selection among species. Community evolution must sometimes result from this competition and selection. Just as is true of the competition of species, however, the winner is not always the more highly evolved or, from one's personal viewpoint, the more desirable of the competitors.

Freedom from raids and from war is undoubtedly an important factor in the orderly evolution of the culture of every kind of community. Disturbances caused by conflict with neighboring tribes or nations, and especially the resulting loss of resources and of wealth, will produce an environment unfavorable for cultural improvement. The high development of the arts among the Maya Indians in Yucatan, for example, is believed by Stewart (1947) to have been possible only because of many centuries of peace. The isolation of the lower Nile valley by the adjacent deserts, cataracts in the upper river, and the Mediterranean Sea permitted early Egypt a large degree of freedom in the development of its distinctive type of early culture (Wilson, 1951: 11).

A successful conquest, on the other hand, may provide a predatory people with surplus resources that enable it to expand its culture. The outpouring of wealth during a time of war, moreover, may produce temporarily an evolution of culture, especially in the military arts, but sometimes including other aspects of culture as well. During each of the two recent world wars, for example, there was a rapid evolution of aviation, and the improvements in transportation by air have proved very useful in peace times.

Toynbee (1946: 80–139) suggested that adverse conditions in the physical, biotic, or social habitat may serve as the stimulus that leads to the origin of new elements of culture or to the emergence of a new civilization. In support of this suggestion he points out that many past civilizations are known to have arisen in deserts, in tropical jungles, and in other difficult surroundings.

It is difficult to demonstrate, however, that adversity itself is ever a stimulus to community evolution. A society that has evolved a mode of life and technology which is successful in a difficult habitat may be able, it is true, to enlarge its population and perhaps to expand into more favorable areas where it can be still more successful. As a result of successful adaptation to its habitat, such a community may continue to evolve its culture over a long period of time. This continuing evolution, however, may not be a response to the stimulus of adversity, but may rather be due to the surplus of resources made available by its first successful inventions.

The precise course of evolution of any human community must necessarily follow chance to a considerable degree. Certain types of inventions can be produced on demand, but most inventions occur at unpredictable times and places. The acquirement by diffusion of new cultural elements also must be largely unpredictable. Similarly, the loss of old cultural elements must be in part subject to chance. Even though the culture of every community must be in general adapted to the conditions of its habitat, there is a wide range of possible adjustment. Two human societies of common parentage which become isolated from one another, for example, are certain to diverge more or less in certain aspects of their culture. This will be true even if they occupy similar types of habitat. An illustration is the evolution of differences in dialect between populations which are separated only by distance. Chance may be assumed, therefore, to be responsible for the evolution of many of the details of every culture.

Rate of community evolution

The possible rate of improvement in the culture of any given society cannot be predicted at the present meager state of our
knowledge. The numerous physical and biological factors of the
habitat, the heredity of the population, and the cultural history
of the society and of its neighbors are so complexly interrelated
that every situation is a special problem, differing in many ways
from all others.

The rapidity with which certain aspects of culture may
change in adaptation to a new environment, however, is illustrated by the occupation of the Great Plains by white settlers
from the eastern United States. These immigrants or their ancestors had come mostly from northwestern Europe, where
they had a culture adapted to life in a forested region. In eastern North America, they had taken to corn (maize) as a major
crop. But corn is not well adapted to the arid plains of the
West. Neither are there forests in that region. In a relatively
brief period, the immigrants modified their culture and adopted
winter wheat as a staple crop (Malin, 1947: 327).

The rate of cultural evolution which results from local invention is especially difficult to measure. Quantitative information
about the rate of invention is mostly lacking. We can, however,
present some suggestions which would seem logical. Rate of invention undoubtedly is affected by the mentality of the people,
by their state of culture, and by the conditions of the environment. An imaginative people will be expected to exhibit more
inventiveness than a dull people. Innovations will perhaps be
less welcomed in a highly formalized culture than in a less con-
ventionalized one. Adverse conditions of the habitat may possibly stimulate new adaptive inventions by certain persons
(though it is not certain that inventions are stimulated by adversity). It seems more likely that inventions occur under condi-

192 Man's Nature and Nature's Man

tions that permit at least some leisure time to the more imaginative members of the society concerned. In our modern North American communities, invention proceeds at a rapid rate because it is encouraged by financial and social rewards.

The rate of cultural evolution caused by the assimilation of elements of culture derived from neighboring societies is also difficult to measure. We know that foreign cultural elements are sometimes adopted rapidly. Certain elements of European culture, for example, have been quickly assimilated by native peoples who have come into contact with it. On the other hand, not all elements of a foreign culture are adopted at the same rate by a given people, and some may be completely rejected.

Under the conditions of primitive society each tribe may be presumed to develop a culture suited to its heredity, and to its own particular set of local conditions. With the spread of modern industrial civilization, however, many of these local primitive cultures find themselves out of adjustment with the larger world culture of which they now form a part. Thus, of the numerous different cultures present in North America before the arrival of Europeans, most have been severely altered by contact and competition with European culture, and some have been completely destroyed (James, 1935: 164). The rate of change of the culture of many native peoples has been very rapid, but other peoples, such as the Hopi (Thompson and Joseph, 1944), have modified their culture very little in certain of its important features, and this in spite of several centuries of more or less continuous contact with European civilization.

That the amount of energy put to use within a given community in the service of man is related to the stage of cultural evolution has been pointed out by numerous authors (see Chap. XI). Cultural evolution took a long stride forward when a local society of primitive men learned to grow cultivated crops, and thus augmented the available food energy. Another important step was the exploitation of the energy of domestic animals. Our modern standard of living is very largely based on the large amount of energy consumed per capita. Cultural evolution is undoubtedly in part dependent upon the amount of energy in the ecosystem which can be directed to man's use, and to the efficiency with which this energy is put to work. Culture evolves as the productivity of human labor increases (White, 1943).

The amount of energy available to a human society is only one of many factors that influence cultural evolution. Nevertheless, it is logical to assume that any invention or any application of knowledge which relieves man from the drudgery of physical labor will provide him with increased opportunity to advance his culture in artistic and intellectual directions as well as in technology.

The rate of evolution of human communities cannot ever be constant. One community may be rapidly improving its culture and heredity, while another community is stagnant or retrogressing. Likewise, a community that for a long period of time has made little or no progress may suddenly enter a period of rapid evolution.

The factors that control community evolution are only in part contained within the organisms that compose the community. The heredity of the human members, and also the hereditary characters of the plants and animals that are associated with man, must be an important factor in the evolution of any community; but heredity cannot express itself except as it interacts with the environment. The conditions of the environment at any particular moment, and especially the relationship between the resources of the habitat and the requirements for existence of the human inhabitants, must play a very large role in the rate of community evolution.

History records many examples of the extremely rapid flowering of particular cultures. When the evolution of a culture has
produced improvements in the utilization of the resources of
the habitat, it will increase the resources available to the people, which may operate to increase still further the rate of improvement in the culture. The process of cultural evolution of
a given people may, therefore, often be expected to accelerate
rapidly for several generations or several centuries after a new
resource has been discovered or put to use (Kroeber, 1948: 391).
This may explain why in so many historical instances cultures
have for a time expanded so rapidly. Following the domestication of animals and plants in the Near East, for example, many
great civilizations arose and advanced rapidly (Linton, 1938:
245).

Town-centered ecosystems (see Chap. XV) are able to
utilize their resources more efficiently than are more simple
types of human communities. Through division of labor and
through social and economic organization, these more complex
types of human communities may thus in their early history
be blessed with a surplus of resources, which may in part be
used for still further evolution of culture. Childe (1939) calls
this process "urban revolution." The period of most rapid evolution of many early civilizations seems in fact to have coincided
closely with the first development of cities.

The factors in community evolution

My general conclusion, then, is that the evolution of human
communities is controlled by the interaction of numerous complexly interrelated factors. Among these factors, the characters
of the physical and biotic habitat are of great importance. A
habitat that is unfavorable to the health of the people or low
in basic resources can usually support only a scanty population,
at a low level of culture. A habitat that is rich in resources may,

on the contrary, support a dense population which may for a time rapidly improve its culture.

A society whose average heredity is poor may not be able to develop a high culture, even though its habitat is rich in natural resources. Again, a society whose heredity is excellent may not be able to reach a high level of culture if its habitat is unfavorable. The level of hereditary ability in the society may be assumed to become increasingly important in the evolution of culture as the technology and organization of the society grow more complex.

The evolution of life on earth has not proceeded in a direct line toward any predetermined goal. This is well brought out by G. G. Simpson (1949) in his book *The Meaning of Evolution*. The evolution of each species has at least in part been directed by factors which are different from those that have directed the evolution of all other species.

Each human community, likewise, may be presumed to follow a course of evolution which is different from that of every other community. This must be true because there is variation from place to place in the physical conditions of habitats, in the kinds of plants and animals that are associated with man, in the heredity of human populations, in cultural history, and in the relation of social groups with their neighbors. The evolution of human communities may for a time follow roughly parallel courses in widely separated regions, but the details of evolution both of heredity and of culture must inevitably be highly individualistic for each local area (Steward, 1953).

The thesis is here supported that conditions are especially favorable to cultural advance when there is available in the habitat a surplus of resources beyond those needed for bare sustenance. Also, it is postulated that cultures stagnate or deteriorate under conditions of poverty, such as may be produced by human overpopulation.

Evolution in human communities is shown especially by change in culture. The evolution of culture profoundly affects every aspect of community life. Every society may be assumed to invent from time to time new tools, new customs, new techniques, and new types of social organization. Societies also acquire improved ways of living from their neighbors by cultural diffusion. The various possible elements of culture which are presented to a given society by local invention and by cultural diffusion are constantly exposed to a process of natural selection. In this process, certain elements compete more or less directly with one another. Every society exhibits a certain amount of conservatism in clinging to its old customs. This conservatism, if not overdone, is justified in that it allows time for the adjustment of desirable new elements to the main body of culture. The culture of every society may be presumed to have a tendency to evolve, usually in an orderly progressive manner, toward making the most effective use of the resources available to it.

Neighboring human communities may affect the rate of community evolution by supplying needed materials through trade, by the diffusion of new elements of culture, by supplying new hereditary factors through interbreeding, or by creating disturbances through raids or through war.

Various types of barriers may impede communication between adjacent human societies. Of these barriers, difference in language is often most effective in preventing intercommunication. But no barrier is ever completely effective. The evolution of every human community is affected more or less directly by its neighbors.

A culture must not be changed too rapidly or confusion in its social organization may result (Wissler, 1929: 368). Even the simplest human culture has very complex customs that affect almost every phase of human life. A human society reacts slowly to any change in mode of thinking or acting. Any too-rapid alteration of customs may result in demoralization.

The changing of an established culture into one of a new and different type is always a difficult process for the individuals concerned. The transition period is likely to be filled with uncertainty and pain for many persons. Our own industrial culture is still in a very immature stage, as is indicated by the many maladjustments in our society.

No stabilization of our present industrial culture seems to be possible just now because of the rapid advances being made in agricultural and industrial technology, transportation, human health and hygiene, and human institutions. We can look forward to a continuing period of uncertainty during which all the cultures of the world must of necessity be in a state of greater or lesser change. So far as I can now foresee, the world is not likely ever to evolve a fully stabilized culture. I expect and hope that there will be continual progress for at least many millennia in the betterment of human life. Nevertheless, well organized series of human cultures, reasonably well adapted to each of the various regions of the world, will ultimately be developed, I feel sure, even though these cultures will constantly be in process of further improvement.

SELECTED REFERENCES

Carter, George F. 1945. Plant geography and culture history in the American southwest. Viking Fund Publ. Anthrop., 5: 1–140.
Childe, V. Gordon. 1939. Man makes himself. New York: Oxford University Press. (Originally published in 1936.)

Childe, V. Gordon. 1951. Social evolution. London: Watts and Co.
Herskovits, Melville J. 1948. Man and his works: the science of cultural
    anthropology. Part VI. New York: Alfred A. Knopf.
Herskovits, Melville J. 1952. Economic anthropology . . . New York:
    Alfred A. Knopf.
Kroeber, Alfred L. 1948. Anthropology: race, language, culture, psy-
    chology, prehistory. Chaps. 9–13. New York: Harcourt, Brace
    and Co.
Simpson, George G. 1949. The meaning of evolution: a study of the history
    of life and of its significance for man. New Haven: Yale Uni-
    versity Press.

The Deterioration of Human Communities

CHAPTER XIII

Human communities may not only exhibit progressive evolution and become more efficient in the use of their resources—they may also deteriorate. The history of the world is replete with examples of local communities, and whole civilizations, that for a time attained a high level of culture, only to sink back into mediocrity or into inferiority. We may mention Assyria, Babylonia, Egypt, Greece, and Rome. In the New World, the Aztecs, the Mayas, and the Incas each evolved highly complex empires, all of which later practically disappeared. New communities have from time to time appeared in all parts of the world, have flourished for a little while, and have then disappeared into obscurity, to be remembered only by archeologists or historians.

Deterioration of a human community has occurred whenever the utilization of its available resources has decreased in efficiency, the ability of its social and political organization to maintain a working balance among its several economic and social classes has declined, or the level of its arts and science has retrogressed. These several criteria are related, and the deterioration of a community in one feature usually is accompanied or followed by deterioration in the others. Most of our knowledge about the decline of the communities of the past, however, pertains to art and other aspects of culture; we know relatively little about the resources and internal organization of most past civilizations.

In discussing the deterioration of communities it is recognized that no past community has ever been a fully integrated unit (Sorokin, 1947: Chap. 43). Many inconsistent beliefs and practices occur in every society. Also, many elements of our modern languages, laws, religions, and other features of culture derive from ancient civilizations which, therefore, are not fully extinct. Nevertheless, communities of all ranks are subject to deterioration in their effectiveness as social and economic units.

Causes

The factors that may cause the decline of human communities have been discussed by many authors, but no agreement on the relative importance of the several possible factors has been reached. Every community that exists at any given place and time must be affected by many diverse and often complexly interrelated factors. Space does not permit a discussion of all the possible factors that might cause it to decline. We shall only consider briefly several of the more important hypotheses that have been proposed to explain community deterioration.

Cycles of cultures   Plato and other early Greek philosophers (Mees, 1946) believed that civilizations rise and fall in recurrent cycles. This view has also been held by some modern scholars. Careful studies, however (Kroeber, 1944: 761; Sorokin, 1947, Chaps. 44–45), have shown that the growth and decline of cultures does not follow any detectable recurrent cycle or pattern.

Cultural senility   Another related hypothesis is that nations and their cultures grow, reach maturity, and after a time decay from old age. This analogy of culture with the individual organism, however, has little evidence to support it (McDougall,

1920: 201). Cultures seem to have little uniformity in their rate of evolution, size of original home, type of territorial expansion, or rate of decline. Some past cultures have flourished for only a few centuries, while others have endured for thousands of years. No biological factor is known which might cause a civilization to deteriorate from old age. It cannot be maintained that any people have ever reached in their culture the limit of their hereditary ability. It seems probable, therefore, that the rise and decline of communities is not in any way homologous with the birth, growth, and death of a single organism.

Natural catastrophe It also has been suggested that a natural catastrophe might destroy a civilization. It is true that a catastrophe such as an earthquake, volcanic eruption, flood, or drought, may sometimes destroy a local human community. No known kind of natural catastrophe, however, could possibly wipe out a civilization which was distributed over any considerable area. Some parts of such an extensive region would escape the catastrophe, and there the culture would survive, probably to spread again over the whole area. The hypothesis of natural catastrophe, therefore, cannot explain the decline of any major civilization.

Climatic change Climatic changes which have occurred since man has been on the earth may have reduced the productiveness of certain regions of the world, thereby producing a deterioration of the cultures of the peoples affected (Huntington, 1907, 1914, 1945; Taylor, 1937). Even a brief series of drought years in middle North America during the 1930's, for instance, caused severe distress among the people and temporarily produced significant changes in the local cultures. The emigration of the Pueblo Indians, part of whom lived in cliff dwellings on Mesa Verde of southwestern Colorado and in adjacent areas, seems to have been correlated with a long period of years of decreased rainfall culminating in a great drought from A.D. 1276 to 1299 (Douglass, 1935). According to Bryan (1941), a prolonged drought during that general period caused a deterioration of the vegetation, in consequence of which the flood-plain fields where many of the natives grew their crops were destroyed by erosion.

The decline of highly organized communities, however, has occurred also in areas for which there is no good evidence of any important climatic change (Wulsin, 1953). The ancient decline of culture in Palestine, for example, is considered by Bennett (1939: 25) to have been due to soil erosion or to factors other than climatic change. Cultures that cover a considerable geographic area are usually able to survive fairly long periods of temporarily adverse climatic conditions. Our knowledge of the climates that prevailed during the early periods of human history is very inadequate, and so it is difficult to find convincing evidence that climatic change has been responsible for the decline of any important ancient civilization. Deterioration of climate, nevertheless, has probably been a factor contributing to the decline of many local cultures (Sears, 1953).

Diseases or pests The addition to a human community of a new disease organism which attacks either man himself, or an associated species of plant or animal on which man depends for some important service, may cause serious damage. The introduction of a virulent disease such as plague or cholera may result in the death of many persons, and may disrupt the organization of the whole community. Disease organisms or parasites that attack a cultivated crop, domestic animal, or important natural food species may seriously reduce a previously available resource, and so bring about profound modifications in customs related to that resource.

The potato blight in Ireland during the nineteenth century, for example, produced a disastrous famine which greatly reduced the population and forced many people to emigrate to

North America and other parts of the world (Salaman, 1950). The potato plant was introduced into Ireland late in the sixteenth century. It is well adapted to the cool and wet climate of the island and supplies a large yield of food for little labor. In response to this new source of food, the population of Ireland had increased from about 5,000,000 in 1800 to 8,175,124 in 1841 and was still growing. In 1845 and 1846, however, the potato blight, a fungus (*Plytophthora infestens*), appeared and destroyed most of the potato crop. In the resulting famine and disease a million persons are estimated to have died. Between the years 1841 and 1855, over two million persons are estimated to have emigrated, mostly to the United States (Harkness, 1931: 265). In later years that were less favorable for the blight, the potato crop was again a success. The damage caused by the blight was decreased also by growing resistant varieties of potato. The human population of Ireland, however, gradually declined and has now for many years been stabilized at about four million (Salaman, 1949).

It has been suggested that malaria may have been a factor in the decline of Greek civilization (Jones, 1909) and that a blood fluke (*Schistosoma*) may have played a part in the decline of Egyptian civilization (Bernstein, 1947). We do not know whether or not malaria was present in Greece during the period of evolution of Greek culture, nor do we know when the blood fluke was introduced into Egypt. A disease or parasite that is native to a region where a particular culture has arisen would not be likely later to cause the decline of that culture. The culture could not have evolved unless it possessed some method for escaping serious damage. On the other hand, the presence of a serious endemic disease may be a handicap that contributes to the decline of a local community when other factors become unfavorable. Thus, the prevalence of malaria must have contributed to the depopulation of the once-fertile

Pontine Marshes, near Rome, though social and economic factors were also involved (Hackett, 1937: xi–xvi).

History reports numerous disastrous epidemics of human disease. The spread of plague over medieval Europe, for instance, created panic in many cities and destroyed many people. In the present century, an epidemic of influenza which spread over almost the whole world led to the death of many persons and for a time disrupted the operations of some societies. There is no convincing evidence that disease has been the actual cause of the decline of any major civilization. Nevertheless, epidemics of various diseases undoubtedly contributed to the decline of the Roman Empire (Zinsser, 1935, Chap. VII), and similar epidemics have been severe handicaps to many other communities.

Evolution sometimes occurs rapidly in certain of the pests which are members of human communities. Under experimental conditions, house flies, for example, are able in a few generations to evolve a strain which is relatively resistant to DDT, a chemical that is currently being used for fly control (Lindquist and Wilson, 1948). Likewise, when a rust-resistant strain of some domestic plant, such as wheat, is developed by man, a new strain of rust to which the wheat is not resistant may appear by mutation or immigration, and may cause much damage until a new strain of wheat, resistant to this new strain of rust, is developed (Stakman, 1947). Should no satisfactory control be developed for a new pest, then the affected crop is likely to be severely damaged or driven out of the region, and the resulting change in the human communities affected may be considerable.

Loss of plant or animal associates The disappearance from any community of a species of plant or animal which is valuable to man inevitably means a greater or lesser decrease in available resources. The elimination of any member species from a community is most commonly due to the introduction of a parasite or a competitor. The destruction in the early part of the twentieth century of practically all the native chestnut trees in the hardwood forests of eastern North America, for example, was due to the chance introduction of the chestnut blight (Keever, 1953). It is also possible that a species or variety of plant or animal valuable to man is temporarily or permanently eliminated from a given area through extreme swings of climate, such as a freeze, a drought, or a flood. During the great drought of the 1930's, for example, most species of the valuable pasture grasses of the western North American prairies were greatly reduced, and some were temporarily eliminated from local areas (Weaver and Albertson, 1936).

Deterioration of heredity That the culture of a people may decline due to a deterioration in the heredity of the population has been suggested by several authors. These authors, however, are not agreed on the factors that may produce such a deterioration in heredity.

Several authors have emphasized the possibility that the crossing of races may result in a deterioration of heredity. This, of course, is the direct opposite of the hypothesis that race crossing may improve heredity. Nilsson (1921), for example, argues that the decline of the Roman Empire was in considerable part due to race mixture. He assumes that the mixing of numerous peoples, each having a heredity adapted to a different type of habitat, resulted in the production of many disharmonies. He further assumes that the original Roman stock had a heredity superior to that of the subject people with whom they interbred later. The birth rate of this original stock is assumed to have declined, so that the population came to be composed mostly of foreign immigrants and their children and of inferior hybrids of these peoples with the Romans.

Other authors have expressed somewhat similar opinions

about the possible damaging effects of race crossing on culture. Petrie (1919), for example, believes that the crossing of races initiates an expansion of culture, but that continued race crossing results in cultural deterioration.

The argument that the decline of past civilizations was caused by race mixture, however, is not supported by satisfactory evidence (Fisher, 1930: 238). It could not be expected that all the early Romans were blessed with superior heredity. Although some of them were able men, others were certainly mediocre, still others no doubt below the world average of ability. The original Romans, furthermore, undoubtedly were themselves to some degree hybrids of various tribes. Just what the proportions of good and of bad heredity were either in the original Romans, or in the immigrants to that country, we do not know and shall never be able to find out. Some of the foreigners who immigrated into Italy or who were brought there as slaves, however, doubtless carried heredity as good as that of the majority of the original Romans. The more competent families in a dominant world culture, such as that of Rome, would not be likely to intermarry with inferior immigrants. If they were to marry foreigners at all, it would be those of superior ability and elevated social station. Like attracted like, in ancient times just as now.

There is, moreover, no good evidence that hybridization itself leads to a degeneration of heredity. Certainly, in North America hybridization among many diverse branches of the white race has not resulted in any deterioration of heredity. After a careful analysis of race crossing, Muller (1936) concluded that there is no theoretical justification for assuming that mixed races of men should for that reason alone be in any way inferior.

Certain authors have suggested that mixed races should be more variable than "pure" races. If this were true it might be expected that a part of a mixed population would be unadapted to the local environment. Such an increase of variability actually appears in the second generation hybrids, and in later generations of a population of laboratory animals formed by crossing two parent stocks, each of which is homozygous for a different hereditary factor. Careful studies have shown, however, that mixed races of man fail to exhibit the expected increase of variability (Herskovits, 1927). This failure can be well explained by Mendelian theory (Muller, 1936). The original parent races in any racial cross are themselves undoubtedly variable rather than uniform in heredity. The hybrid offspring of such variable stocks would be expected to be little, if any, more variable than the parent stocks.

I do not deny that interbreeding with individuals of inferior heredity from other races would probably result in deterioration. But this would be due to the inferior heredity of the individuals concerned rather than to the mixing of the races. No convincing evidence has been presented that any considerable proportion of the members of a mixed population are actually unadapted to their environment. There is no evidence, therefore, to support the hypothesis that lack of adaptation due to racial mixture with immigrant peoples has caused the decline of any ancient culture.

Several authors have advanced the hypothesis (Fisher, 1930, Chap. XI) that a decrease in the fertility of the more able classes in a society may produce a decline in the general level of hereditary ability of a population, resulting ultimately in a deterioration of the culture. That the leaders in a highly organized society, such as our own, often are relatively infertile is well known. The professional classes in our society are generally less fertile than skilled laborers, and skilled laborers in turn are less fertile than unskilled laborers (Lorimer and Osborn, 1934).

A differential birth rate, under which those persons in the

population who carry superior heredity multiply more slowly than those of poorer hereditary ability, will inevitably result ultimately in a deterioration of the heredity of the society. Furthermore, such a deterioration of heredity would in turn almost certainly cause a decline of the culture.

Ability, insofar as it is hereditary, is undoubtedly based on many different genes, which in proper combination may produce a superior individual. It can hardly be denied, therefore, that many of the genes responsible, in proper combination, for the production of superior ability, must be widely distributed in every human population (Pearl, 1927). The loss of some of these genes, through a lowered fertility of the "higher" classes, would not be expected to result immediately in any great reduction in the hereditary ability of the whole population, though such a loss continued for many generations would certainly have most serious results.

The professional classes in a democratic society are continually being recruited from among the sons and daughters of industry and agriculture. Thus, the scientists of the United States come mostly from middle-class families and from the smaller centers of population and rural areas (Knapp and Goodrich, 1952: 278–79). Many of the children of professional people enter business or industry rather than a profession. There is then, at least in the United States, a frequent interchange of heredity among the several classes.

The extent of interchange of heredity among the social and economic classes is undoubtedly greatest in a democracy, but there are always certain limitations. It is probably rare, for example, even in a democracy, that the son of a professional man becomes an unskilled laborer. It is probably equally rare for the son of an unskilled laborer to achieve eminence, though more publicity may be given to the latter event than to the former.

Differential fertility among the several classes in a human population is undoubtedly a potential threat to the continued success of the society, but we do not know how serious this threat is in any particular instance (Penrose, 1948, 1950; Landis and Hatt, 1954, Chaps. 12–14). It is impossible, therefore, to secure reliable evidence about the effect which differential fertility among the classes may have had on the decline of any past civilization. It seems unlikely that differential fertility could have been a major factor in the cultural decline of every ancient community, but it cannot be denied that deterioration in heredity may have been a factor contributing to the decline of some of them.

Adverse selection due to war has been presumed by some authors to result in á deterioration of heredity, which in its turn produces a decline in the culture of the people affected. David Starr Jordan (1915) has been among the most vigorous proponents of this hypothesis. During war, officers of all grades, except the highest ones, suffer a heavier rate of mortality than the men of the lower ranks. On the average, the officers must be more intelligent and have a higher degree of hereditary ability than the men of the ranks. Furthermore, all the men in an army have been selected for military fitness, and this selection has rejected many men who carry hereditary defects, as well as many men who are defective from a military standpoint because of nonhereditary factors (Hunt, 1930). The deduction cannot be avoided that war must in general have a dysgenic effect, and that exposure to war over several successive generations might seriously lower the level of hereditary ability of a population.

It is not certain, however, that the dysgenic effects of war would manifest themselves rapidly enough to be the major cause of those rapid declines of culture which are so conspicuous a feature of human history. The deterioration of heredity caused by the adverse selection of war, serious though it may be, must usually be a slow process. Theoretically, a number of generations of such adverse selection would be required to produce any considerable deterioration of heredity. It is likely, therefore, that the adverse effects of war in producing community deterioration are expressed mostly through its destruction of resources and its disorganization of economic and political machinery rather than through its immediate dysgenic effects.

The dysgenic effects of long-continued war may nevertheless contribute to a cultural decline initiated by other agencies. These effects will theoretically be especially serious if the leaders of a conquered nation are put to death or sent into exile by the conquerors. Any deterioration of heredity, whether produced through adverse selection by war or other agents, might prevent a society from recovering from the effects of war, or from other types of disaster.

The celibacy of the clergy in certain religious organizations is another factor that may produce a deterioration of the heredity of a people and, therefore, may have some effect in producing a decline of the culture of the society concerned. The practice of celibacy of the clergy has grown up especially in the Roman Catholic Church. The men who become priests or monks in this church may be assumed to be intellectually superior to the average in their societies. Such an adverse selection against ability, if continued over many generations, must have a serious dysgenic effect on the population (Holmes, 1921: 361). The celibacy of the clergy might theoretically contribute, therefore, to the decline of cultures. There is no good evidence, however, that the celibacy of the clergy actually has been the principal factor leading to the decline of any particular culture.

In certain human societies, competition among the members is often very strong. Under such conditions there is some pressure toward the evolution of characters and types of behavior that benefit the individual, even though these characters may be detrimental or even harmful to the species (Carr-Saunders, 1938: 115).

In past geologic ages, many species have evolved highly specialized horns, antlers, or other appendages, and subsequently have become extinct. These elaborate special structures may have been of value to the individuals but detrimental to the species (Haldane, 1932: 124). Thus, a large set of antlers may give a male an advantage over other males in competing for females, but handicap him in escaping from predators. Competition among the members of a human population might, to take a hypothetical illustration, favor those persons who are most selfish in seeking their own advantage, but this characteristic would likely be harmful to the society. So little is known, however, about the heredity of human traits that nothing worthwhile can be said about the possible effects of individual competition in causing deterioration of human heredity. In fact, it is probable that a certain amount of competition among the individuals forming a human society may contribute to progressive evolution.

Another agency that may operate to cause deterioration in human heredity is mutation. It is known that mutations occur in certain human genes at a rate estimated to range between one in 6,000 to one in 75,000 births. Mutations are generally said to be spontaneous, although the rate of mutation is affected by various environmental factors, of which one of the most important, under experimental conditions, is high-energy radiation (Muller, 1950). Most mutations cause deterioration in heredity, although the effects of a particular recessive mutation may not appear for a number of generations. Deleterious mutations that occur in nature are in time eliminated by natural selection. In modern human populations, however, selection is presumed to be relaxed, and unfortunate mutations may consequently fail to be eliminated (Carr-Saunders, 1942). Diabetes, for example, can be compensated for by taking insulin, defective vision by wearing eyeglasses. If such harmful genes continue to accumulate, all our descendants are likely to have to wear eyeglasses, dentures, and hearing aids, and to carry a pocketful of hypodermic syringes. This is not a cheerful prospect.

Deterioration in the intelligence of a people could admittedly in time result in the decline of their cultures. It has not been proved, however, that the average level of intelligence of any modern community has declined (Penrose, 1949: 121). Actually, it would be very difficult to prove such a decline, because of our lack of suitable methods for ascertaining the heredity of intelligence. It is probable, nevertheless, that valuable genes have been and are now being lost from certain populations through the failure of their carriers to leave offspring. Also, the heredity of certain local populations may actually now be deteriorating. On the other hand, it is equally possible that those agencies which promote deterioration in heredity are more than counterbalanced by other agencies, such as assortative mating and decreased mortality rate, which in certain cases may operate to improve the general level of hereditary competence. Nor has it been demonstrated that deterioration in heredity has been the cause of the retrogression of any past civilization. It is very doubtful, moreover, that such deterioration could occur with sufficient rapidity to produce the sudden decline in culture which has been recorded by history in numerous regions. Deterioration of heredity, nevertheless, may in certain countries possibly have contributed to a decline of culture caused mainly by other factors.

Conquest The conquest of one people by another has in many historical instances resulted in the destruction or severe modification of the culture of the conquered. Thus, the culture of the Carthaginians, the Aztecs, and the Incas was destroyed or greatly altered as a result of their conquest by others. It is not always easy, however, to distinguish the effects of the conquest itself from the effects of the imposition of the culture of the conquerors. When all the men, women, and children of a conquered people are put to death, their local culture is of course destroyed. But if the conquered people are allowed to continue to live as subjects, they will nearly always retain at least some elements of their former culture.

A high type of culture has not infrequently been destroyed by the invasion of a warlike people who have introduced a different and often lower level of culture. Subject peoples, however, do not always suffer a decline in culture because of their subjugation. There are numerous instances of enlightened political management in which the culture of a subject people has even been improved by their rulers.

The conquest of a civilization by outsiders is preceded sometimes by internal disruption. Thus, Toynbee (1946: 245) finds reason to believe that any civilization which is the victim of a successful invasion is no longer in a state of active growth but has already broken down internally. Whatever may be true of highly evolved civilizations, it is evident that many native cultures have been overwhelmed by foreign invaders when their cultures were still in a state of progressive evolution. The culture of the American Indians in many parts of the New World, for example, was still in process of development at the time white men first appeared.

Depletion of natural resources The depletion of an important natural resource is a frequent cause of the deterioration of a human community. The exhaustion of a mine which formerly was a source of wealth, for example, may result in a considerable decline of local culture. The pathetic condition of a worked-out mining town is obvious to every beholder. The effects of the exhaustion of a single mine or group of mines, however, are usually only felt locally, because in our modern era of trade essential minerals can always be obtained elsewhere. The world culture as a whole, therefore, is not seriously affected by the exhaustion of one mining region. In looking at the tragic local results, we nevertheless see an illustration of what might happen to the culture of the United States, or to that of any other nation, should its whole supply of petroleum or any other essential nonrenewable resource suddenly become depleted. Although substitutes for such resources can usually be found, they will often be less satisfactory for many uses. Usually they will be more expensive and therefore less available to the persons who need them. Each loss or serious reduction in availability of a valuable resource will perforce require important modifications of the culture of the people affected. Should the loss of the resource be a very serious one, the level of culture of the society can hardly fail to be depressed.

The depletion of a biotic resource can be at least equally as serious in its effect on the cultural level of a community as that of a mineral resource. The near extermination of the bison in North America during the last century, for example, deprived the Plains Indians of a most important resource and rendered meaningless many of their colorful and formerly important customs relating to the bison hunt. Although the deterioration of the native Plains cultures was certainly influenced by other numerous and diverse factors, the loss of the bison resource undoubtedly exerted a considerable pressure toward their decline. Similarly, the depletion of the northern whale fisheries resulted in the elimination from our own culture of certain materials and practices based on whale products.

Destruction of the productive capacity of the habitat through overgrazing by domestic animals, excess cutting of forest lands, unwise exploitation of fish or game crops, or similar overuse of the biotic resources, must in the course of history often have reduced the resources of a people and forced them either to migrate to new territory or to suffer a decline in their culture. There is evidence that the decline during ancient times of many local colonies, and even powerful cities, was due in considerable part to overuse of the habitat, with a consequent serious decline in its productivity.

Soil fertility is an important natural resource whose loss may have contributed to the cultural decline of certain communities. Improper agricultural practices often result in the depletion of some soil element which is essential for plant growth. In many parts of our own country the unfortunate effects of soil exhaustion are painfully evident. In many sections of the southeastern states, for instance, the local level of culture of the inhabitants is at a low level because of the impoverishment of the soil by overuse and improper management.

The milpa system of agriculture widely practiced in the moist tropics quickly exhausts the agricultural resources of a local area. After the forest is cleared, crops can be grown only for one to three years before grasses take over and choke out the crops. This is true even where the soil fertility has not been seriously depleted. Before crops can again be grown, the forest must regenerate sufficiently to shade out the grass. Morley (1946) believes that this inherent limitation to the agricultural resources of Central America, together with overpopulation, was the cause of the decline of the Mayan civilization.

Improper farming practices have ruined many lands for the production of any kind of worthwhile crop. By the use of proper agricultural technics, however, it is possible in most regions to grow crops continuously with no deterioration in the productivity of the soil. In China, large areas are said to have been under continuous cultivation for over four thousand years with not only no deterioration in fertility, but actually some increase in productivity (Wilcox, 1947: 128). A certain sugar-cane field in Cuba is said to have continued to produce heavy cane crops for thirty years without the addition of any fertilizer. The secret of the continual productiveness of that field seems to be that the leaves and the other debris from the cane harvest are left on the ground and now form a knee-deep mulch (Ackerman, 1946). Not every field, perhaps, can be made as productive as this cane field. It is safe to say, however, that the productivity of the soils of most parts of the world could be greatly increased by farming practices that would utilize so far as possible the natural ecologic processes.

The decline of many ancient civilizations is ascribed by H. H. Bennett (1939) in considerable part to soil erosion. Through overgrazing, overbrowsing, and other unwise agricultural practices much of the topsoil may be lost from agricultural land by erosion. Often so much of the covering soil is lost that the land becomes worthless for growing crops.

Under natural conditions, centuries are required for the formation of good topsoil, but only a few years of poor land management for its loss. Furthermore, through the clearing of mountain forests and the overuse of pastures, the soil may be eroded from the uplands and deposited on the lowlands, where it may overwhelm the naturally productive soils found there. In arid regions, wind erosion may be fully as destructive as water erosion. Bennett presents evidence that the decline of the civilizations of certain sections of Mesopotamia, Palestine, Greece, and numerous other ancient regions was at least in part due to soil erosion. The decline of the Maya civilization of Central America may also have been due in part to overuse of the land, with a resulting loss of the fertile soil (Cooke, 1933; Bennett, 1939).

As was pointed out in Chapter VII, wasteful agricultural practices have already resulted in the loss of the topsoil of many millions of acres of the best farm land of the world. Land that is under cultivation is particularly liable to erosion (Graham, 1944: 107), being considerably more susceptible to damage than pasture lands covered by a grassy sod or forest lands protected by trees. Destructive fires in forests and grasslands also have caused much loss. Fire not only destroys the crop of timber or other plants and the resident wild animals, but often seriously injures the soil. Overgrazing, too, has greatly injured the vegetation in many communities, and sometimes initiated destructive erosion. Much progress has been made in recent years in the development and application of soil conservation measures. Considerable areas of the world, unfortunately, have already been denuded of their vegetation and soil, and this destruction has not yet, by any means, been stopped even in our own country.

The role of soil erosion in lowering the living standard of a whole people, however, may have been overemphasized, for instance by some of the authors who have written about the "dust-bowl" area of the Great Plains. Malin (1947: 131–48) has pointed out that some erosion occurred naturally in the Plains area even before its occupation by white settlers. Furthermore, much of the land in the dust-bowl area produced bumper crops in the wet years of the 1940's. A fluctuation in the climatic cycle was involved here, rather than a permanent deterioration of the productivity of the soil. This in no way contradicts the evidence for the harmful effects of overuse and erosion in this and other parts of the world.

We must not, however, assume that soil erosion was the major factor or even an important factor in the decline of all ancient civilizations. Professor Arthur E. R. Boak has pointed out to me that soil erosion was undoubtedly a factor in the decline of certain local civilizations of the past, but that it alone cannot explain the breakdown of a widely extended civilization such as that supported by the Roman Empire. At least in certain parts of the Roman Empire, France for example, the soil did not deteriorate, but remained at a high level of fertility and may even have been improved as time went on, through the application of organic fertilizers. In many parts of the Nile Valley, also, the soil probably did not deteriorate appreciably during the period of decline of the ancient Egyptian civilization.

The exhaustion of forest resources is still another factor that can have a most unfortunate effect on a community. The over-exploitation of forests has in the past deprived many communities of adequate supplies of lumber, fuel, forest-inhabiting game, and other valuable forest products. The removal of the natural forests may have still other unfortunate effects on human communities. For example, forests assist in storing the water that falls as rain or snow. The removal of the forests on watersheds may result in increased soil erosion, increased damage from floods, and a decreased water supply in those seasons when the rainfall is scanty.

In many parts of the world, forest resources have aided in the development of complex human communities. This is particularly true in the cold Temperate Zone where tight habitations are needed as protection against rain and cold. Such habitations can very easily be constructed from forest products. Wood is also a valuable fuel for heating small houses. Many cold temperate regions are uninhabitable for primitive peoples except where wood is available for food and other uses.

Wherever any large aggregation of men has lived for any considerable period of time, however, the local forests are likely to have been overutilized and destroyed. A large city can continue to exist in a cold climate only by bringing in forest products from a long distance, or by developing substitutes for wood for building and for fuel. The immediate environs of every

large city are usually denuded of their forests. It may be suspected, therefore, that in the course of history the exhaustion
of their forest resources may well have contributed to the deterioration of certain local communities.

The exhaustion of a valuable mineral resource may also have
been a factor in the decline of certain past communities. The
working out of a mine or group of mines has frequently resulted
in the decline or abandonment of a local mining town. In a few
cases the working out of certain mines may have contributed
to deterioration of larger communities. Thus, when the silver
mines at Laurium became exhausted, the resulting loss of income was probably one of the numerous factors which led to
the decline of Athens as a center of old-world culture (Fairfield Osborn, 1953: 10).

Waste of resources The resources which are available to a
community are often inefficiently used or may be in part wasted.
Some of this waste will be caused by faulty technology, but at
least a part of it may be due to poor community organization
and harmful customs. If the waste of resources is very great,
the community may in time be in danger of deterioration. This
danger will be especially acute in those recurrent periods when
the productivity of the habitat in food and in other resources
is for any reason temporarily reduced.

Bizarre religious beliefs often result in practices that are
especially wasteful of resources. Religious practices seem, in
fact, to be more likely than other elements of culture to evolve
along economically nonadaptive lines. The practice, which appears in numerous religions, of inflicting pain on one's own
body is an example of such a nonadaptive item of culture. The
priesthood, if strong enough, is likely to demand an ever-increasing proportion of the wealth of the community in order to
support more and more elaborate rituals. Personal sacrifices
are often required, such as abstention from certain kinds of

food, the prohibition of certain types of behavior (tabus), the observance of certain holy days with elaborate ceremonies, gifts or destruction of food and other wealth, the burying with the dead of objects of value including perhaps wives and retainers, and human sacrifice. The individuals sacrificed may be not only prisoners of war, but sometimes first-born infants or other valuable members of the community. Such religious practices may absorb or destroy an appreciable part of the wealth of a community, and often may seriously handicap its progressive evolution or even threaten its existence (Herskovits, 1952: 491).

Religious intolerance often accompanies adherence to peculiar religious beliefs. As a result, social pressure, the enactment of laws, or force may be used in an attempt to compel all members of the community to adopt the code of behavior advocated by the sect which happens to be in control. Nonconformists may be punished, or banished, or killed as heretics or infidels. Whether or not a dominant sect may be able to impose its code of behavior on the whole society, the group of believers comes to be set apart from the other members of the community. Such a schism must often be a handicap to the orderly operation of a community.

The rulers, nobility, military officers, priests, economic royalists, and other privileged classes in a society often absorb a great proportion of the community income, thereby weakening the community (Muller, 1952). To be sure, the administrative officers and other essential leaders of a community require support. Unfortunately, an overprivileged class often manages to absorb so large a proportion of the available wealth that the underprivileged classes are often forced to live in poverty. We do not have to search far among our modern communities to discover some that are handicapped by the burden of supporting one or several largely unproductive privileged classes.

The continued existence within any tribe or nation of a

hereditary aristocratic or ruling class may be an important factor leading toward the decline of that community. The most important concern of any class has always been and must always be to perpetuate and to increase its own power and perquisites. Public-spirited aristocrats do of course appear from time to time, but they are exceptions to the general rule that each class first of all considers its own interests. Where a conflict develops between the interests of the whole population and those of the ruling class, the rulers will seldom find it difficult to convince themselves that the best interests of the state are identical with their own.

Every ruling class has a tendency to absorb more and more of the resources of the commonwealth, leaving a continually smaller proportion of the annual productivity to be distributed among the other classes which compose the human society. For a time, perhaps for a number of generations or centuries, a nation ruled by a dictatorship or aristocracy may thrive, especially if it is able to exploit continuously new sources of internal or external wealth. By building of temples, monuments, and public works, the culture may actually appear to progress in the arts. Painting, sculpture, music, literature, and other arts also may thrive because they are supported by the rulers, by the churches, and by wealthy people, even while the majority of the citizens are in poverty. In time, however, such a community will inevitably deteriorate, because it lacks effective regulatory mechanisms to keep the various classes in the society in adjustment with each other.

It has not been demonstrated that the absorption of an undue proportion of the available resources by a particular privileged class has been solely responsible for the decline of any past community, large or small. The drain due to the support of one or more largely useless privileged classes, nevertheless, may logically be assumed to be among the factors that have aided in the downfall of numerous past communities. Even if a community has the resources to support an overprivileged class without serious damage to itself, those same resources, put to constructive use, could aid in improving the standard of living of the other classes in the society, and might support further evolution of the community culture.

An autocracy probably causes its greatest damage to a human society by the suppression of freedom of thought and activity among its subjects. New ideas among the common people may be dangerous to a dictator or to a ruling class. In a police state, the people can be forced to conform to almost any type of conduct decreed by the masters. Even beliefs and ideals may be controlled to a considerable degree by propaganda combined with punishment of those who deviate. Those who have original ideas that fail to be accepted by the rulers, or who are nonconformists, will probably be imprisoned, banished, or executed. Under such conditions progress is unlikely to continue, except along lines that support the control of the tyrants. In time, therefore, deterioration of the community is inevitable. In the opinion of Muller (1952), the decline of many past states has been due to the concentration of autocratic power in the hands of a small fraction of the population.

Even if there is no hereditary privileged class in a community, the cost of government may become so great as to be a severe handicap. The inefficiency of bureaucratic government is notorious. The excessive cost of military and civil services, for instance, may have been an important factor in the downfall of the Roman Empire (Louis, 1927: 21; Boak, 1947: 365).

The cost of government becomes especially great when the administration is corrupt. There is always a tendency for the relatives, friends, and followers of those in power to secure unearned income and perquisites at the expense of the public. They may receive a salary or special fees without an adequate return in service. Even worse is political graft, in which the officials responsible for the welfare of the community profit by its despoliation. No community can long continue in a state of health under a corrupt government. The common people of a nation which is burdened by an oppressive ruling class have frequently welcomed alien invaders as liberators. Thus, when the barbarian hordes overran the provinces of the Roman Empire, they encountered no strong resistance from the people (Boak, 1947: 457).

The construction of magnificent monuments may have been a factor in the decline of certain past civilizations. The construction of schools, courthouses, highways, canals, water systems, and similar types of productive public works constitutes an asset to a community. Most monuments, however, are unproductive of anything but esthetic enjoyment. Beauty is, of course, an important factor in any advanced culture. Too frequently, however, an expensive structure is erected by a society in which the common people live in poverty (Clough, 1951: 6). This seems to hold true for some of the beautiful cathedrals of Europe as well as some of the monuments of more ancient civilizations. Resources used for the construction of excessively expensive buildings are withdrawn permanently from the community. Their loss may prevent the further evolution of a community, and under certain conditions might contribute to its decline.

Every normal person desires to be well thought of by his associates. The desire to acquire prestige among one's fellows is a powerful incentive to endeavor, which often results in the enrichment of the culture. Community approval generally is given to those persons who obey the written and unwritten code of behavior of the group, and who avoid those acts which meet with group disapproval. Certain persons often enjoy particular prestige by reason of their wealth, political or economic power, noble or aristocratic birth, heroic behavior, philanthropy, beauty or histrionic ability, inventiveness, or other special abilities.

A man's desire to achieve prestige, however, sometimes results in acts that are not to his own best advantage and may constitute a danger to his society. The potlatch of certain of our northwest coast Indians, for example, is inspired by the desire of individuals, or families, to acquire prestige in their society by giving a feast at which expensive presents are distributed (Herskovits, 1952: 476). In consequence, some individuals or families may save for many years and impoverish themselves in order to acquire the valuable presents which are to be given away at the potlatch. The withdrawal from use for considerable periods of a large part of the wealth of such a society is not to its best interests and may delay or prevent the evolution of the culture in other more desirable directions.

The vulgar display of wealth, which is occasionally seen in every society including our own, is apparently also an attempt to achieve social prestige (Veblen, 1912). Wastage of wealth in this manner, unless extreme and widespread, may not result in an immediate deterioration of the culture concerned, though it must always be harmful.

Aggressive or defensive war always results in lowering the productivity of a country by the destruction of wealth, natural resources, and manpower. War often disrupts the economic and political organization as well, and thereby still further lowers productivity. A protracted war may so seriously reduce the productivity of a country that it can no longer support as dense a population, or as high a culture, as before. If the population density is not concurrently reduced, it could happen, then, that war might initiate a cultural decline from which the society may be unable to extricate itself. If its resources have not been destroyed, however, a defeated nation often has risen again quickly.

History is filled with accounts of peoples who for a time have been successful at aggressive warfare. With the booty in treasure, captives, or colonies obtained by conquest, military societies have often for a time expanded their populations and sometimes also their cultures. Certain military empires have thus flourished for centuries. Eventually, however, every nation whose success was based primarily on military conquest has been overthrown. War exhausts the resources of even the richest country to such an extent that finally it is open to conquest by its neighbors (Toynbee, 1947: 331–49). Wars among states, cities, or districts often ruin all concerned, as was true of ancient Greece (Robertson, 1912). The known history of the world up to and including the present time, nevertheless, shows constant attempts at military conquest by one people or another, with only brief interludes of peace.

Aggressive warfare is at times a symptom of maladjustment between population density and available resources. When the resources are deficient in relation to population density, a part of the people, in the attempt to increase their resources, may become bandits, or rise in revolt, or wage war against a neighboring people. When misery is widespread, any demagogue who promises relief through violent action is likely to find a following, even though the action proposed is sheer folly.

That a culture may decline in spite of continuous peace, however, seems to be demonstrated by the history of the Old Empire of the Maya in Central America (Morley, 1946: 70). There is no evidence of any extensive civil war or foreign conquest during the period when the culture of the Old Maya Empire declined. War is, therefore, to be treated only as one of the factors which may be related to the decline of a civilization.

Internal disorders may seriously weaken a community through the destruction of wealth and capital and the disrup-

tion of processes of production. When such disorders occur frequently in a local community, a state, a nation, or the world
community, it may be assumed that faulty organization is
largely to blame. In a perfectly organized community of any
rank, each class or geographic district would theoretically receive a correct proportion of the community resources and
duties, and with it a corresponding degree of responsibility.
Various regulatory mechanisms would serve to adjust any inequalities that might arise from time to time among the several
classes or districts within the community. In such a perfectly organized community, disorders should never occur.

Internal disorders may aggravate an already existing maladjustment of organization and may thus be a contributing factor
in producing degenerative changes of such a serious nature that
they lead to the collapse of the community. Such a weakened
community is often in its final stage overwhelmed by attacks
from its neighbors (Toynbee, 1947: 579).

Relations among factors of deterioration

If it is to continue to exist, each human community must constantly adjust itself to its resources, the conditions of its habitat,
and the activities of the neighboring communities. In Chapter
IX, I have discussed some of the regulatory mechanisms that
operate to maintain a tolerable balance between a human society and its environment. Community welfare is maintained
only as a result of complex interaction of many diverse factors
within the community and in its environment. Because of the
complex interrelations between each highly organized human
community and its habitat, deterioration in the community usually results from an unfortunate combination of unfavorable
factors, rather than from any one single factor.

The attempts to explain the decline of the Roman Empire, for
example, or of any other past civilization by a single cause have

been notorious failures. The damage caused by local catas-
trophes of drought, flood, fire, storm, disease, pests, soil erosion, or overpopulation is often quickly repaired if the community is otherwise in a thriving condition. Recovery from the
destructive effects of war may also at times be rapid. It may be
suspected, however, that a community which is already seriously weakened may succumb to a relatively minor adversity.

Overpopulation Overpopulation in relation to the available
resources has undoubtedly played a considerable role in the
stagnation or decline of at least certain cultures. The conditions that are most suitable for the improvement of human culture are exactly those that encourage an increase in population
density. Wherever there is a surplus of resources that allows
scholars, artists, and inventors to thrive and thereby to improve
the culture, there also the population has a tendency to expand
rapidly.

Every human population tends to increase in numbers to the
limits of the capacity of its habitat (Chapter V). However, when
a population has reached or exceeded the limit of density that
its habitat can easily support, it cannot also support the inventors, scientists, scholars, and artists who have been responsible
for the growth of its culture. Once the density of the population
has increased beyond the level at which a surplus of the necessities of life is available, the culture must, according to this hypothesis, inevitably retrogress.

A too dense population not only operates to produce stagnation in the culture of the society concerned, but is likely also to
cause a decrease in the carrying capacity of its habitat. A population which is too large to be easily supported by the available
resources overutilizes its habitat and thereby destroys to some
extent the productive capacity of its ecosystem. The overuse
and ruinous exploitation of forests, mineral wealth, and soils has
greatly reduced the capacity of many parts of the world to sup-

port human populations. Overpopulation, together with the resultant overutilization of the resources of the habitat, has
undoubtedly been an important contributing factor in the deterioration of many of the local cultures of the world, though it
has not been demonstrated that any widespread culture was
destroyed by overpopulation alone.

In certain parts of the world, we at present can observe the
effects of overpopulation causing a relatively low state of culture. In certain rural parts of the United States there is, according to Lorimer and Osborn (1934: 343), an accumulation of
surplus population in agricultural areas with limited natural
resources. This holds down the standard of living, including the
levels of education and of health. Similarly, low standards of
living are evident in such overpopulated areas as Puerto Rico,
and parts of India and China.

It may be argued that it is the low level of education in these
areas which produces the low level of culture. In reply, it may
be pointed out that the areas concerned have too few resources
in relation to their populations to be able to provide an adequate number of schools and of teachers and that the children
cannot be supported through a long period of schooling. Lack
of educational facilities, therefore, is often correlated with a
population density that is too great in proportion to the available resources.

It seems unlikely that any country which is greatly overpopulated in relation to its resources can long support a culture
which contains many nonessential elements. Even a dictatorship must eventually find it impossible to extract from an overpopulated people sufficient income to support a high state of
culture in a privileged class.

In many parts of the world, natural resources have become
seriously depleted. Wasteful exploitation is still continuing in
numerous regions. Many countries are already overpopulated,

yet population densities continue to increase almost everywhere. A recent review by Fairfield Osborn (1948) indicates that the standards of living in many countries are now in peril of being lowered still further. This can hardly fail to result in a decline of culture. If the population density of a country can be controlled so that it does not exceed the carrying capacity of the habitat, that country will have conquered one of the major factors leading toward cultural decline.

Ineffective regulatory mechanisms The population density that can be supported in any given state or nation is dependent not only upon the available resources, but also upon the efficiency of their utilization, and upon the effectiveness of those mechanisms which control the community. Good social organization often encourages progressive evolution of culture, particularly of technology. A dense population, consequently, may thrive on resources that in the absence of good organization could only support far fewer people. This is demonstrated in an outstanding manner in North America, where the increase in population since the coming of the Europeans may be ascribed in considerable part to the superiority of their economic, social, and political organization over that of the native Indians.

A type of community organization that is well adapted to, or at least tolerable for, a small and simple community in its youth may be inefficient when the community has grown in size and complexity. It may be suspected, consequently, that the decline of many of the larger human communities of the past has in part been due to the failure of their community organizations to evolve rapidly enough to maintain control over the enlarged size and increased complexity of their societies. Furthermore, certain inefficient elements in community organization which can be tolerated when the resources are abundant in relation to the size of the population may become severe handicaps as a society begins to approach the limit of its resources.

In its early youth, for example, Rome was mostly a nation of small farmers, with few city dwellers. It could then operate effectively as a republic, which was governed by a Senate composed of elder statesmen and an Assembly of all the citizens. The prosperity of the small farmers, however, was destroyed by the importation of hosts of slaves captured in wars of conquest, and by the policy of the government of selling food below cost, or giving it away free to the citizens of Rome. The simple political organization of the original republic was not effective in an empire. Rome was later ruled by a succession of rulers, many of whom exercised dictatorial power. On imported captured wealth and slaves, and on taxes and supplies received from her provinces, Rome continued to exist and to expand her culture for many centuries. During most of this time, however, the standard of living of most of the citizens of Rome was deplorable, though the wealthy classes lived luxuriously (Haskell, 1939). The soil of Rome was not sufficiently productive to feed and clothe her inflated population (Louis, 1927: 3). When easy wealth could no longer be secured by conquest, nor high taxes be collected from its colonies, the Empire found itself with inadequate resources to support its population. Internal regulatory mechanisms capable of adjusting the community to the changed conditions were lacking. Because of these and other maladjustments, the Empire collapsed.

Fortunate indeed is the human society whose institutions continuously evolve in harmony with the growth of its population, and whose resources and internal regulatory mechanisms are always adequate for those periods of crisis that are certain to occur from time to time. History, however, affords many examples of internal dissension and disorder indicating serious maladjustments in the organization of particular communities. The decline of the Roman Empire was no doubt due in part to faulty social and economic organization, which resulted ultimately in the ruin of the small farmers and businessmen. The remedies attempted by the later emperors included severe restrictions on trade and on personal freedom, excessive taxes, and a great expansion of the bureaucracy. Although certain of the emperors were able and devoted men and did the best they could, they were unable to prevent the disintegration of the Empire (Walbank, 1953).

Many ancient civilizations which for a time expanded rapidly may have failed ultimately because the evolution of their human institutions did not keep up with the expansion of their geographic area and the growth of their populations. Many of them were ruled by dictators or oligarchies, types of government which are notoriously conservative. Unless a civilization is able continually to evolve new methods and new institutions, it cannot adjust to the changes in relation to its habitat produced by its own growth. It may accordingly be concluded that one important factor in the decline of cultures in the past may have been their inability to evolve their institutions rapidly enough to meet their expanding needs.

Haskins (1951) believes the totalitarian type of government to be particularly vulnerable to changes in the environment. By totalitarian is meant a highly centralized type of government which tolerates no opposition. This form of government may be very effective in meeting a crisis. During war, for instance, most peoples will accept a considerable degree of regimentation, even though in peacetime they operate as democracies. A totalitarian government may be especially successful in military adventures that enrich it at the expense of its neighbors. Consequently, it may acquire resources that for a time enable the people to expand their culture rapidly. Ultimately, however, it is almost certain to produce stagnation of culture, because it stifles initiative among its citizens and attempts to make everyone conform to a specified type of thought and of conduct. Any

serious change in the conditions of the habitat, or any increase
of competition from its neighbors, is likely to mean disaster to a
totalitarian society.

The partial breakdown of the primary social groups (Cooley,
1925: 23), particularly the family and the neighborhood, may
also predispose to deterioration. Group opinion can play a large
role in the integration of a small community whose members
are well known to each other. In a large city, however, it is possible for an individual to become almost completely socially isolated, with only few or no close associates. Should the breakdown of family and neighborhood become widespread, without
replacement by some other type of intimate social group, damage to the organization of the larger community would seem
certain to occur (Barnes, 1952: 510–15).

Community decline usually due to multiple factors The decline of Rome, and of every other past empire or smaller community, was undoubtedly caused by a combination of unfortunate factors, rather than being due to any single cause.
Temporary or local disasters like drought, flood, fire, storm, disease, or pest, and even widespread damage caused by war, soil
erosion, or depletion of certain resources can often be overcome
if the community is otherwise in thriving condition. A community which is weak in internal organization or in resources, however, may succumb to an adversity which would cause only
minor difficulty to a more vigorous community.

A decline in culture once initiated in a complex human community may be impossible to stop short of complete disaster. As
the organization of the community deteriorates, the population
density earlier built up can no longer be supported at the old
standard of living. Starvation or emigration may ultimately re-
lieve population pressure, but during the period of scarcity the
reserves of the community may have become exhausted and
much of its working capital may have been consumed or wasted.

If stress continues, the community may retrogress to a relatively primitive state of culture and technology.

The balance between community success and failure must often be precarious. It may be suspected, however, that disintegration of community organization will seldom proceed far in those ecosystems in which there is at least a small surplus of available resources. Contrariwise, any community whose population density is at the limit of the carrying capacity of its habitat is vulnerable to every fluctuation of productivity and every minor or major catastrophe.

The continued existence of all human communities is dependent upon the simultaneous operation of many favorable factors both within the human society and in its habitat. No community can be expected forever to evolve to higher and higher levels of culture. The unfavorable factors to which every community is exposed are many and powerful. Only a marvelous concordance of happy circumstances will permit any community to thrive over a long period of time. It is not surprising, therefore, to read in the pages of history that many of those communities which in the past had evolved a high level of culture have since deteriorated, and that some have completely disappeared.

SELECTED REFERENCES

Bennett, Hugh H. 1939. Soil conservation. New York: McGraw-Hill Book Co.
Boak, Arthur E. R. 1947. A history of Rome to 565 A.D. New York: Macmillan Co.

Hankins, Frank H. 1926. The racial basis of civilization. New York: Alfred A. Knopf.

Haskell, H. J. 1939. The new deal in old Rome . . . New York: Alfred A. Knopf.

Haskins, Caryl P. 1951. Of societies and men. New York: W. W. Norton and Co.

Hawley, Amos H. 1950. Human ecology . . . Part IV. New York: Ronald Press Co.

Huntington, Ellsworth. 1945. Mainsprings of civilization. New York: John Wiley and Sons.

Kroeber, Alfred L. 1948. Anthropology: race, language, culture, psychology, prehistory. Chap. IX. New York: Harcourt, Brace and Co.

Lorimer, Frank, and Frederick Osborn. 1934. Dynamics of population . . . New York: Macmillan Co.

Morley, Sylvanus G. 1946. The ancient Maya. Stanford: Stanford University Press.

Sorokin, Pitirim A. 1947. Society, culture, and personality . . . New York: Harper and Bros.

Toynbee, Arnold J. 1947. A study of history. New York: Oxford University Press.

Interrelations Among Communities

Communities of every rank necessarily have various relations with their neighbors. A change in one community ultimately affects all the others in the same region at least slightly.

Any improvement, from man's point of view, that is attempted in a community is likely to be resisted by the natural controls in the community itself and those adjacent to it. This frequently happens on the human frontier, where newly planted crops may be damaged by raids of the animal inhabitants of adjacent natural communities. Such crops are safe only after all the troublesome elements in the natural communities have been eliminated. This means, of course, that these natural communities themselves often will be greatly altered and their controlling mechanisms interfered with.

If natural predators have been eliminated from a region, the native herbivores may greatly increase, invade man's cultivated fields, and damage his crops. These herbivores must in turn be controlled. Man the planner must consequently consider not only those ecosystems in which he himself dwells and those that directly produce his food and other essentials, but he must also be concerned with the neighboring communities.

Interchange

Ecosystems that adjoin one another are related by the interchange of materials, individual organisms, genes, and ideas. Inorganic soil particles, organic debris, and small living organisms, for example, are often carried from their place of origin to neighboring ecosystems by the action of wind and water, or the activities of animals (Dice, 1952, Chap. XVIII). Of particular importance to man is the interchange of commodities, persons, hereditary factors, and elements of culture.

Of commodities Commodities are interchanged between adjacent communities by either of two methods: robbery or trade. Both methods are operative from time to time not only in primitive societies, but also in certain modern civilizations.

Some primitive tribes and barbarous nations have in times past obtained a portion of their livelihood by robbing their neighbors. Even relatively peaceful tribes sometimes make raids on their neighbors to secure food, weapons, commodities, or slaves. In the recent past, unprovoked attacks by one nation on another to secure lands, mines, treasure, or strategic advantages have unfortunately occurred all too frequently.

In trade, as contrasted to robbery, some item or items of real or presumed value are given in exchange for those items which are obtained. Participation is generally voluntary. Trade articles which originated in many diverse parts of North America, for example, were widely distributed among the Indian tribes before the continent was occupied by Europeans (Herskovits, 1952: 198). Articles of value may through trade become dispersed over vast distances.

The exchange of articles between tribes often involves barter. Very few nonliterate tribes have any common medium of exchange, such as money. Sometimes no actual barter occurs and the operation is treated as an exchange of gifts (Herskovits, 1952, Chap. 8).

Trade between two primitive tribes is sometimes carried on at the tribal boundaries. Often, however, a trader enters the territory of his clients, where he is perhaps received with suspicion, but is not molested so long as he conforms to the accepted rules of behavior for a trader. Trade may even be carried on between hostile tribes by leaving items intended for exchange at some designated post. In this "silent" trade, there is no personal contact between the members of the two communities concerned (Herskovits, 1952, Chap. 9).

To an industrial community trade is essential, both to secure the raw materials out of which goods are manufactured and to dispose of the fabricated articles. The United States thus buys rubber from the East Indies, tin from Bolivia, diamonds from South Africa, petroleum from Venezuela, and similar essential materials from practically every part of the world. Automobiles, tractors, and many other manufactured articles are sent in return. Modern trade, moreover, is by no means a simple barter of raw materials for manufactured articles, but involves manufacturers, wholesalers, jobbers, retail merchants, commission merchants, purchasing agents, salesmen, customs brokers, railroads, shipping lines, banks, insurance companies, and many similar agencies.

Nor are the commodities that are exchanged between communities limited to those which are essential for human existence. Many of the articles of trade are luxuries, such as spices and other special items of food, jewels and other articles of personal adornment, paintings and similar works of art, scientific and technical books, religious paraphernalia, and many other items. No matter whether the articles exchanged between communities are essential or are luxuries, the community that receives them thereby enriches its culture.

Of persons Persons who go to a foreign community for only a few days, weeks, or months may be considered as tourists. Those who remain in a foreign community for a year or more, but with no expectation of staying permanently, may be classed as semipermanent visitors. Those who leave one community in order to make a permanent home in another community are emigrants from their place of origin, and immigrants in the community where they take up residence.

A wide variety of persons are interchanged between communities. In primitive communities, the most common interchange of persons presumably involves prisoners of war, who later may be sacrificed or become slaves. At times, wives are secured from neighboring tribes by capture. Apart from these, the most common interchange of persons among primitive and barbarous communities is presumably that of tradesmen.

When a nation has reached a high level of culture, certain of its citizens may temporarily become members of other neighboring or distant societies. Some of these may simply be tourists, but others will be traders, businessmen, missionaries, teachers, students, journalists, writers, artists, engineers, scientists, diplomats, politicians, and military personnel, or they may have still other special reasons for their travels. Such interchange of persons may take place between two communities which are equally advanced in culture; the citizens of a community well advanced in culture may become temporary members of a more primitive community; or conversely, certain citizens of a primitive community may visit a more advanced community.

Persons who go as visitors to a foreign land sometimes remain as permanent residents. Others who for any reason are dissatisfied in their homeland may go as settlers to a foreign land where the chances of success seem to them more promising. In recent centuries, thousands of persons have thus changed their places of residence.

Of hereditary factors An important result of the interchange of persons among communities is the transfer of hereditary factors (genes) from one population to another. Immigrants or their descendants often marry into the resident population. Tourists and visitors often form temporary alliances with native women. The heredity of a small tribe may be greatly changed by outbreeding with a more numerous neighboring population. By intermarriage with whites, continued for a number of generations, for instance, certain of the native North American Indian tribes have become considerably hybridized.

Interchange of genes may be presumed as a rule to increase the hereditary variability in the populations affected. Some of the newly introduced genes may prove to be valuable in combination with other genes already present in the population, and may thus provide the basis for progressive evolution.

Not all the hereditary factors received by a population through outcrossing, however, will be valuable additions. The individuals involved in miscegenation are often of inferior social status, and often may be suspected of carrying a heredity which is below the average of their race. The mixed-breed descendants of such outcrossing, accordingly, have a strong chance of being inferior in heredity.

Of cultural elements The diffusion of cultural elements is one of the most conspicuous interactions among communities. New ideas may be acquired from visitors or immigrants, or may be brought back by members of the community who have traveled in foreign lands. Communities that have developed the arts of communication may also acquire new cultural elements from newspapers, magazines, books, radio, and motion pictures.

Only a few of the new cultural ideas to which a community is exposed will be accepted by it, as has been pointed out in Chapter XII. This is fortunate, because many of the items which are a part of the culture of one people will not be suited to another

people in a different type of habitat. One of the interesting results of the acceptance of a new item of culture is that it may
produce a demand which previously did not exist for certain
trade goods. Thus, the adoption by certain societies in the north
cold Temperate Zone of the custom of drinking coffee necessi-
tates the purchase of coffee berries which grow only far to the
south.

Centers of interchange Interchanges between two adjacent
communities may occur all along the common boundary. The
amount of interchange may be greater at certain localities than
at others. Thus, a seaport usually is a place where trade and interchange of persons with foreign communities is concentrated.
Certain inland cities also are centers of trade with nearby foreign communities. If a trade route crosses a country, foreign
commodities and foreign customs may be spread all along its
path.

Barriers to interchange The barriers that separate human communities are of two main types: physical and cultural. Both
types of barriers have been in the past, and in many places still
are, of considerable effectiveness in preventing interchange
among human communities.

The physical barriers between human communities that are
perhaps most important of all are the oceans and other large
bodies of water. To an island community, water may form a barrier on every side. When ocean-going vessels are available, however, the ocean becomes a highway that may connect even
distant communities.

On the continents, high mountain ranges and extensive deserts often form barriers between human communities. These
barriers are never complete, for there are always passes across
the mountains and routes through the deserts, though passage
may be difficult or hazardous. Nevertheless, physical barriers
are often of considerable effectiveness in isolating human com-

munities. Thus, a community that occupies a mountain basin may be strongly isolated from its neighbors by the difficult and often hazardous trails across the mountain ridges (James, 1935: 343).

Differences between two peoples in religion, technology, and other features of culture may form strong barriers. A particular barrier here is that each people comes to believe that its own beliefs and customs are the only proper ones, and that any other type of behavior or of ideals must of necessity be inferior.

Of all the cultural barriers between communities, difference in language is perhaps the most effective. Two human populations that are unable to understand each other can have little intercommunication. It is true that certain persons learn to talk both languages and can thus serve as interpreters. The use of an interpreter, however, is a handicap which greatly hinders communication and understanding.

Special artificial types of barriers are often established to prevent or restrict certain kinds of interchange between communities. Nearly every industrial country, for example, has special regulations to govern the import and export of commodities. Often fees are charged which are sufficiently high to discourage the interchange of certain articles. The United States, for instance, has a high import tariff on many kinds of goods. This tariff is designed in part to secure revenue, and in part to hinder the entry into this country of those commodities which compete with domestic articles of similar kinds.

Another type of artificial barrier restricts the movements of persons between communities. Passports, and immigration and emigration regulations may restrict or at times completely prevent the interchange of persons. At present, for instance, the borders of certain countries behind the Iron Curtain are closed, and only rarely is any person permitted either to enter or to leave. Restrictions on the movements of persons across its national boundaries are sometimes essential for a prosperous nation if it is not to be overwhelmed with an excessive number of immigrants. Immigration restrictions are especially needed to prevent the entry of known criminals or of those persons who carry hereditary defects.

Still another kind of artificial barrier between human communities are currency differences. The money of each nation usually differs in kind and value from that of all other nations. These differences themselves impose barriers to the interchange of goods and credit. In addition, many countries impose other restrictions on the movements of currency or credit across their boundaries. It is almost impossible at the present time (1955), for instance, to send money out of certain countries.

Competition

Human communities that come into contact will almost inevitably compete with one another. When the two populations differ in their racial origins and/or in their types of culture, their competition is often severe. The resulting antagonism may sometimes result in war. War with neighbors was frequent among many primitive tribes, though often only in the form of raids rather than organized fighting. Most modern nations also have had a long history of war which may be assumed to have sometimes been because of competition.

Competition for land and resources   Competition among communities most frequently concerns land (living space) and resources. It is usually difficult to distinguish clearly between competition for resources and competition for the land to which the resources are related. A human society whose home region is densely populated, in proportion to its resources, is likely to exert heavy pressure on the surrounding societies. If such a people is inclined to violence, and unable or unwilling to solve its own problems of overpopulation, it is likely to devise some more or less plausible pretext for attempting to annex some of the lands or resources of its neighbors.

Competition among cultures Cultures also compete with one another through the competition of neighboring communities which differ in language, technology, customs, or religion. A major difference in religion between two neighboring communities, for example, leads often to misunderstanding and sometimes to open conflict. Many of the wars waged in the past ostensibly for religious purposes, however, have had economic and other aims in addition to those related to religion. Many of them have, in fact, been prompted primarily by simple motives of robbery.

Competition among communities that differ in culture, however, does not entirely prevent the diffusion between them of cultural elements, as has been pointed out earlier in this chapter. Communities that are in more or less close contact with one another for any considerable number of human generations will presumably become progressively more alike in their cultures.

Succession

One type of human community sometimes is replaced by a different type of community. This process constitutes community succession (Hawley, 1950, Part IV). A distinction must be made here between community succession and community evolution, although the two processes are closely related. When a community is replaced by another community whose human population differs in heredity or in culture, it is clear that succession has taken place. A minor change in the heredity of a population or in its culture, however, would not be community succession, but might perhaps be a step in community evolution. A major evolutionary change in a community, such as the discovery and utilization of a new important resource, on the other hand, might possibly be considered to have produced a new type of community and consequently would constitute succession, even though no change had occurred in the human population. No sharp line between evolution and succession can be drawn any more than sharp lines can be drawn between most biologic concepts or entities.

Succession does not always lead from a more primitive to a more complex community. Sometimes retrogression occurs—a well organized community may be replaced by a simpler one. Many a boom town, for example, has flourished for a time as a center of industry, only to relapse later into a small trade center or even to disappear completely. Succession is consequently not to be considered synonymous with progressive development.

Succession of peoples Sometimes an invading people completely displaces the former people and its culture. The victors may often be assumed to have a culture that is more efficient than that of the vanquished for utilizing the resources of the habitat. But this is not always so. A warlike nation may conquer and replace a nation which is much more advanced in the peaceful arts than is its conqueror.

Succession in type of community organization Pioneer human communities are usually succeeded by better integrated communities, and these by still more highly organized and more complex communities (Billington, 1949, Chap. 1). The exact sequence of succession in any given situation varies, however, with the resources of the local habitat, the heredity and culture of the people, and other factors. Much more study is needed in order to understand all the factors involved in the succession of human communities. We are yet far from being able to predict the future succession that is likely to take place in a given situation. In fact, it is unlikely that succession in human communities ever follows as regular a sequence as is presumed to be true in general for natural communities.

Succession in metropolitan land use   Numerous authors have called attention to the succession in local land use that often occurs in a metropolitan area. Every large city becomes divided into districts which are devoted, respectively, to retail trade, wholesale produce markets, wealthy residences, apartment houses, slums, manufacturing, and similar specialized uses (Burgess, 1926; McKenzie, 1926; Firey, 1947). As a city grows, certain of these districts may expand or shift their location. A district that at one time contains expensive residences, for example, may later be taken over by apartment houses, and still later may become an overcrowded slum. A manufacturing district, likewise, may encroach upon and eventually displace a residence district. Some of these replacements of one type of local community by another are clearly successions, because the human population often changes entirely in the process, and frequently there are important differences in culture and even in race among the successive local populations.

Succession in land use is inevitable as a city grows, but it has not been demonstrated that the trend of succession in a growing city is toward any particular climax type of land use. The succession of land use in an expanding city seems thus only remotely related to the ecologic succession that occurs in natural communities.

Cooperation

The relations between two adjacent communities is not restricted to competition. Cooperation also is a regular occurrence. In the process of trade, for example, the communities concerned may usually be presumed to secure mutual benefit. One community is often wholly dependent upon a neighboring community for some commodity essential for its welfare. This is particularly true of modern industrial communities, which import materials from all parts of the world.

Organization of communities into larger units If there is a considerable degree of cooperation among two or more small communities, they may together form a larger, more complex unit. Such a larger unit of community organization may operate wholly on the economic level; no political or cultural affiliation of its component subcommunities is necessarily involved. But communities that are closely related economically are likely in time to grow close together culturally, politically, and racially, though this does not always happen. Many communities that are adjacent to one another physically and cooperate by the interchange of commodities, may remain distinct and even antagonistic in certain other features.

The organization of several small communities into a larger political unit brings numerous advantages. A large political unit is able to protect itself more adequately against aggression from its neighbors and can ensure domestic tranquility more firmly than can a small community working alone. A large community is likely to contain a diversity of types of habitats and resources, and will therefore be more self-sufficient than a small community. By division of labor among its citizens, moreover, a large community can function more efficiently in the production of goods than a small one. Disasters that befall part of a large community also can more quickly be remedied than those that affect the whole of a small community. The advantages derived from the organization of small communities into larger political units become of increasing importance as technology and culture grow complex. In fact, any considerable complexity of technology would be impossible in a community of very small size.

A large political unit, however, has certain inherent disadvantages as well. It is harder to make democracy work in a complex large community than in a small one. Large political organizations are often autocratic, with the result that some of the smaller constituent communities may be discriminated against. Some large political units are inefficient, though many small community enterprises are equally ineffective. In general, it may be presumed that the advantages to be derived from the organization of small communities into larger ones often outweigh the disadvantages, especially when precautions are taken to retain the individuality of each subcommunity.

Influence on neighbors

The influence a human community exerts on its neighbors is related to its size, the vigor of its people, and the distance between them. Communities may continue to exert an influence long after they have lost their individuality.

Size and influence A large community will in general have more influence on its neighbors than a small one (Semple, 1911, Chap. 5). The greater the number of individuals making up a community, the greater, as a rule, its productivity of commodities, the stronger the population pressure it will exert, and the greater the respect or perhaps fear it will enjoy among its neighbors.

A large community will nearly always produce more commodities than a small one with the same level of culture, and consequently will have more goods available for exchange if there is a surplus at all of production above current needs. The volume of trade of a large community, therefore, will almost always be greater than that of a small one. Furthermore, a large community will almost always produce a greater diversity of commodities than a small one.

The larger a population, the greater in general its pressure on the surrounding populations. It is not certain, however, that this rule always holds for human communities. A large community whose human population has a high level of technology but is still at a relatively low density may for a time exert little population pressure on its neighbors. This condition, for example, seems to have held for the United States in the past.

Because of its potential economic, political, and military power a large human community commands a certain amount of respect from its neighbors. Even though small communities do not always treat a larger neighbor with particular deference, the possible exercise of power by the large community must always be in their minds. A small community, however, need not always fear a particular larger neighbor. Small communities have often depended very largely on a more powerful neighbor to defend them against attack.

Human vigor and community influence A highly vigorous human community will have more influence on its neighbors than a less vigorous one. By vigor I here mean the relative degree of activity of the people in the arts either of war or of peace. A people who are active in war may greatly affect their neighbors by overrunning their lands, robbing them of their resources, or perhaps enslaving them. A people active in cultural matters may affect their neighbors by supplying new items for cultural diffusion.

Community influence and distance The influence of a human community decreases with distance. Contiguous communities must affect each other more strongly than those not in direct contact. Nevertheless, the influence of a community may extend far beyond its immediate neighbors. Travelers and emigrants may carry their heredity a considerable distance from their home communities. Trade goods are often carried many miles from their places of origin. Cultural elements may be diffused for great distances, and in the process they may cross many separate human communities.

The general rule that the influence of a natural community decreases with the square of its distance (Dice, 1952, Chap. VIII), however, is probably not generally applicable to modern human communities, though it may apply to primitive ones. Routes of trade, and special means of communication in the modern world, have extended the influence of every community to practically all the parts of the inhabited earth.

The influence of past times The influence of a community does not always end when the community itself has ceased to exist. Many communities of the past still continue to influence our modern ways of life. The code of law developed by the Roman Empire, for example, still serves as the basis for the laws of many European nations. The precepts of the Mosaic code also still exert tremendous influence. Inventions, religions, and customs developed by ancient peoples constitute a considerable part of the culture of all modern societies. Writing is an especially potent means for a community to influence those which come after it.

The influence that communities of the past still exert is particularly well illustrated by our domestic animals and cultivated plants. The human communities of today are largely dependent for their success on their use of such domestic animals as the horse, cow, sheep, goat, and pig, and of such cultivated plants as wheat, barley, oats, rye, maize, potato, and cotton. All of these and many other valuable animals and plants were domesticated by men so long ago that the wild ancestors of many of them are either extinct or are unknown. In fact, very few of our most valuable species have been domesticated within the past one thousand years. Every modern community consequently is dependent for its very existence on contributions made by communities which disappeared thousands of years ago.

It is safe to say, therefore, that every human community influences its neighbors in numerous ways. The influence of each community spreads out in circles of decreasing effectiveness, but a valuable new invention made in a remote place may ultimately spread to every inhabited part of the world. All existing human communities are directly or indirectly interconnected. The whole world, past and present, constitutes the largest unit of community organization.

SELECTED REFERENCES

Dice, Lee R. 1952. Natural communities. Chap. XVIII. Ann Arbor: University of Michigan Press.
Hawley, Amos H. 1950. Human ecology . . . Part IV. New York: Ronald Press Co.
Herskovits, Melville J. 1952. Economic anthropology . . . Part III. New York: Alfred A. Knopf.
Keith, Arthur. 1947. Evolution and ethics. New York: G. P. Putnam's Sons.
Semple, Ellen C. 1911. Influences of geographic environment . . . Chaps. 5–9. New York: Henry Holt and Co.

Human Ecosystems

CHAPTER XV

A human community consists not only of men, women, and children, but, as a minimum, it includes also certain plants that supply food to man, either directly, or indirectly through animals. Every human community is actually far more complex than this; it includes food chains of numerous kinds, domestic animals and perhaps crop plants, parasites, diseases, and numerous other species of organisms, some of which serve as regulatory mechanisms or perform other ecologic functions.

When the habitations and related structures built by man, and the soils, climate, and other non-living features of the habitat are considered along with the organisms, each human community together with the lands it occupies forms an ecosystem. From the ecologic point of view the interrelations between a human society and its biotic and physical environment are of great significance. Any complete ecologic classification, consequently, must consider ecosystems, rather than human societies alone.

In a region which has only a sparse human population living in a low state of culture, man will be only one species among those which compose the several natural communities. The ecosystems of such an area may consequently be classified in much the same manner as natural ecosystems (Dice, 1952, Chaps. XIX and XX). Where, on the other hand, the human population is relatively dense and its state of culture is advanced to a point where man controls the habitat either partially or completely, the classification must include also those modified ecosystems which are formed as a result of man's activities.

Social groups composed of numerous persons will modify the natural ecosystem to a greater degree than an isolated family. Within any area that is occupied by a fairly dense human population, many of the ecosystems will be very different from those that occur in a state of primitive nature. In a densely populated area, certain nearly natural communities may still remain, but most of the area will be severely modified by man's activities. Villages, towns, and cities and their associated grazing lands, cultivated fields, orchards, clearings, forest plantations, mines, factories, highways, and other artifacts clearly require a different ecologic classification than natural ecosystems.

Some early students of human ecology have pointed out that primitive human communities can be classified according to whether the people: (1) depend for their livelihood on fishing, hunting, or food gathering, (2) exist as pastoral nomads, or (3) are agriculturalists (Bews, 1935). Industrial communities would form a fourth category. This classification of human communities has much to commend it, but it is an obvious oversimplification. A human community is rarely dependent upon a single type of food and seldom limited to a single kind of activity (Herskovits, 1948: 601). Agriculture, for example, often is combined with the herding of domestic animals and sometimes also with hunting, fishing, or the gathering of wild foods.

A more comprehensive classification of human ecosystems is greatly needed. Human societies, however, vary so greatly in their organization and culture and have such diverse relationships to their associated species of plants and animals, their physical habitats, and other human societies that no simple classification seems possible. Several ranks of ecosystems that seem to be of particular importance to man, nevertheless, may be pointed out.

Tribal ecosystems

Because of his social habits, man usually lives in aggregations. In a society with a primitive state of culture, the band constitutes the smallest social and economic unit (Linton, 1936: 210; Steward, 1936). A band may consist of a single family, or may in part be composed of less closely related individuals. Under a primitive type of culture, each band must be small in numbers because the habitat will not support a dense population.

Each band may for a time constitute a self-sufficient economic and social unit, capable of finding or growing all the food it requires, making the tools and clothing it needs, and constructing its own habitations. No single band, however, can long exist as a biologic unit. If close inbreeding is to be avoided, wives and husbands for the young must be secured from outside the group. Incest tabus nearly always operate to prevent the mating of near relatives. The tribe, rather than the band, therefore, is the biologic unit of organization for primitive human societies.

A tribal ecosystem may be defined as the sum of the men, women, and children who make up a tribe, together with all their associated native and domestic animals and plants, and all the physical features of the tribal habitat. A great deal more than the human population, therefore, is contained in a tribal ecosystem. The human society, nevertheless, is from our viewpoint the most significant part of such a unit.

Each tribal ecosystem is a generally self-sufficient unit which contains one tribe of men. This tribe may be either nomadic or sedentary; and it may subsist either on food obtained from gathering and hunting, from its domesticated herds, or from its agricultural crops. The success of each tribe depends to a large extent upon the efficiency with which its heredity and culture are adapted to its habitat. The habitat, in turn, is modified by the activities of the tribe.

Tribes vary in the number of members. Some tribes are small and feeble, others large and vigorous. Large tribes often are divided into smaller subunits, each of which may ultimately evolve into a tribe. Feeble tribes, on the other hand, are likely to become extinct, especially if they are under heavy pressure from more vigorous neighbors.

The political organization of a tribe may be based upon a chief, an assemblage of elders, or a loose democracy among the members, but presumably it is always sufficient to preserve the autonomy of the group and to separate it from neighboring tribes.

The reactions of a tribesman toward a member of his own group are very different from those toward a member of a foreign tribe (Spencer, 1892; Keith, 1947). The members of a tribe nearly always cooperate with and assist each other to survive and to prosper. By contrast, a person who is a member of a different tribe is nearly always met with suspicion if not outright hostility. Within the tribe there is often a sharing of resources, but in many societies it is not accounted a crime to outsmart, or steal from, an outsider—or even to murder him.

All the members of a single tribe speak as a rule the same language, and are similar in most other features of their culture, although dialects and peculiar fashions may distinguish local subdivisions. Between adjacent tribes, on the other hand, there may be striking differences in customs and often in language. The greater the difference in language and other aspects of culture between any two tribes, the greater the amount of isolation of each of them, as has been pointed out in Chapter XIV.

Adjacent tribes compete for land and for resources. Even though open warfare between adjacent tribes may be absent, there is nevertheless a constant pressure on their boundaries. In such a struggle, the tribe that has the best weapons, the best tactics of offense and defense, the most vigor, or the largest number of members is likely to win out.

A tribe that has eliminated a neighbor and thereby acquired additional lands may then be able to expand its numbers and/or improve its culture. A warlike tribe may destroy all the members of a conquered tribe, but is more likely to preserve and to absorb certain individuals as slaves, wives, or adopted children. The tribe, therefore, is an extremely important unit for the evolution of both heredity and culture.

Because of the great variations among tribes in culture and population density, their habitats are affected by human occupancy in various ways and to varying degrees. Each tribe, together with its biotic associates and physical habitat, consequently, constitutes a more or less distinctive ecologic unit, which is here called the tribal ecosystem.

Camp-centered ecosystems A minor center of human influence is established locally wherever an individual person or band sets up a camp. In ancient Wales, for example, the homes of the people were not collected into villages but were scattered along the edges of the woods, and from time to time they were moved. This distribution of habitations enabled the Welsh, who were a pastoral people, to take effective care of their herds (Seebohm, 1915: 187).

Each human band commonly lives in a camp or home, which may be a natural cave or shelter or an artificially constructed dwelling or cluster of dwellings. Wherever a band establishes a temporary camp or a more permanent home in a primitive area, the natural ecosystem that formerly occupied the site will of necessity be altered, as has been discussed in Chapter VIII. This is true whatever the type of human culture, though the state of culture may greatly affect the degree to which the natural ecosystem near the camp becomes altered.

The native species of plants and animals which supply human needs for food, building materials, fuel, and other essentials must soon become more or less depleted around every camp-site. Dangerous large carnivores also will probably be reduced in numbers. Scavengers, commensals, and human parasites, on the other hand, may increase in abundance. The domestic plants and animals which man brings with him may cause considerable changes in the local densities of the native species with which they compete or on which they feed. The camp and its associated domestic species may also attract certain kinds of predators and parasites.

The extent of change produced in a natural ecosystem by the presence of a camp will depend upon the number of persons in the society, the area over which the camp is spread, the time it remains at one location, and the state of culture of the people. The camps of a nomadic people seldom remain long in one place. Such camps, consequently, may be assumed to produce fewer alterations in the local natural ecosystems than the more permanent habitations of agricultural peoples. Every gradation between temporary camps and fixed homesteads, however, may occur, and it is difficult to draw any sharp dividing line between them.

Biotic provinces and tribal ecosystems The regional community that occupies an area of relatively uniform climate, physiography, and soil is a useful unit of classification for human communities, as it is for natural communities. When the physical features of the regional habitat are included together with the living organisms, the unit is called a biotic province. Every continent may be divided into a limited number of biotic provinces, each distinguished by its climate, physiography, soil types, vegetation, flora, and fauna (Dice, 1943). In each biotic province, succession leads toward one or several particular types of ecologic climaxes.

The plants and animals of each biotic province form an assemblage of species and races which differs in at least certain important characters from the assemblages of neighboring provinces. Many of the domestic varieties of plants and animals that thrive best in a particular biotic province will be peculiar to that province. The human population which thrives best in each province must also have a hereditary constitution that is adapted to the climate and resistant to the common diseases of the area.

The culture of the human population of each biotic province must be tolerably adapted to the climate, physiography, and soil of the area, or the population cannot survive. Culture areas (Kroeber, 1948: 785–94) that are more or less concordant with biotic provinces may thus be recognized. Man is a very adaptable animal, however, and may be able to live in a particular province in spite of a culture that is imperfectly suited to the habitat. Furthermore, many elements of human culture have little or no obvious dependence upon the habitat. As a result, tribes with dissimilar cultures may, at least for a time, live in the same climatic region.

Between adjacent climatic regions there are often wide areas of intergradation. For this reason, the limits of biotic provinces and of culture areas are seldom very sharp (Dixon, 1928: 24; Dice, 1943).

Each human tribe may be assumed to have a tendency to expand the area it occupies to and beyond the limits of the biotic province in which it lives. Beyond the boundaries of its biotic province, the climate may be unfavorable to the members of the tribe. Furthermore, the tribe may there come into competition with other tribes whose heredity and culture are better adapted to the conditions in the adjacent provinces.

The whole area of a biotic province, on the other hand, may not always be occupied by one particular tribe. Even if the province is wholly occupied by a tribe, the area may be shared in part with one or more alien tribes. Many tribes, moreover, have ranges which extend into or across several biotic provinces.

The failure of a tribal ecosystem to coincide with the limits of a biotic province is often due to historical accidents. The encroachment of another tribe or group of tribes may drive a tribe from part or all of its ancestral home, and force it into another province. The displaced tribe may have the adaptability to survive in its new environment. Very rarely, unfortunately, are we able to ascertain the precise place of origin of a particular tribe. Deductions about the relationship between tribal evolution and geographic areas are consequently mostly theory.

Homestead ecosystems

In certain regions in which the inhabitants live in generally permanent residences, the homesteads may be scattered singly over the area. Such a pattern of scattered homesteads is exhibited in many parts of the United States, both in areas devoted to livestock pasturage and in areas where agricultural crops are grown. As a rule, each homestead is occupied by a single family together with its retainers. The pastures and/or cultivated fields usually lie immediately adjacent to the habitations and outbuildings of the family, often surrounding them. The result of this type of human occupancy is that each homestead forms a minor ecosystem.

Homestead ecosystems may in turn be subdivided into still smaller ecologic units. The edificarian community, for example, is composed of those animals and plants that live in the buildings constructed by man, or in their immediate vicinity (Chapter VII). Each type of pasture land, woodlot, orchard, and cultivated field likewise supports a special kind of community. These man-modified communities vary so greatly from place to place, however, that attempts to classify them seem at present to be impractical.

Village-centered ecosystems

A different type of human occupancy is exhibited where the inhabitants of a local area group their homes to form hamlets or villages. Where there is danger from bandits or raids by outsiders, such village aggregations may provide better protection than a series of isolated homesteads. The habit of farmers and others of living in small aggregations, however, is evident also in many regions where personal safety seems not to be a factor. The satisfaction that is derived from frequent social contacts with neighbors is undoubtedly one of the reasons why many people prefer to live in groups.

In many parts of early agricultural Europe, the homes of the people were commonly grouped around the villa of the landlord. This is the origin of the term village. In England, for instance, the village type of community seems to have been characteristic from the earliest times down to the present (Seebohm, 1915). The lord of the manor, however, was not an autocratic owner; the people had certain rights. Many villages, furthermore, are composed solely of the homes of the villagers, without any residence of landlord or overseer.

Surrounding each village lie the pastures, fields, forests, and waters which produce the food and other materials needed to support the villagers. Each village and its supporting lands together constitute an integrated ecosystem, whether part or all of the lands are owned in common, whether the lands are owned by the farmers individually, or whether they are owned by landlords. The conspicuous feature of such a village, as contrasted with more complex types of human communities, is that all its families perform essentially the same routine labors.

It should be pointed out that the term village is here used in its older sense, to denote an aggregation of the homes of agriculturalists, and that it carries no implication about the number of its inhabitants.

At the present time village-centered ecosystems still function in many parts of the world. The village of El Cerrito, New Mexico, for example, is a small aggregation of humble houses, barns, and other accessory outbuildings, a school, and a church. Domestic stock and agriculture supply the basic economic needs of the villagers, but the men sometimes go for a time to other communities and work for wages. The inhabitants are all of Spanish-American descent and are closely integrated socially by family ties and by membership in the Roman Catholic Church (Leonard and Loomis, 1941).

Pastoralists and hunters also sometimes live in groups in especially favorable situations. These aggregations of dwellings may be occupied only at certain seasons. The aggregations of peoples in a primitive state of culture may nevertheless consist of a surprising number of families. Thus, among the Eskimos, a few settlements have populations in excess of 200 persons each (Weyer, 1932: 205).

Town-centered ecosystems

Under a simple type of culture each family that lives in a hamlet or small village may be nearly self-sufficient and may produce essentially the same kinds of foods and other materials as all the other families. In an advanced state of culture, however, no family can any longer be fully self-sufficient, but must secure certain tools, supplies, and services from outside its circle. Even in fairly small social aggregations there may consequently be some specialization of labor (Chapple and Coon, 1942, Chap. 11), so that certain persons serve as blacksmiths, merchants, teachers, priests, or in other special capacities.

A town-centered ecosystem may be defined as one which has as its nucleus a small center of human population in which specialization of labor is conspicuous. In this definition the term "town" refers to the complexity of economic organization, rather than to the number of inhabitants. The number of people who live in such a center of trade and service varies; in the United States, the center might consequently be called either a town, a village, or even a hamlet (Loomis and Beegle, 1950: 177).

Where the homesteads of farmers or ranchers are distributed singly, as in most parts of the United States, there also are often aggregations of population which constitute important local centers of trade, service, and culture. Such centers will usually have stores, repair shops, schools, churches, and other establishments that serve the surrounding area. The town, in its turn, receives food and other materials from the farmers and ranchers. Certain of the farmers, especially those who are retired, may live in the center. Each such aggregation together with its surrounding homesteads and fields constitutes a town-centered ecosystem.

As an example of a town-centered ecosystem may be cited the one which centers in the town of Irwin, Iowa (Moe and Taylor, 1942). In 1942, this town-centered ecosystem included about 1,500 human inhabitants. These dwelt in the town itself and in parts of four surrounding townships. Located in the town and serving the community were stores, garages, blacksmith shops, grain dealer, bank, telephone exchange, doctor, hamburger shop, school, church, movie houses, beer hall, pool room, and other service units. Certain schools and churches that served the community, however, were located elsewhere in the ecosystem than the town. Members of the community frequently went to other towns or cities to purchase supplies and secure certain special services. Nevertheless, the town of Irwin is an important center of community activities, and together with its surrounding homesteads, fields, and inhabitants it forms a recognizable ecologic unit. Other examples of town-centered ecosystems were described by Loomis and Beegle (1950: 175–203).

Few rural social aggregations in the United States, however, are as simple as the term "town-centered" community implies. Certain local communities that center around a church or school, for example, may share the trading center with other local communities. Furthermore, the automobile has so greatly increased the mobility of country folk that a given farm family may belong to several different types of social group at the same time (Bell, 1942). Even among such a clannish and conservative people as the Old Amish of Lancaster County, Pennsylvania, there is much complexity of community patterns: some local communities are based on church affiliations, while others are centered in villages or towns (Kollmorgen, 1942).

A great weakness of the present arrangement of human communities in the United States is that their political organization nearly always fails to conform to natural economic or social groups. Township and other political boundaries rarely coincide with ecologic or social divisions. A group of people who have interests in common may consequently have great difficulty in cooperating for their mutual benefit. As has been pointed out by Galpin (1915) the natural unity between a town and its surrounding rural lands is disrupted by organizing the town under a different political unit than the rural areas. When a farmer comes to town, for example, he enters a politically foreign, though not a hostile, area. Inadequate provision is made by most city governments for the comfort and welfare of such essential visitors. For some purposes, urban and rural areas may require different kinds of administration, but they have many interests in common and it would be to the best interest of both to work together much more closely than is possible under our present political system.

City-centered ecosystems

In a city there is much greater specialization of labor than in a town. The offices of government, large mercantile houses, major manufacturing plants, and centers of transportation are usually located in cities. To its surrounding area, a city furnishes machinery and other manufactured goods, public administration, police protection, advanced educational facilities, various forms of entertainment, medical facilities, and many other kinds of special services, all of which are essential for the maintenance of a complex culture. The farms, villages, and towns which surround the city supply it in return with articles of food and with raw materials. The city and its hinterland thus form a closely integrated economic, social, and cultural unit.

A metropolis has been considered by some authors to constitute an economic and social organism (McKenzie, 1933). In a large city the interrelations among the various parts of a human society reach their highest degree of complexity. A city, however, is never self-sustaining. Most of the food of its inhabitants, much of the raw materials for its factories, and many items included in its trade must be drawn from the surrounding area or from more distant regions. The city, in its turn, serves its surrounding area in many ways. While we may treat the city as one kind of community, any complete treatment of its ecology must consider the larger regional community of which it forms only a part.

A city-centered ecosystem is seldom organized in a simple manner. The surrounding homesteads, villages, and towns are not just subdivisions of the city-centered unit. Rather, they are complexly interrelated among themselves and with the city. Special suburban ecosystems, which serve primarily for residence, manufacture, or other purposes, nearly always surround a large city, and these suburban units also may be complexly interrelated among themselves, with the city, and with the neighboring village-centered and town-centered ecosystems.

National ecosystems

A nation is a political unit composed of a number of tribes or city-centered societies. The societies that form a nation may vary in racial stock, language, and culture. The political boundaries of a nation, moreover, may bear no close relationship to natural climatic or physiographic divisions. The boundary between Canada and the United States, for instance, cuts across many natural areas.

Each nation, nevertheless, does form something of a unit, at least in its economy. Barriers to trade are usually less restrictive within than between nations. For example, most modern nations restrict the import and export of numerous types of commodities, while restrictions on trade between states within the nation are much less rigid. The national organizations required for the circulation of money, collection of taxes, law enforcement, national defense, and internal security of necessity impose a certain amount of unity on each nation.

International ecosystems

Various types of international organization have been attempted in the course of history. Military empires have been common in the past, but more recently the trend is toward voluntary associations of nations. An empire may be considered ecologically as merely a large example of a national ecosystem. A voluntary association of nations will usually be somewhat more loosely integrated than a single nation or an empire.

In its economy, the whole world is rapidly becoming a single unit. Foods for our tables and raw materials for our factories come from abroad and frequently from distant lands. Trade in all kinds of commodities between countries is extensive, and steadily increasing. Only a few of the most isolated and primitive tribes are fully or nearly independent of their neighbors. The largest unit of ecologic classification, consequently, is the world ecosystem. Unless life exists on other planets, or unless space travel to another inhabitable heavenly body becomes possible, the ecosystem which covers the earth is the maximum possible ecosystem.

The complexities of economic and social interrelations among the various parts of the world ecosystem make the classification of human communities very difficult. In a primitive state of culture, a tribal ecosystem may be a clearly defined unit; but this unit becomes of decreasing importance as industry and trade advance. Farmsteads, villages, and cities are significant centers of ecologic organization even in the most highly industrialized parts of the world. It often is difficult, however, to delimit these units clearly, because of the many interactions among the various ranks and sizes.

Another impediment to classification is that many existing human communities are in process of change. Although certain types of communities that appear to be fairly stable recur frequently and thus might form the basis for a classification, many others are evidently intermediate between these types. The result is that only a part of the communities in any given area will fit any proposed system.

In our present state of knowledge, therefore, no complete classification of human communities seems possible. The units described in this chapter are intended to serve only as examples of some of the most obvious types of human ecosystems.

SELECTED REFERENCES

Brownell, Baker. 1950. The human community . . . New York: Harper and Bros.

Dice, Lee R. 1943. The biotic provinces of North America. Ann Arbor: University of Michigan Press.

Dice, Lee R. 1952. Natural communities. Chaps. 19 and 20. Ann Arbor: University of Michigan Press.

Hawley, Amos H. 1950. Human ecology; a theory of community structure. Chaps. 12–15. New York: Ronald Press Co.

Kroeber, Alfred L. 1948. Anthropology: race, language, culture, psychology, prehistory. Pp. 785–94. New York: Harcourt, Brace and Co.

Loomis, Charles P., and J. Allan Beegle. 1950. Rural social systems . . . Chaps. 6–8. New York: Prentice-Hall.

Quinn, James A. 1950. Human ecology. Chap. IV. New York: Prentice-Hall.

Philosophy of the Human Community

CHAPTER XVI

The innumerable types and ranks of human communities that now exist on the earth, or have existed in the past, vary tremendously in the number of individual persons composing them, in the kinds of associated plants and animals, in the complexity of their social, economic, and political organizations, and in their stability. Each minor or major community, furthermore, is nearly always also a component part of some larger unit of community organization. Nevertheless, each small or large interacting group of persons, together with its associated plants and animals, forms a more or less perfectly integrated unit.

Unity Every human community, no matter what its size or rank, has a unity and an individuality of its own. Although the particular plants, animals, and persons of which it is composed must ultimately die, or more rarely may migrate away, they are usually replaced by other individuals of the same general kinds, and the community continues to exist. Because of its internal regulatory mechanisms the community, furthermore, is able to survive considerable fluctuations in the conditions of its physical habitat.

Small human communities nearly always constitute a unit in

some larger and more extensive community. Each such larger community has again a unity of its own, even though it is composed of several smaller units. We see this illustrated by the village-centered ecosystems grouping to form city-centered ecosystems, and these city-centered units in their turn grouping to form national ecosystems. Each community of low rank forms an integrated unit that performs certain functions, while other functions are delegated to the larger communities. In those primitive societies which have no large communities, the small community units must perform all the functions necessary for the successful existence of the whole society.

Each self-sufficient human community, irrespective of its rank, must include a sufficient number of plants and animals to provide man with food, shelter, and other necessary materials and services. The population densities of each species, including man, must also be adjusted to the resources of the ecosystem. Suitable regulatory mechanisms must be present to keep the various parts of the community in proper adjustment with each other and with the conditions of the habitat. The culture of the human society, furthermore, must be adapted to the conditions of the physical habitat, to the resources of the ecosystem, and to the associated species of plants and animals. Every continuing community must, accordingly, be a more or less well integrated unit.

A human community is more than the sum of its parts   Every human community is composed of individual persons, other animals, and plants, all of which have numerous ecologic interrelations. Certain of these species cooperate to promote their mutual welfare. Those species that man has domesticated, for instance, profit from the association by thriving better than they could in a state of nature, though at the price of their individual freedom. The mutual interdependency of the members of the community is in no way lessened by the fact that one species—man—dominates the others and is able to some extent to control the whole ecosystem.

Through their combined efforts and abilities, the human members of a community are able to accomplish results which are far beyond the capacity of any one individual. An industrial community, for example, produces goods and services that are wholly inaccessible to an unorganized group of men. Even a small band of men in a primitive state of culture may be able to exist where a single individual would perish. A human community, also, by providing care and training for its young, not only makes possible the reproduction of the human species, but also ensures the transmission from generation to generation of the cultural heritage of the group. Most important of all, each human community offers a basis for still further evolution both in human heredity and in community culture. In many ways, then, each community constitutes a unit that differs from the sum of the individual men and other organisms of which it is composed.

Complexity All kinds of human communities are complex in their organization. Even the simplest kind of human community (consisting of a single human family together with its associated species of plants and animals) has a very complex structure. The members of the family vary in sex and age. They perform different functions in the family community, and have different responsibilities.

The food supply of the human members of a primitive community will usually be obtained from certain species of plants and of animals that form part of the same ecologic aggregation. In each community there occur also competitors, herbivores, predators, parasites, and beneficial symbionts, which form many diverse food chains and often have highly diverse ecologic interrelations with one another. Even the simplest community is thus highly complex.

A modern human community is tremendously more complex than a primitive community. The complexity is particularly great in a metropolitan community where numerous kinds of goods are manufactured. In such a community one will find very great specialization of labor among the human inhabitants, resulting in almost innumerable types of skilled occupations. In the list of human occupations must be included the unpaid workers and those disreputable or even illegal occupations which nevertheless are part of the life of the city (Hawley, 1950: 217).

A modern community contains a great number of economic, religious, political, and social groups which often have overlapping membership (Angell, 1941). Even to list the great variety of organized and unorganized social groups that exist in a city of any size is difficult, and a complete consideration of the interrelations between these numerous units is perhaps impractical at present.

A city, moreover, is never a self-sustaining ecologic unit. Its food, the raw materials for its factories, and much of its manufactured goods must be secured from outside sources. A considerable portion of its labor will also be furnished by commuters who live outside the city boundaries. The city exists because it supplies certain services needed by the larger unit which includes its environs (Hawley, 1950: 216).

Adaptations to community life All species of plants and of animals exhibit numerous adaptations to life in the particular communities in which they have their being. A carnivore, for example, must have adaptations for capturing the individuals of those suitable prey species which are members of the same community.

The most important special adaptations to community life exhibited by man are those which lead to social cooperation with his fellows. It is through social cooperation that man is able to dominate to a high degree those ecosystems which he inhabits. A considerable part of man's social cooperation is due to training in youth, and to social pressure. Training in cooperation can be only successful, however, because man, along with many other primates, inherits a high degree of social aptitude. The heredity of social aptitude is itself presumably the result of evolution, based on the survival of those individuals who were most easily trained to cooperate with other members of their groups.

Another set of adaptations exhibited by man are those that make him resistant to the common disease-producing organisms which also are members of his communities. This disease resistance is seldom perfect, but it enables man to live in more densely crowded populations than otherwise would be possible. Life under crowded conditions has many disadvantages for man. The major past advances in technology and in the arts have been achieved, nevertheless, in highly concentrated societies. Thus, the development of disease resistance which permits man to live in large groups has been an important factor in the development of human communities.

Philosophic basis of the community concept

Certain students of human communities are of the opinion that human societies and their cultures are largely controlled by the characters of the local environments. According to another view, each culture is largely a chance aggregation of customs. Disagreement also exists concerning the effects heredity may have on the evolution of human culture, and the importance of the individual man in the development of human societies.

Environmental determinism The hypothesis that the major features of each human culture are adapted to the physical and biotic characters of the habitat is called environmental determinism (Herskovits, 1952: 489–91). In earlier chapters I have pointed out that no human society can long endure unless it has customs which enable it to make tolerably efficient use of the available foods and other essentials for human existence which are supplied by the associated plants and animals. Neither can a society succeed unless the habits of its people are adjusted to the climate and the local changes of weather.

The character of its physical habitat must necessarily affect and control every human community in many ways, as has been pointed out in Chapter XI. The climate, physiography, and soil affect both directly and indirectly the lives of the people themselves and of the wild or domestic plants and animals that provide them with food and other necessities for life. In a consideration of the Indian tribes of the great Basin-Plateau area of western United States, for instance, Steward (1938: 236) concluded that each primitive society has to conform to the physical and biotic factors of its habitat.

In a habitat with scanty resources, the character of these resources largely determines the type of culture of the human inhabitants. Tribes with meager and scattered food resources on different continents and among peoples of diverse racial ancestry have developed subsistence patterns of culture that are very similar. To obtain adequate food, such people must live in single, scattered families during the greater part of the year. Larger groups can be formed only temporarily in places where food is locally abundant. In a habitat with abundant resources in relation to population density, on the other hand, a complex culture can be developed. Under such conditions, many of the aspects of culture may not be closely dependent upon the type of food or other resources of the habitat (Steward, 1941).

The dependence of culture upon environment is, consequently, most evident in extremely rigorous types of habitats. Thus, the inhabitants of the frigid zone and those who live in hot deserts exhibit many special adaptations of culture to the natural resources and the extreme physical conditions of their respective habitats. In temperate climates and in regions with an abundance of natural resources, on the contrary, the success of a given tribe may not be closely dependent upon the co-ordination of its culture with the conditions of its habitat. Even in the best habitats, nevertheless, it may be assumed that environment has considerable influence on the evolution of culture (Bennett, 1944). The character and resources of the habitat at least limit the amount of cultural advance which is possible (Meggers, 1954).

The most ardent advocate of the importance of environment in the evolution of culture would not likely maintain that all elements of culture are environmentally controlled. Many elements of religion, language, art, and social organization are evidently not directly dependent upon the environment. The technologic and economic elements of culture are far more responsive to the characters of the habitat than are the non-material elements (Herskovits, 1952: 490). Even so, many social, religious, and artistic elements of culture are affected indirectly or directly by the environment (Huntington, 1945; White, 1949b).

A striking illustration of cultural features which are non-adaptive in relation to the environment are those customs that result in the destruction of valuable property in order to gain personal or family prestige (Herskovits, 1952: 491). Not only primitive societies exhibit such noneconomic customs. In our country, an expensive wedding or funeral is often a severe strain on the finances of the family. Environmental determinism evidently is not a complete explanation of human cultures, although it does explain many of their features.

Cultural drift Opposed to the hypothesis of environmental determinism is that of cultural drift (Herskovits, 1948: 581).

This hypothesis assumes that many or perhaps all of the elements of a culture have arisen by the piling up of a series of minor changes. Such changes may not be entirely haphazard; instead they often move in a particular direction, one step in cultural evolution leading to the next. According to this hypothesis, historical accidents play a large role in the evolution of culture. The discovery of the use of fire, for example, may be assumed to have been such an accident.

There can be little doubt that new inventions, the acquirement of new cultural elements by diffusion, and minor modifications of fashions and customs have been very important in the evolution of every culture. Certain items of culture may be assumed to be neither directed nor controlled by anything in the environment or heredity of the people concerned. In fact, customs that are to some degree unadaptive may evolve, such as the habit of women in the northern United States to wear silk or other lightweight stockings on bitterly cold days. Cultural elements that seriously handicap the success or survival of individual persons or a social group, however, would not be expected to become established. Unadaptive cultural drift may consequently be expected to occur most frequently in religion, art, and other nonmaterial elements of culture.

The hypothesis that culture may evolve independently of the characters of the environment, or of the heredity of the people, seems then to apply mostly to the nonmaterial elements of culture, and perhaps only to certain ones of these. Nevertheless, historic accidents undoubtedly are responsible for many of the particular features of every culture. Adaptation to any given environmental feature can nearly always be obtained in a number of ways. Which way is actually adopted may be largely a matter of chance.

Culture and heredity   Whether the evolution of culture is related in any way to the heredity of the people is a matter of much dispute. The hypothesis has been advanced that each race has a tendency to evolve a particular type of culture, distinct from that of all other races. Certain authors assert that the highest types of culture and of community organization can be evolved only by races of generally superior heredity. This hypothesis has often been associated with the further assumption that the best heredity and the best culture of all are the monopoly of the race or nation of the writer.

At the other extreme we are told that heredity has nothing whatever to do with the evolution of culture. This hypothesis seems to be very popular just now among social anthropologists, many of whom deny in particular that culture is in any way dependent upon race (Opler, 1944).

Actual information is mostly lacking about the general level or variability of ability in the numerous diverse populations who inhabit the world. Nor do we possess any satisfactory method for ranking the level of culture in any particular community. It is consequently impossible to make any critical comparison between group heredity and level of culture. But some comments on this subject are possible nevertheless.

Judging by what we can observe of the persons who make up the society in which each of us may happen to live, there is a considerable amount of variation in innate ability among individuals. It may be assumed that the level of culture possible to any society is related at least in part to the proportion of persons in the population who inherit superior ability. A human society in which the majority or all of the members have inherited inferior ability cannot be expected ever to evolve, or to be capable of using, a highly complex culture. We may suspect that such inferior populations have existed in the past, and that a few still exist in local, isolated areas. On the other hand, a society with a high proportion of able persons may not be able to develop a high culture if it lacks natural resources, or if it is subjected to a series of misfortunes. Very able individuals occur at times in almost every population. We seem to be justified, consequently, in concluding that heredity may be an important factor in the organization and evolution of human communities, but that no one society or race has a monopoly of ability.

The heredity of each human band or larger unit of population is in part affected by the customs and ideals of the group. The custom of destroying defective children at birth will reduce the frequencies of those hereditary factors which are discriminated against. On the other hand, selection toward particular ideals of personal beauty, bravery, or special ability such as might make for success in hunting, would increase the proportion in the population of those among these traits which are inherited.

The assemblage of hereditary traits possessed by a human population also indirectly affects its culture. An aggressive or quarrelsome band, for instance, would be expected to develop a culture very different from that of a peaceful and cooperative folk. It is difficult to disentangle differences in culture resulting from the heredity of behavioral traits and differences that have been imposed by training. There is good evidence, however, that breeds of dogs, chickens, and other domestic animals differ in aggressiveness and in other features of behavior and temperament. Certain races of the native North American deermice of the genus *Peromyscus,* for example, exhibit distinctive types of behavior. It seems highly probable, then, that at least part of the variation in behavior and temperament among the tribes of men may be based on hereditary factors, and that these features may in their turn affect certain elements of culture.

The individual and his society Persons who live as members of a human society are able to exist with far more ease and satisfaction to themselves than they could have if they were compelled to wrest their living from the primitive earth without assistance from their fellows. Social life thus promotes the survival and pleasure of human beings. Complex societies can provide the necessities and luxuries for a larger number of persons than can simple societies, although ease and pleasure of living do not necessarily increase in proportion to the size or complexity of the society.

Philosophers have proposed extremely diverse hypotheses of the basic relationships between the individual man and his society. It is not necessary here to consider these several views in detail. We must reject the hypothesis of Hegel that the individual exists to supply the needs of the state, and equally the contrary hypothesis of Spencer that the state exists to protect the liberties of the individual (Keith, 1947: 39). A better viewpoint is that political institutions are most useful when they are voluntary organizations by citizens to promote their mutual welfare.

One important question that may be asked is: How much actual influence does each individual person have on the evolution of the culture of his group? White (1948) takes the position that the individual is unable to affect the evolution of culture in any appreciable way, although he agrees that human effort produces consequences which are part of the current culture of his group. It undoubtedly is true that the influence of any one individual on his culture is slight, and that almost every discovery, invention, and new concept which is ascribed to a certain historic personage is really the product of numerous contributors. It also is helpful to consider that each human community, together with its culture, is an integrated unit or superorganism, whose functioning and whose evolution obey laws which in part are different from those biologic and psychologic laws that govern the behavior of individual men. It does not follow, however, that the effect of the individual man on his culture is negligible. On the contrary, I firmly believe that the continued existence of every human society and the possibility of its further evolution is dependent upon the efforts of its individual members.

Environment, heredity, and culture   Environment, human heredity, and culture influence each other in innumerable ways, as has been pointed out in earlier chapters. Some of the changes which man makes in his physical and biotic environment, for instance, are directed by the culture of the local society. Thus, the raising of particular kinds of decorative plants such as flowering cherries or chrysanthemums, or of particular breeds of pets, such as goldfish or dachshunds, are responses to esthetic values which are esteemed or at least tolerated by a particular human society.

Since environmental influences, heredity, and culture all interact to control the evolution and continued existence of each human community, it is foolish to ask which of them is the most important. All are essential, and none can be considered apart from the others. Any change in one produces more or less important changes in each of the others. Culture, however, is able to change more quickly and to a relatively greater degree than either the environment or human heredity. But the influences of environment and of human heredity on every human community are nevertheless of high significance.

Dynamic nature of the community

The organization of every community, considered only as a static structure, is so enormously complex that such a unit is extremely difficult to describe. When we add to this complexity a consideration of the dynamic character of the interrelations within and between its numerous constituent units, we are likely to be overwhelmed in our attempts to comprehend the operation of any large community.

Changes The nature of the changes that may occur in the social organization of a city community, for example, has been described by Hawley (1950). These changes include the subtraction of an individual from a subsidiary social unit by migration, retirement, or death, and his replacement by some other individual. Such a replacement will usually require some slight readjustment within the group concerned, but the social unit itself continues to operate with little change.

A more serious change in a social unit may take place through its growth. Through the addition of new members, the unit may expand, and in so doing may evolve a greater degree of complexity in its internal organization. The relationships of such a growing social unit to its neighbors will also become altered in time.

A social unit may also contract in size. Through the loss of one or more of its members the unit may become smaller than before, which may force a simplification of its organization. Likewise, the contracting unit will almost certainly develop altered relations to adjacent social units.

Still another type of change in a social unit is its partial or complete replacement by a unit of a different kind. Such a process is known as succession and has been described in some detail in Chapter XIV. Succession in human communities seems to be much less regular than in natural communities. The concept of cultural climax in human communities corresponds only in part to that of climatic climax in natural communities.

Internal regulatory mechanisms Each community, if it is to continue to exist, must continually adjust itself to the fluctuations in the conditions of its physical habitat. The oscillations of climate, such as produce wet, dry, warm, or cold years, may for a time greatly modify the productivity of food, and may adversely affect the health and welfare of the people. But the internal regulatory mechanisms which every community possesses will nearly always produce adjustments to the altered conditions, with only slight disruption of the functioning of the community (Chapter IX).

Continuing nature of community evolution   Communities tend to evolve continually toward more perfect adjustment to their habitats and toward a more efficient utilization of their resources. Because of man's ability to modify his culture, human communities are able to evolve far more quickly than natural communities. Certain elements of human culture, notably those concerned with religion, may evolve along lines that are in part irrational and unadaptive or even harmful to the human society. The material elements of culture, however, generally evolve toward an adaptive relationship to the characters of the physical and biotic environment.

Some early anthropologists expected community evolution to proceed everywhere in an orderly fashion, with certain clearly marked stages repeated in each cultural sequence. This, however, does not happen. Cultural evolution in one region or in one human society has no necessary relation to the sequence of stages, or to the cultural climax, of any other region or society. The trend of cultural evolution is directed, as has been explained in Chapter XII, by the characters of the local environment, by the heredity and past history of the people, by interactions and interchanges of cultural elements with neighboring communities, and by the chance acquirement or loss of cultural elements. The evolution of culture proceeds differently in each climatic region, and differently for each tribe of men. Consequently, we cannot predict the future course of evolution for any given community. Nevertheless, the concept of community evolution is of high descriptive and theoretical value (White, 1947).

The rate of cultural evolution is often so rapid that customs which an individual may have learned in his youth are out of date by the time he has reached old age. It is difficult for an old person to change his habits or point of view, and older persons in a rapidly evolving culture are thus likely to be disturbed by the changes that are taking place. We frequently are exhorted, therefore, to return to the old-time religion, or to restore other aspects of the "good, old" ways of life. It is rarely possible, however, to reverse the trend of evolution, nor would it usually be for the best interests of the community to do so. It is not to be denied, however, that certain fashions which for a time are widely accepted in a particular community may be nonsensical or even harmful. Not all changes in custom are necessarily beneficial.

Place of the human community in the evolution of life

In the evolution of the living world, the ecologic community is a unit that occupies a very high level (Dice, 1952). Inasmuch as every community is composed of numerous species of plants and animals, it occupies a higher level of integration than any individual species.

Among the types of communities which have developed on earth, human communities of various types are the most complex and most advanced, because they exhibit far greater specialization of labor than the societies of any other species, and because man has learned to control his own environment to a very high degree. We may conclude that the human community represents the highest level of organic evolution that has yet appeared on the earth.

The concept of communities derives its chief justification from the emphasis it places on the organization into an operating unit of each aggregation which is composed of several species. Each community, irrespective of its size or rank, constitutes an operating unit because it possesses numerous internal regulatory mechanisms which keep it constantly adjusted to the changing conditions of its habitat.

Integration and evolution inherent in life The tendency of every human community to operate as a unit and to become adapted to its habitat is not unique in the biological world. Every individual organism forms an integrated unit, and every species has the possibility of evolution in the direction of increased adaptation. Each organism is able to continue to exist because its regulatory mechanisms enable it to operate as a unit in adjusting to the vicissitudes of its habitat. A human community is far more complex than any single organism, but the general biologic principles of integration, regulation, evolution, and adaptation apply to every human community just as they do to the lowliest one-celled protozoan. Every community constitutes a more or less perfectly unified whole (Smuts, 1926).

The ability of each organism to coordinate its several parts to operate as a unit is inherent in life itself. Furthermore, all living organisms, societies, and communities are able through progressive evolution continually to improve their degree of adaptation to their habitats. We may be confident that the evolution of human communities is not yet completed, but that so long as man exists on earth progress will continue toward ever-higher levels of community integration.

SELECTED REFERENCES

Dice, Lee R. 1952. Natural communities. Chap. XXIII. Ann Arbor: University of Michigan Press.
Hawley, Amos H. 1950. Human ecology . . . Part III. New York: Ronald Press Co.
Herskovits, Melville J. 1948. Man and his works . . . Chap. 34. New York: Alfred A. Knopf.
Huntington, Ellsworth. 1945. Mainsprings of civilization. New York: John Wiley and Sons.
Smuts, J. C. 1926. Holism and evolution. New York: Macmillan Co.
Steward, Julian H. 1938. Basin-Plateau aboriginal sociopolitical groups. Bull. U.S. Bur. Amer. Ethnol., 120: 230–62.
White, Leslie A. 1949b. Ethnological theory. *In* Philosophy for the future, edited by R. W. Sellars and others. New York: Macmillan Co. Pp. 357–84.

Moral Codes

CHAPTER XVII

The success of every human community depends upon the behavior of the men who compose it. This is true because man has the power to control, at least to some degree, those communities of which he is a member. Having developed some ability to reason, and accordingly being able to choose between diverse modes of action, man must assume responsibility for conducting himself in a manner that will contribute to the well-being of himself and his associates.

Freedom of choice

I here assume that man has at least some degree of freedom of choice (free will), and that he is to that extent responsible for his actions. The Calvinist doctrine of predestination in its extreme form, therefore, is rejected. I reject also the philosophy of the mechanistic concept of life, which in its most extreme expression would consider all manifestations of life to be due solely to the operation of physical and chemical laws. True, many of the activities of man are carried out mechanically, whether they are based on simple types of inherited reactions and instincts, or on individual training and experience. At least occasionally, however, every man is confronted with a situation where he must choose between two or more possible lines of conduct.

Any choice between possible alternative modes of action will of course be strongly influenced by the training and experience of the individual, by his inherited reflexes and instincts, and by the customs of the society of which he forms a part. We only delude ourselves if we think that we have complete freedom of choice in any instance. On the other hand, every man encounters from time to time situations when he is aware that he has some power of deciding upon his course of action. The classification of certain acts as good and others as bad is a recognition that a choice of conduct actually is possible.

Diversity of moral codes

During the long history of man, various moral codes have been proposed as a basis for discriminating between right and wrong behavior. Nearly all of them are based in large part on the customs of the human societies which originated them (Hollingshead, 1940: 361; Firth, 1951, Chap. III). Part of the moral code of each society becomes incorporated into its religion, another part into its civil laws, but a considerable part is expressed only in the customs and beliefs of the people.

Every code of morals has had a long period of evolution. It is not surprising, therefore, that there are considerable variations among the moral codes of the diverse peoples of the world, nor that there is some degree of variability of moral behavior within each human society.

Some criterion is evidently needed for judging which acts are most likely to benefit the person and society concerned, and which may be contrary to his and his society's best interests. We need in particular to be able to say beforehand whether any proposed human act should or should not be performed.

Scientific basis for moral codes

The best basis for a scientific judgment of whether a specific act is good or bad is to consider its effect on all mankind. If the action will benefit mankind as a whole, including the present and all future generations, then it is good. If, on the contrary, it will be harmful to mankind broadly considered, then it is to be classed as bad. This gives a scientific basis for ethics, which is lacking if reliance is placed on any other criterion.

That we should "take as the standard of morality the general good or welfare of the community" was expressly stated many years ago by Charles Darwin in his book *The Descent of Man* (1874, Chap. 4). Many scientists have since reiterated this logical conclusion (Gerard, 1942; Holmes, 1948a: 48). Many moralists and students of ethics, however, have continued the futile attempt to derive a code of morality from other criteria.

In order to predict whether any proposed action may be beneficial or harmful to mankind, consideration must of course be given not only to its possible effects on the health and happiness of the person involved, but also to its effects on all his neighbors, including ultimately all the individual men in the whole world and in all future generations. Consideration must also be given to the possible effect of the action on all the communities that might be involved. The whole of science and of art, therefore, is included in every moral judgment.

As an example of a moral deduction based on scientific evidence may be cited the conclusion of Aldo Leopold (1933) that it is ethically wrong to despoil a forest or to allow soil erosion to occur, because this despoliation decreases the productivity of the land and thereby harms the future generations of mankind.

The course of action that will produce the greatest good for mankind, however, may not always result in the greatest amount of pleasure for the particular individual concerned. The community often demands great sacrifices from certain individuals. A soldier, for example, must be willing to suffer injury, or, if need be, death. A mother must relinquish many temporary pleasures in order to care for her children. The lower animals also often make great individual sacrifices for the sake of their young or for the pack or herd of which they are members. But pleasure can be found also in labor and in sacrifice. Very satisfying and abiding pleasure is in fact often derived from the performance of service for others.

The basis for ethics outlined above is frankly avowed to be conceived from the viewpoint of man's welfare alone, with no consideration of the welfare of any other species. When the welfare of any other species of plant or animal runs counter to that of man, any rational human being must choose the welfare of his own species rather than that of an alien form. Nevertheless, insofar as possible, man should also give due consideration to the welfare of other forms of life. He should do this to avoid needless suffering of any kind. Besides, it will often be to man's own best interest to conserve the plants and animals of the earth, for many of these are beneficial to his own welfare in one way or another.

Regulatory effects of a moral code

In each human society, conformance by the members to the accepted moral code operates to maintain the organization of the group (Emerson, 1954: 78). Moral conduct thus serves much the same kind of function in a society as cooperation between the several organs of the body serves in maintaining a state of individual health (Holmes, 1948a: vii). Each organ of the body must perform its functions at the proper times and to the proper extent to carry on the life and activities of the organism. In the living organism, chemical hormones and nerve impulses serve to coordinate the operations of the whole individual.

In a society, likewise, the activities of the individuals must be coordinated so that the group may thrive. Excessive individualism in the behavior of one member of a society may have results unfavorable for the whole group. Instincts or tropisms may serve to coordinate the operations of the individual members in societies where the actions of the individuals are directed mostly by these simple types of inherited behavior. But in societies such as the human society, where the individual members are able to choose to some extent their own course of behavior, the moral code must coordinate the acts of the individuals, so that the society itself may function properly and may continue to exist.

A highly organized society sets up formal laws, administrative officers, and courts in order to compel conformance with its customs (Hollingshead, 1940: 361). These social institutions, however, do not deal with all of the more essential features of the moral code. Most customs never become incorporated into formal laws, but have authority only by the force of public opinion.

The moral code of every human society operates, in fact, as a powerful stabilizing influence. Departures from the accepted moral code are often frowned upon severely, and may invite reprisals or punishment. Certain infractions of the moral code may result in imprisonment or even capital punishment. Ostracism and banishment are some of the very severe punishments sometimes meted out to offenders against the accepted standards of a society. Public opinion, especially in a small community, is not lightly to be flouted.

Conscience   Feelings of right or wrong on the part of any person may be presumed to be associated with his conformity or failure to conform to the customs of the society of which he is a member. These rules of conduct often deal with very trivial matters. For example, one may be acutely distressed at finding himself the only person wearing full dress at a party. The feelings of discomfort and chagrin of the person caught in such a situation are probably the same in kind, though undoubtedly less in degree, as the feeling of guilt of the person who is caught stealing watermelons or robbing a bank.

A person who is aware that his actions are in accord with the customs of his social group will have a feeling of self-satisfaction, while he who knows that he is acting contrary to social custom will usually be uncomfortable. In other words, behavior which is in accord with custom is felt to be right, while behavior which fails to accord with custom is felt to be wrong. The feelings of the individual about the rightness or wrongness of his actions perhaps constitute what is usually spoken of as conscience.

In stating thus simply that there is a correlation between feelings of right and wrong and the degree of conformity of the person concerned to the behavior required by the customs and ideals of his social group, I do not overlook the fact that some individuals seem to derive satisfaction from behavior which is contrary to that required by custom, seem actually to enjoy flouting the opinion of their neighbors. Others make a practice of attempting to see how near they can come to breaking the law without being caught. I doubt, however, that such persons are completely without a sense of guilt.

On the other hand, certain persons deliberately violate the majority public opinion and perhaps also the laws of the commonwealth, to act in accordance with a set of standards which they have set up themselves, or which they have adopted from a religious sect or a political party. A few strong-minded persons seem actually to enjoy becoming martyrs. They derive satisfaction from acting in accordance with their own moral codes.

It is probable that the capacity to have feelings of right and of wrong will evolve in any kind of social animal with a highly developed nervous system. If a social group is to thrive, each member must know with a high degree of reliability how the other members will behave under the usual conditions of existence, and in emergencies.

In an animal such as man, which often has the possibility of diverse types of response to a given stimulus, one good way to secure relative uniformity in social behavior would be to endow the individuals with feelings of right and wrong. Natural selection should favor the survival of those who conform to the general type of behavior of their social group. We may assume, consequently, that basic nervous mechanisms capable of producing the feelings of right and wrong will have a tendency to become fixed in heredity, and to grow more and more efficient from generation to generation until they reach a high level of effectiveness.

Necessity for changes in moral codes

It may often happen that acts which are desirable at one time and in one place may under other circumstances be harmful. All types of customs and practices must, accordingly, be subject to modification if a human society is to adjust itself to changes in its environment.

A good illustration of the necessity for the moral code to adjust itself to a change in the ecologic relations of a community is afforded by the increase of the deer population in the state of Michigan. During the early part of the twentieth century, the population of white-tailed deer in Michigan and other parts of the United States had become seriously depleted. Laws were passed and the custom inculcated of permitting the hunting only of adult male deer (bucks) during a short season each fall. It then became morally wrong for any person to kill a female deer (doe) or a fawn at any season of the year, or to kill a buck at any other time than the legal hunting season. This code of hunting behavior acted as an artificial regulatory mechanism and proved very successful in increasing the number of deer—so successful, in fact, that after some years the deer populations grew so dense that their food resources became depleted and in certain localities many deer starved to death during severe winters. Under these altered circumstances, a reduction in the whole deer population was desirable. Yet when the Michigan Game Division proposed changing the regulations to allow the killing of adult does as well as of bucks, many hunters strenuously objected. The previously inculcated moral code that classed the killing of a doe as a moral wrong could not easily be changed. Yet, from the standpoint of man, it certainly is better to harvest the surplus does for food rather than to let them starve in the woods. From the point of view of the deer population it is best that the population density be reduced to the level of the carrying capacity of the range, since otherwise the food producing capacity of the range will in time be reduced by over-browsing until few deer can survive.

This example illustrates the fact that morals can never be fixed and final. On the contrary, the moral code of each people must constantly change to meet the needs of its ever-changing ecosystem. Morals can no more be static than life itself.

Evolution of moral codes

Morals and customs are to be considered as purely natural phenomena which can be explained wholly in scientific terms (Holmes, 1948a: 15). Its type of behavior is just as much a characteristic of a species or a strain of animals as is its body form or its physiology. The mental processes of man, in spite of their present high complexity, must have evolved from simpler patterns. Customs and moral codes must likewise have had a natural origin.

The moral code of every people may be assumed to have evolved toward a more or less harmonious relationship with the conditions for human life in the area concerned. No people with a moral code that is seriously maladjusted to its habitat could long survive. A type of behavior that results in the waste of any considerable part of a food resource, for example, would be a serious handicap. Any social group carrying such a handicap would probably not survive in competition with another people whose moral code demanded careful food conservation.

In stating that morals are subject to evolution I do not refer primarily to the evolution of inherited instincts, or of inherited behavior of any kind. Instincts undoubtedly are subject to selection and consequently to evolution. But evolution based on changes in heredity is necessarily a slow process. On the other hand, the evolution of customs can occur rapidly, because it is not necessary for the newly evolved types of behavior to become fixed in heredity. The transfer of culture from generation to generation accomplishes much the same result in certain aspects of human behavior as does biological heredity, but permits a very much faster rate of evolution.

Responsibilities of the individual man   It is largely because of his social organization that man is able to control to some extent those communities of which he forms a part. This control is effected through common action with his fellows. Too often, unfortunately, the laws and the unwritten customs of a local society are not those which are best for the full utilization of the resources of its habitat. Every human society, therefore, should strive continually to improve its laws, its customs, and its morals, to the end that the community may adapt itself more perfectly to its habitat.

It is the responsibility of the individual man to conform in his behavior to those precepts of the moral code of his society which are generally accepted as being best for the welfare of the community. But it is also his responsibility to seek improvements in the moral code to the end that the best interests of humanity may be advanced.

SELECTED REFERENCES

Darwin, Charles. 1874. The descent of man, and selection in relation to sex. Rev. ed. Chap. 4. New York: Rand McNally and Co.

Firth, Raymond. 1951. Elements of social organization. Chap. VI. London: Watts and Co.

Gerard, Ralph W. 1942. A biological basis for ethics. Philosophy of Science, 9: 90–102.

Hollingshead, A. B. 1940. Human ecology and social society. Ecol. Monog., 10: 354–66.

Holmes, Samuel J. 1948a. Life and morals. New York: Macmillan Co.

Sumner, William G. 1940. Folkways . . . Boston: Ginn and Co.

Westermarck, Edward. 1932. Ethical relativity. London: Kegan Paul, Trench, Trubner and Co.

Epilogue: What Lies Before Us

CHAPTER XVIII

This modern era with its frequent wars, economic depressions, and domestic unrest is full of trouble for mankind. Many parts of the world are overcrowded with people and poverty-stricken. The future of our civilization looks very unpromising to many thoughtful persons. There have been forebodings that techno-logical advances are so far ahead of improvements in culture and in heredity that destruction of our existing civilizations is imminent, and that the world may again pass into a dark age. There have even been predictions that the human species itself might become extinct, so that some other species, perhaps the rat or some type of insect, may become the dominant animal on earth.

To the ecologist, these pessimistic predictions have little jus-tification. Organic life has persisted on the earth for hundreds of millions of years. It could do so because each living individual contains within itself regulatory mechanisms that keep it con-stantly in tolerable adjustment with its environment. Human communities also have this power of self-regulation, though it does not always operate at full effectiveness.

The position of dominance in nature now held by man has not

been reached without a struggle. During his whole course of evolution he has been exposed to adverse circumstances that have often filled his life with misery. It may well be questioned whether anything in modern life can be worse than some of the conditions under which primitive men have existed. The possibility that man, after surviving all these trials and threats to his existence, should succumb to the adversities that now assail him is unthinkable. The worst conceivable war or pestilence would leave some remnants of human population alive in remote corners of the world. From these remnants, a new evolution of culture would begin which would in time replace the civilization that had been destroyed. I am in full accord, consequently, with Conklin (1937: 602) and Muller (1952) in believing that the long course of evolution that has led to man and to our modern cultures is not yet finished.

The troubles that beset man today are, from the point of view of the ecologists, only symptoms of a lack of proper adjustment in those communities of which man is the dominant member. They will not soon pass over to usher in a millennium of peace and plenty. Man is yet far from having arrived anywhere at a satisfactory adjustment between the resources of his habitat, his own hereditary nature, and the state of his culture. There is in fact no likelihood that peace and plenty will ever reign on the earth, except perhaps in local situations and only for very brief periods of time. Man's constant and highly laudable striving to better his condition and improve his standard of living can never lead to achievements that are not somewhat short of his ideals. The time will not soon come when every person born on earth can be assured of a safe and comfortable existence.

In spite of the great advances that have been made in the improvement of the conditions for human life on earth, still further advances are not only possible but almost certain. This is true not only for backward districts, but even for the most progressive countries. Even the best communities in the world to-day can be greatly improved.

Man has both the ability and the power to improve greatly his culture, so as to use the resources of the earth with much greater efficiency than he does at present. The productivity of fields and herds can be much increased. Improvements in industrial operations, and in mechanical devices, will without question increase the production of material goods and expand the comforts of human life. Greater control of disease, and more adequate diet, will greatly improve the health of every individual.

The stability of every ecologic system is dependent upon the effective operation of its internal regulatory mechanisms. Human communities are continually becoming more and more complex and consequently have an ever-increasing need of internal controls. Improvements in political and economic organization can greatly increase the efficiency of every human community. The fairness and effectiveness of free competition as a regulatory mechanism can be greatly improved. So can the amount of cooperation within and among human societies. There are also great possibilities for the expansion and development of other regulatory mechanisms that will aid in keeping the various parts of human communities of every rank and kind in balance with one another. Each community that is provided with a wide variety of effective regulatory mechanisms is likely to enjoy a high degree of stability.

A very important feature which should be included in every type and rank of human community is provision for further improvement. Progressive evolution can occur only when the possibility exists for considering and testing new suggestions. If the control of a society happens to lie in reactionary hands, suggestions for changes are not likely to be given serious consideration. On the other hand, too great a readiness to accept new modes of thought or behavior without adequate testing may lead to chaos. In our own country, at the present time, improvements in technology are welcomed and eagerly accepted. Handsome financial rewards are provided to the inventors and sponsors of useful mechanical innovations. In the fields of political and social organization, education, and fundamental science, however, the existing community machinery is, in general, inadequate for the most effective promotion of further evolution.

This "cultural lag" in the evolution of social, economic, and political processes and institutions compared to technological progress is a basic cause of many of the major disorders that plague the modern world (Ogburn, 1922; Barnes, 1948: 144–69). The productivity of our farms and factories has greatly increased, but there has not been an equal increase in methods for the distribution of goods. Surpluses consequently pile up at the same time that many people in other parts of the world and even in our own country are inadequately nourished and are unable to acquire those products of our factories which would add greatly to their efficiency. Nations have devised no generally effective method for settling their differences, so that the threat of war is constantly present and the heavy burden of military preparedness absorbs a large share of the world's productiveness. Strikes and threats of strikes by labor often disrupt the orderly production of goods. Discrimination against racial minorities is the rule in many parts of the world. It is true that some progress has been made in recent years in the evolution of our social and political institutions to meet modern needs, but progress in these matters is by no means keeping up with the rate of progress in natural science and in technology.

The greatest problem of all in planning for the advance of human communities is how to secure improvement in the heredity and training of man himself, to make him a better world citizen willing to cooperate with his fellows in building and

maintaining stable societies. There is no question but that potentialities exist for improving the heredity of man so that he
will become more healthy, more intelligent, and more capable
of social cooperation. By education and training he can be
made skillful in the use of tools and language, and can be led to
conform more or less satisfactorily to the customs of his local
community. Unfortunately, material progress in our cultures
often far outruns the use that people make of their opportunities.

Human communities cannot be expected ever to become uniform in type throughout the whole world. Climates and resources vary from place to place. Heredity and customs also
vary among peoples. Diversity of heredity and of culture among
the communities that exist in the world is highly desirable since
it permits adaptation to local environments and affords a basis
for progressive evolution. But the standardization of certain
items of culture such as language, measurements, calendar, and
currency is desirable in order to permit free trade and interchange of ideas.

Man is not an isolated species living alone, but is dependent
upon numerous associated species of plants and of animals for
food and for many of the other essentials of life. Man also is directly or indirectly dependent upon the physical conditions that
occur in the habitats in which he lives. All the biotic and physical factors that affect man are complexly interrelated. In order
to improve himself and his cultures, therefore, man must build
on a firm basis of scientific knowledge so that he may make full
use of all the organic and inorganic resources of every part of
the earth. Well planned research is greatly needed in every
phase of human ecology.

When adequate regulatory mechanisms are successfully put
into operation in all human communities, a long period of world
peace and prosperity should ensue. But if, on the contrary, the
growth of human populations fails to be controlled, and if other

suitable regulatory mechanisms are not invented and placed in operation, then we may anticipate a future in which domestic distress and foreign wars will initiate a vicious cycle of cultural deterioration that may spread over the whole world. A decline in any particular human community is always a possibility, for history shows that cultures can retrogress as well as improve.

A series of well-integrated and well-regulated world communities is not likely to be constructed soon nor without tremendous effort and travail. Nevertheless, the evolutionary trend is toward this end. Selfishness, ignorance, and bigotry may be able to delay the discovery and application of scientific principles to human communities, but no kind of antisocial force will be able, I believe, to prevent the ultimate evolution of a series of orderly world communities which will continually advance toward ever-higher levels of culture. If effective efforts are made to discover and apply the natural laws that affect human affairs, the time required to construct a well organized group of world communities can be greatly shortened. Our future is in our own hands.

Literature Cited

This list includes only books and articles cited in this work, and does not purport to be a bibliography of the very extensive published materials dealing with human communities.

Ackerman, Edward A.
  1946 The geographic meaning of ecological land use. Journ. Soil and Water Conservation, 1: 63–67.
Adolph, Edward F.
  1943 Physiological regulations. Lancaster, Pennsylvania: The Jacques Cattell Press.
Adolph, William H.
  1944 The protein problem of China. Science, 100: 1–4.
Aiton, Arthur S.
  1951 The impact of the flora and fauna of the new world upon the old world during the sixteenth century. Chronica Bot., 12: 121–25 (Biologica, 2: 121–25).
Allan, Philip F.
  1942 Defensive control of rodents and rabbits. Journ. Wildlife Management, 6: 122–32.
Allee, W. C.
  1943 Where angels fear to tread: a contribution from general sociology to human ethics. Science, 97: 517–25.
  1951 Cooperation among animals; with human implications. New York: Henry Schuman.
Allee, W. C., A. E. Emerson, O. Park, T. Park, and K. P. Schmidt
  1949 Principles of animal ecology. Philadelphia: W. B. Saunders Co.

Allee, W. C., and Karl P. Schmidt
    1951 Ecological animal geography. 2d ed. New York: John
        Wiley and Sons.
Anderson, A. W., and E. A. Power
    1947 Fishery statistics of the United States, 1943. Statistical
        Digest, U.S. Dept. Interior, Fish and Wildlife Service,
        14: 1–241.
Angel, J. Lawrence
    1945 Skeletal material from Attica-Hesperia. Journ. Amer.
        School Class. Studies, Athens, 14: 279–363.
    1946 Social biology of Greek culture growth. Amer. Anthrop.,
        48: 493–533.
Angell, Robert C.
    1941 The integration of American society: a study of groups
        and institutions. New York: McGraw-Hill Book Co.
Baker, O. E.
    1928 Population, food supply, and American agriculture.
        Geog. Rev., 18: 353–73.
Baldwin, Paul H., and Gunnar O. Fagerlund
    1943 The effect of cattle grazing on koa reproduction in Hawaii
        National Park. Ecology, 24: 118–22.
Barnes, Harry E.
    1925 The new history and the social studies. New York: Cen-
        tury Co.
    1940 The new history, archeology, and cultural evolution. *In*
        Contemporary Social Theory, edited by H. E. Barnes,
        H. Becker, and F. B. Becker. New York: D. Apple-
        ton-Century Co. Pp. 543–97.
    1948a Historical sociology: its origins and development. The-
        ories of social evolution from cave life to atomic bomb-
        ing. New York: Philosophical Library.
    1948b An introduction to the history of sociology. Chicago:
        University of Chicago Press.
    1952 Society in transition. 2d ed. New York: Prentice-Hall.
Bates, Daisy
    1939 The passing of the aborigines; a lifetime spent among
        the natives of Australia. New York: G. P. Putnam's Sons.
Bell, Earl H.
    1942 Culture of a contemporary rural community, Sublette,
        Kansas. Rural Life Studies, U.S. Dept. Agric., no. 2
        (mimeographed).
Bennett, Hugh H.
    1939 Soil conservation. New York: McGraw-Hill Book Co.

Bennett, J. W.
 1944 The interaction of culture and environment in the smaller societies. Amer. Anthrop., 46: 461–78.
Bernstein, Joseph
 1947 The worm that ruined a nation. Nat. Hist., 56: 368–69.
Bews, J. W.
 1935 Human ecology. New York: Oxford University Press.
Billington, Ray
 1949 Westward expansion: a history of the American frontier.
   New York: Macmillan Co.
Boak, Arthur E. R.
 1947 A history of Rome to 565 A.D. 3d ed. New York: Macmillan Co.
Boas, Franz
 1920 The methods of ethnology. Amer. Anthrop., 22: 311–21.
 1924 Evolution or diffusion? *Ibid.*, 26: 340–44.
Boulding, Kenneth
 1945 The economics of peace. New York: Prentice-Hall.
 1948 Economic analysis. Rev. ed. New York: Harper and Bros.
Bowen, Howard
 1937 Capital in relation to optimum population. Social Forces,
   15: 346–50.
Bowman, Isaiah, editor
 1937 Limits of land settlement. A report on present-day possibilities. New York: Council on Foreign Relations.
Boyd, M. F., and W. K. Stratman-Thomas
 1933 Studies on benign tertian malaria. no. 4. On the refracto-
   riness of negroes to inoculation with *P. vivax*. Amer.
   Journ. Hygiene, 18: 485–89.
Brody, Samuel
 1945 Bioenergetics and growth. New York: Reinhold Publishing Corp.
Brown, Harrison
 1954 The challenge of man's future: an inquiry concerning
   the condition of man during the years that lie ahead.
   New York: Viking Press.
Brownell, Baker
 1950 The human community; its philosophy and practice for
   a time of crisis. New York: Harper and Bros.
Bryan, Kirk
 1941 Pre-Columbian agriculture in the southwest, as condi-
   tioned by periods of alluviation. Ann. Assoc. Amer.
   Geog., 31: 219–42.

Burgess, E. W., and Paul Wallin
    1944 Homogamy in personality characteristics. Journ. Abnormal and Social Psychol., 39: 475–81.
Burnet, Macfarlane
    1953 Natural history of infectious disease. 2d ed. Cambridge: Cambridge University Press.
Burrow, T.
    1953 Science and man's behavior: the contribution of phylobiology. New York: Philosophical Library.
Burt, William H.
    1946 The mammals of Michigan. Ann Arbor: University of Michigan Press.
Cannon, Walter B.
    1939 The wisdom of the body. Rev. ed. New York: W. W. Norton and Co.
    1941 The body physiologic and the body politic. Science, 93: 1–10.
Carbine, William F.
    1945 Growth potential of the northern pike (*Esox lucius*). Papers Mich. Acad., 30: 205–20.
Carpenter, C. R.
    1934 A field study of the behavior and social relations of howling monkeys. Comp. Psychol. Monog., 10: 1–168.
    1942 Societies of monkeys and apes. Biol. Symposia, 8: 177–204.
Carr-Saunders, A. M.
    1922 The population problem; a study in human evolution. Oxford: Clarendon Press.
    1938 Human evolution and the control of its future. *In* Evolution: essays on aspects of evolutionary biology presented to Prof. E. S. Goodrich on his seventieth birthday, edited by G. R. DeBeer. Oxford: Clarendon Press.
    1942 The biological basis of human nature. London and New York: Oxford University Press.
Carter, George F.
    1945 Plant geography and culture history in the American Southwest. Viking Fund Publ. Anthrop., 5: 1–140.
Chapple, Eliot D., and Carleton S. Coon
    1942 Principles of anthropology. New York: Henry Holt and Co.
Childe, V. Gordon
    1939 Man makes himself. London and New York: Oxford University Press. (Originally published in 1936.)

1951 Social evolution. London: Watts and Co.
1953 What is history? New York: Henry Schuman.

Clark, J. G. D.
1952 Prehistoric Europe. The economic basis. New York: Philosophical Library.

Clements, Frederic E., and R. W. Chaney
1936 Environment and life in the Great Plains. Suppl. Publ., Carnegie Inst. Wash., 24: 1–54.

Clough, Shepard B.
1951 Rise and fall of civilization. An inquiry into the relationship between economic development and civilization. New York: McGraw-Hill Book Co.

Conklin, Edwin G.
1937 Science and ethics. Science, 86: 595–603.

Cook, Robert C.
1947 Puerto Rico marches on. Journ. Heredity, 38: 45–48.
1951 Human fertility: the modern dilemma; with an introduction by Julian Huxley. New York: William Sloane Associates.

Cook, S. F.
1937 The extent and significance of disease among the Indians of Baja California, 1697–1773. Ibero-Americana, 12: 1–39.
1946 Human sacrifice and warfare as factors in the demography of pre-colonial Mexico. Human Biol., 18: 81–102.
1947 Survivorship in aboriginal populations. Human Biol., 19: 83–89.

Cooke, C. Wythe
1933 Possible solution of the Maya mystery. Sci. Monthly, 37: 362–65.

Cooley, Charles H.
1925 Social organization. A study of the larger mind. New York: Charles Scribner's Sons.

Coombs, J. W., Jr., and Kingsley Davis
1950 The pattern of Puerto Rican fertility. Population Studies, Cambridge, 4: 364–79.

Coon, Carleton S.
1951 Caravan. New York: Henry Holt and Co.

Coon, Carleton S., Stanley M. Garn, and Joseph B. Birdsell
1950 Races; a study of the problems of race formation in man. Springfield, Ill.: Charles C. Thomas.

Craig, Charles F., and E. C. Faust
1945 Clinical parasitology. 4th ed. Philadelphia: Lee and Febiger.

Craven, Avery O.
1925 Soil exhaustion as a factor in the agricultural history of Virginia and Maryland, 1606–1860. Univ. Illinois Studies Soc. Sci., 13 (no. 1): 1–179.

Daniels, Farrington
1949 Solar energy. Science, 109: 51–57.

Darwin, Charles
1874 The descent of man, and selection in relation to sex. Rev. ed. New York: Rand McNally and Co.

Davis, Kingsley
1951 The population of India and Pakistan. Princeton: Princeton University Press.

Day, Clarence, Jr.
1920 This simian world. New York: Alfred A. Knopf.

Day, Gordon M.
1953 The Indian as an ecological factor in the northeastern forest. Ecology, 34: 329–46.

Deevey, Edward S., Jr.
1951 Recent textbooks of human ecology. Ecology, 32: 347–51.

Dice, Lee R.
1920 The land vertebrate associations of interior Alaska. Occ. Papers Mus. Zool. Univ. Mich., 85: 1–24.
1940 Ecologic and genetic variability within species of Peromyscus. Amer. Nat., 74: 212–21.
1943 The biotic provinces of North America. Ann Arbor: University of Michigan Press.
1952 Natural communities. Ann Arbor: University of Michigan Press.

Dice, Lee R., and Philip M. Blossom
1937 Studies of mammalian ecology in southwestern North America, with special attention to the colors of desert mammals. Publ. Carnegie Inst. Wash., 485: 1–129.

Dixon, Roland B.
1928 The building of cultures. New York: Charles Scribner's Sons.

Dobzhansky, Theodosius
1951a Genetics and the origin of species. 3d ed., revised. New York: Columbia University Press.

1951b Human diversity and adaptation. Cold Spring Harbor
       Symposium Quant. Biol., 15: 385–400.
Dobzhansky, Th., and M. F. Ashley Montagu
  1947 Natural selection and the mental capacities of mankind.
       Science, 105: 587–90.
Dodd, Alan P.
  1940 The biological campaign against prickly-pear. Brisbane,
       Australia: Commonwealth Prickly Pear Board.
Douglass, A. E.
  1935 Dating Pueblo Bonito and other ruins of the southwest.
       Nat. Geog. Soc. Pueblo Bonito Ser., 1: 1–74.
Dublin, Louis I., A. J. Lotka, and M. Spiegelman
  1949 Length of life; a study of the life table. Rev. ed. New
       York: Ronald Press Co.
Duley, F. L.
  1946 Progress in soil science. Amer. Sci., 34: 633–42.
East, Edward M.
  1923 Mankind at the crossroads. New York: Charles Scrib-
       ner's Sons.
Ekblaw, Elmer
  1921 The ecological relations of the polar Eskimo. Ecology,
       2: 132–44.
Emerson, Alfred E.
  1941 Biological sociology. Denison Univ. Journ. Sci. Lab.,
       36: 146–55.
  1943 Ecology, evolution, and society. Amer. Nat., 77: 97–118.
  1946 The biological basis of social cooperation. Trans. Ill. St.
       Acad. Sci., 39: 9–18.
  1954 Dynamic homeostasis: a unifying principle in organic,
       social, and ethical evolution. Sci. Monthly, 78: 67–85.
Evans-Pritchard, E. E.
  1940 The Nuer; a description of the modes of livelihood and
       political institutions of a Nilotic people. Oxford:
       Clarendon Press.
Fairchild, Henry P.
  1939 People. The quantity and quality of population. New
       York: Henry Holt and Co.
  1947 Race and nationality as factors in American life. New
       York: Ronald Press Co.
  1952 The prodigal century. New York: Philosophical Library.
Firth, Raymond
  1951 Elements of social organization. London: Watts and Co.

Fisher, R. A.
   1930 The genetical theory of natural selection. Oxford: Clar-
        endon Press.
Fiske, John
   1899 A century of science and other essays. Boston: Hough-
        ton Mifflin Co.
Fitter, R. S. R.
   1945 London's natural history. London: Collins.
Fleure, H. J.
   1951 A natural history of man in Britain; conceived as a study
        of changing relations between men and environments.
        London: Collins.
Forde, C. Daryll
   1934 Habitat, economy, and society: a geographical intro-
        duction to ethnology. London: Methuen and Co.
Gabrielson, Ira N.
   1941 Wildlife conservation. New York: Macmillan Co.
Galpin, C. J.
   1915 The social anatomy of an agricultural community. Res.
        Bull. Agric. Exp. Sta. Univ. Wisc., 34: 1–34.
Gerard, Ralph W.
   1940 Organism, society, and science. Sci. Monthly, 50: 340–
        50, 403–12, 530–35.
   1942 A biological basis for ethics. Philosophy of Science, 9:
        92–120.
Gillin, John P.
   1948 The ways of men: an introduction to anthropology. New
        York: Appleton-Century-Crofts.
Gilmore, Melvin R.
   1919 Uses of plants by the Indians of the Missouri River re-
        gion. Ann. Rept., Bur. Amer. Ethnol., 33: 43–154.
   1932 Methods of Indian buffalo hunts, with the itinerary of
        the last tribal hunt of the Omaha. Papers Mich. Acad.,
        16: 17–32.
Goldstein, Marcus S.
   1943 Demographic and bodily changes in descendants of
        Mexican immigrants; with comparable data on par-
        ents and children in Mexico. Institute of Latin-Amer-
        ican Studies, University of Texas.
Gottlieb, M.
   1949 Optimum population, foreign trade, and world economy.
        Population Studies, Cambridge, 3: 151–69.

Gowen, John W., editor
  1952 Heterosis: a record of researches directed toward explaining and utilizing the vigor of hybrids. Ames: Iowa State College Press.
Graham, Edward H.
  1944 Natural principles of land use. London and New York: Oxford University Press.
Griffin, Clare E.
  1949 Enterprise in a free society. Chicago: Richard D. Irwin.
Hackett, L. W.
  1937 Malaria in Europe; an ecological study. London and New York: Oxford University Press.
Haldane, J. B. S.
  1932 The causes of evolution. New York: Harper and Bros.
  1947 Evolution: past and future. Atlantic Monthly, 179 (3): 45–51.
Hallowell, A. Irving
  1949 The size of Algonquin hunting territories: a function of ecological adjustment. Amer. Anthrop., 51: 35–45.
Halperin, Sidney L.
  1946 Human heredity and mental deficiency. Amer. Journ. Mental Deficiency, 51: 153–63.
Hankins, Frank H.
  1926 The racial basis of civilization. A critique of the Nordic doctrine. New York: Alfred A. Knopf.
Harkness, D. A. E.
  1931 Irish emigration. *In* International migrations, edited by W. F. Wilcox. Vol. II. Interpretations. Pp. 261–82. New York: Nat. Bur. Econ. Research.
Haskell, H. J.
  1939 The new deal in old Rome: how government in the ancient world tried to deal with modern problems. New York: Alfred A. Knopf.
Haskins, Caryl P.
  1951 Of societies and men. New York: W. W. Norton and Co.
Hatt, Paul K., editor
  1952 World population and future resources. New York: American Book Co.
Havemeyer, Loomis
  1929 Ethnography. Boston: Ginn and Co.
Hawley, Amos H.
  1950 Human ecology; a theory of community structure. New York: Ronald Press Co.

Herskovits, Melville J.
   1927 Variability and racial mixture. Amer. Nat., 61: 68–81.
   1929 Social selection and the formation of human types. Human Biology, 1: 250–62.
   1948 Man and his works; the science of cultural anthropology. New York: Alfred A. Knopf.
   1952 Economic anthropology; a study in comparative economics. New York: Alfred A. Knopf.
Herskovits, Melville J. and Frances S.
   1947 Trinidad village. New York: Alfred A. Knopf.
Hollingshead, A. B.
   1940 Human ecology and human society. Ecol. Monog., 10: 354–66.
Holmberg, Allan R.
   1950 Nomads of the long bow: the Siriono of eastern Bolivia. Publ. Inst. Soc. Anthrop. Smithson. Inst., 10: 1–104.
Holmes, Samuel J.
   1921 The trend of the race; a study of present tendencies in the biological development of civilized mankind. New York: Harcourt, Brace and Co.
   1936 Human genetics and its social import. New York: McGraw-Hill Book Co.
   1948a Life and morals. New York: Macmillan Co.
   1948b Organic form and related biological problems. Berkeley: University of California Press.
Hooton, E. A.
   1946 Up from the ape. Rev. ed. New York: Macmillan Co.
Horn, E. E., and H. S. Fitch
   1942 Interrelations of rodents and other wildlife of the range. *In* The San Joaquin Experimental Range. Bull. Univ. Calif. Agric. Exp. Sta., 663: 96–129.
Hsu, Francis L. K.
   1953 Americans and Chinese: two ways of life. New York: Henry Schuman.
Hubbert, M. King
   1949 Energy from fossil fuels. Science, 109: 103–9.
Hunt, Harrison R.
   1930 Some biological aspects of war. New York: Galton Publishing Co.
Huntington, Ellsworth
   1907 The pulse of Asia: a journey in central Asia illustrating the geographic basis of history. Boston: Houghton Mifflin Co.

1914 The climatic factor as illustrated in arid America; with contributions by Charles Schuchert, Andrew E. Douglass, and Charles J. Kullmer. Publ. Carnegie Inst. Wash., 192: 1–341.

1945 Mainsprings of civilization. New York: John Wiley and Sons.

1951 Principles of human geography. 6th ed., revised by Earl B. Shaw. New York: John Wiley and Sons.

James, Preston E.

1935 An outline of geography. Boston: Ginn and Co.

Jenks, Albert E.

1900 The wild rice gatherers of the upper lakes; a study in American primitive economics. Ann. Rept. Bur. Amer. Ethnol., 19: 1013–1137.

Jenness, D.

1922 The life of the Copper Eskimos. Rept. Canadian Arctic Expedition, 1913–18, 12: 1–277.

Jones, W. H. S.

1909 Malaria and Greek history; to which is added: The history of Greek therapeutics and the malaria theory, by E. T. Withington. Manchester: Manchester University Press.

Jordan, David S.

1915 War and the breed; the relation of war to the downfall of nations. Boston: Beacon Press.

Keever, Catherine

1953 Present composition of some stands of the former oak-chestnut forest in the southern Blue Ridge Mountains. Ecology, 34: 44–54.

Keith, Arthur

1947 Evolution and ethics. New York: G. P. Putnam's Sons.

1949 A new theory of human evolution. New York: Philosophical Library.

Keller, A. G.

1915 Societal evolution. New York: Macmillan Co.

Kendeigh, S. Charles, and others

1950–51 Nature sanctuaries in the United States and Canada: a preliminary inventory. Living Wilderness, 35: 1–45.

Kinietz, W. Vernon

1947 Chippewa village: the story of Katikitegon. Bull. Cranbrook Inst. Sci., 25: 1–259.

Kluckhohn, Clyde

1949 Mirror for man. The relation of anthropology to modern

life. New York: Whittlesey House (McGraw-Hill Book Co.).

Kluckhohn, Clyde, and Charles Griffith
1951 Population genetics and social anthropology. Cold Spring Harbor Symposium Quant. Biol., 15: 401–8.

Kluckhohn, Clyde, and Dorothea Leighton
1948 The Navaho. Cambridge: Harvard University Press.

Knapp, R. H., and H. B. Goodrich, editors
1952 Origins of American scientists. Chicago: University of Chicago Press.

Kollmorgen, Walter M.
1942 The old order Amish of Lancaster County, Pennsylvania. Rural Life Studies, U.S. Dept. Agric., no. 4 (mimeographed).

Kroeber, Alfred L.
1919 On the principle of order in civilization as exemplified by changes of fashion. Amer. Anthrop., 21: 235–63.
1939 Cultural and natural areas of North America. Univ. Calif. Publ. Amer. Arch. and Ethnol., 38: 1–242.
1944 Configurations of culture growth. Berkeley: University of California Press.
1948 Anthropology: race, language, culture, psychology, prehistory. New York: Harcourt, Brace and Co.

Kroeber, Alfred L., and Clyde Kluckhohn
1952 Culture: a critical review of concepts and definitions. Papers Peabody Mus., Harvard Univ., 47: i–viii, 1–223.

LaBarre, Weston
1948 The Aymara Indians of the Lake Titicaca Plateau, Bolivia. Mem. Amer. Anthrop. Assoc., 68: 1–250.

Landis, Paul H., and Paul K. Hatt
1954 Population problems: a cultural interpretation. 2d ed. New York: American Book Co.

Lasker, Gabriel W.
1952 Environmental growth factors and selective migration. Human Biology, 24: 262–89.

Lehman, Harvey C.
1953 Age and achievement. Mem. Amer. Phil. Soc., 33: i–xiii, 1–359.

Leonard, Olen, and C. P. Loomis
1941 Culture of a contemporary community, El Cerrito, New Mexico. Rural Life Studies, U.S. Dept. Agric., no. 1 (mimeographed).

Leopold, Aldo
    1933 The conservation ethic. Journ. Forestry, 31: 634–43.
Lindquist, Arthur W., and H. G. Wilson
    1948 Development of a strain of houseflies resistant to DDT. Science, 107: 276.
Linsdale, Jean M.
    1946 The California ground squirrel; a record of observations made on the Hastings Natural History Reservation. Berkeley: University of California Press.
Linton, Ralph
    1933 Tanala; a hill tribe of Madagascar. Publ. Field Mus. Nat. Hist., Anthrop. Ser., 22: 1–334.
    1936 The study of man; an introduction. New York: D. Appleton-Century Co.
    1938 The present status of anthropology. Science, 87: 241–48.
    1945 The cultural background of personality. New York: D. Appleton-Century Co.
Lippmann, Walter
    1937 An inquiry into the principles of the good society. Boston: Little, Brown and Co.
Loomis, Charles P., and J. Allan Beegle
    1950 Rural social systems; a textbook in rural sociology and anthropology. New York: Prentice-Hall.
Lorimer, Frank, and Frederick Osborn
    1934 Dynamics of population: social and biological significance of changing birth rates in the United States. New York: Macmillan Co.
Lotka, Alfred J.
    1948 Physical aspects of organic evolution. Bull. Math. Biophysics, 10: 103–15.
Louis, Paul
    1927 Ancient Rome at work. An economic history of Rome from the origins to the empire. New York: Alfred A. Knopf.
Lovering, T. S.
    1949 The exploitation of mineral resources. Sci. Monthly, 68: 91–95.
Lowie, Robert H.
    1929 Culture and ethnology. New York: Peter Smith.
McDougall, William
    1920 The group mind; a sketch of the principles of collective psychology with some attempt to apply them to the

interpretation of national life and character. New
York: G. P. Putnam's Sons.

MacIver, R. M.
1917 Community; a sociological study; being an attempt to
set out the nature and fundamental laws of social
life. London: Macmillan and Co.

MacKenzie, R. D.
1933 The metropolitan community. New York: McGraw-Hill
Book Co.

Malin, James C.
1947 The grassland of North America. Prolegomena to its history. Lawrence, Kansas: James C. Malin.

Malthus, T. R.
1826 An essay on the principle of population; or, a view of
its past and present effects on human happiness; with
an inquiry into our prospects respecting the future
removal or mitigation of the evils which it occasions.
6th ed. London: John Murray. 2 vols.

Mannheim, Karl
1950 Freedom, power, and democratic planning. New York:
Oxford University Press.

Mather, Kirtley F.
1944 Enough and to spare; mother earth can nourish every
man in freedom. New York: Harper and Bros.

Mead, Margaret, editor
1937 Cooperation and competition among primitive peoples.
New York: McGraw-Hill Book Co.

Mees, C. E.
1946 The path of science. New York: John Wiley and Sons.

Meggers, Betty J.
1954 Environmental limitation on the development of culture.
Amer. Anthrop., 56: 801–24.

Meltzer, S. J.
1907 The factors of safety in animal structure and animal
economy. Journ. Amer. Med. Assn., 48: 655–64.

Moe, Edward O., and Carl G. Taylor
1942 Culture of a contemporary rural community, Irwin,
Iowa. Rural Life Studies, U.S. Dept. Agric., no. 5
(mimeographed).

Morley, Sylvanus G.
1946 The ancient Maya. Stanford: Stanford University Press.

Muller, H. J.
1936 On the variability of mixed races. Amer. Nat., 70: 409–
42.

1950 Our load of mutations. Amer. Journ. Human Genetics, 2: 111–76.

1952 Will science continue? Bull. Atomic Scientists, 8: 301–7.

Murdock, George P.

1934 Our primitive contemporaries. New York: Macmillan Co.

Nansen, Fridtjof

1893 Eskimo life. Translated by William Archer. London: Longmans, Green and Co.

Neel, James V., and Harold F. Falls

1951 The rate of mutation of the gene responsible for retinoblastoma in man. Science, 114: 419–22.

Nilsson, Martin P.

1921 The race problem of the Roman empire. Hereditas, 2: 370–90.

Odum, Eugene P.

1953 Fundamentals of ecology. Philadelphia: W. B. Saunders Co.

Odum, Howard W.

1951 American sociology. The story of sociology in the United States through 1950. New York: Longmans, Green and Co.

Opler, Morris Edward

1944 Cultural and organic conceptions in contemporary world history. Amer. Anthrop., 46: 448–60.

Osborn, Fairfield

1948 Our plundered planet. Boston: Little, Brown and Co.

1953 The limits of the earth. Boston: Little, Brown and Co.

Osborn, Frederick

1951 Preface to eugenics. Rev. ed. New York: Harper and Bros.

Pearl, Raymond

1918 Biology and war. Journ. Wash. Acad. Sci., 8: 341–60.

1927 Differential fertility. Quart. Rev. Biol., 2: 102–18.

1937 On biological principles affecting populations: human and other. Amer. Nat., 71: 50–68.

1939 The natural history of population. New York: Oxford University Press.

1946 Man the animal. Bloomington, Indiana: Principia Press.

Pearson, Frank A., and Floyd A. Harper

1945 The world's hunger. Ithaca: Cornell University Press.

Pearson, Karl

1896 Mathematical contributions to the theory of evolution.

III. Regression, heredity, and panmixia. Phil. Trans.
Roy. Soc. London, 187: 253–318.

1926 On our present knowledge of the relationship of mind
and body. Ann. Eugenics, 1: 382–406.

Pearson, Oliver P.

1948 Metabolism and bioenergetics. Sci. Monthly, 66: 131–
34.

Penrose, E. F.

1934 Population theories and their application, with special
reference to Japan. Food Research Institute, Stanford
Univ.

Penrose, Lionel S.

1933 A study in the inheritance of intelligence. The analysis
of 100 families containing subcultural mental defec-
tives. Brit. Journ. Psych., Gen. Sec., 24: 1–19.

1948 The supposed threat of declining intelligence. Amer.
Journ. Mental Deficiency, 53: 114–18.

1949 The biology of mental defect. New York: Grune and
Stratton.

1950 Genetical influences on the intelligence level of the population. Brit. Journ. Psych., Gen. Sec., 40: 128–36.

Petrie, Flinders

1919 The revolutions of civilization. London: Harper and
Bros.

Pickford, G. D., and Elbert H. Reid

1943 Competition of elk and domestic livestock for summer
range forage. Journ. Wildlife Management, 7: 328–
32.

Pitt-Rivers, G. H. Lane-Fox

1927 The clash of cultures and the contact of races; an an-
thropological and psychological study of the laws of
racial adaptability, with special reference to the depopulation of the Pacific and the government of subject races. London: George Routledge and Sons.

Pound, Charles E., and Frank E. Egler

1953 Brush control in southeastern New York: fifteen years
of stable tree-less communities. Ecology, 34: 63–73.

Price, Grenville

1939 White settlers in the tropics. Publ. Amer. Geog. Soc.,
23: 1–326.

Quinn, James A.

1950 Human ecology. New York: Prentice-Hall.

Ransom, Jay E.
　1946 Aleut natural food economy. Amer. Anthrop., 48: 607–23.
Rasmussen, Knud
　1931 The Netsilik Eskimos. Social life and spiritual culture. Copenhagen: Rept. 5th Thule Exped., 1921–24, 8: 1–542.
Richards, Audrey I.
　1932 Hunger and work in a savage tribe; a functional study of nutrition among the southern Bantu. London: George Routledge and Sons. (Publ. in U.S.A. by Free Press, Glencoe, Ill., 1948.)
Richter, Curt P.
　1952 Domestication of the Norway rat and its implication for the study of the genetics of man. Amer. Journ. Human Genetics, 4: 273–85.
Riley, Gordon A.
　1944 The carbon metabolism and photosynthetic efficiency of the earth as a whole; with an introduction by G. Evelyn Hutchinson. Amer. Scientist, 32: 129–34.
Ritchie, James
　1920 The influence of man on animal life in Scotland: a study of faunal evolution. Cambridge: Cambridge University Press.
Robertson, J. M.
　1912 The evolution of states. An introduction to English politics. New York: G. P. Putnam's Sons.
Robinson, S., D. B. Dill, J. W. Wilson, and M. Nielson
　1941 Adaptations of white men and negroes to prolonged work in humid heat. Amer. Journ. Tropical Med., 21: 261–87.
Roe, Frank G.
　1951 The North American buffalo; a critical study of the species in its wild state. Toronto: University of Toronto Press.
Salaman, Redcliffe N.
　1949 The history and social influence of the potato. Cambridge: Cambridge University Press.
　1950 Influence of food plants on social structure. Nature (London), 166: 382–83.
Schneirla, T. C.
　1949 Levels in the psychological capacities of animals. *In*

Philosophy for the future, edited by R. W. Sellars.
New York: Macmillan Co. Pp. 243–86.

Scott, J. P.
1942 Genetic differences in the social behavior of inbred
strains of mice. Journ. Heredity, 33: 11–15.

Sears, Paul B.
1935 Deserts on the march. Norman: University of Oklahoma Press.
1939 Life and environment; the interrelations of living things.
New York: Teachers College, Columbia University.
1953 Climate and civilization. *In* Climatic change, edited
by Harlow Shapley. Cambridge: Harvard University
Press. Pp. 35–50.

Seebohm, Frederic
1915 The English village community examined in its relations to the manorial and tribal systems and to the
common or open field system of husbandry; an essay
in economic history. 4th ed. London: Longmans,
Green and Co.

Semple, Ellen C.
1911 Influences of geographic environment, on the basis of
Ratzel's system of anthropo-geography. New York:
Henry Holt and Co.

Semple, Ellen C., and Clarence F. Jones
1933 American history and its geographic conditions. Boston: Houghton Mifflin Co.

Shapiro, H. L.
1939 Migration and environment; a study of the physical
characteristics of the Japanese immigrants to Hawaii
and the effects of environment on their descendants.
New York: Oxford University Press.

Simmons, Leo W.
1945 The role of the aged in primitive society. New Haven:
Yale University Press.

Simpson, George G.
1941 The role of the individual in evolution. Journ. Wash.
Acad. Sci., 31: 1–20.
1949 The meaning of evolution: a study of the history of life
and of its significance for man. New Haven: Yale
University Press.

Sinnott, Edmund W.
1945 Plants and the material basis of civilization. Amer. Nat.,
79: 28–43.

Smuts, J. C.
1926 Holism and evolution. New York: Macmillan Co.
Snell, George D.
1951 Hybrids and history. The role of race and ethnic crossing in individual and national achievement. Quart.
Rev. Biol., 26: 331–47.
Sorokin, Pitirim A.
1947 Society, culture, and personality: their structure and
dynamics. A system of general sociology. New York:
Harper and Bros.
Speck, F. G.
1915 Family hunting territories and social life of various Al-
gonquin bands of the Ottawa Valley. Mem. Canadian
Geol. Surv., 70: 1–30.
Spencer, Herbert
1892 Principles of ethics. New York: D. Appleton and Co.
Vol. I.
Spicer, Edward H., editor
1952 Human problems in technological change. A casebook.
New York: Russell Sage Foundation.
Stakman, E. C.
1947 Plant diseases are shifty enemies. Amer. Scientist, 35:
321–50.
Stern, Curt
1949 Principles of human genetics. San Francisco: W. H.
Freeman and Co.
Stern, E. Wagner, and Allen A. Stern
1945 The effect of smallpox on the destiny of the Amerindian.
Boston: Bruce Humphries.
Steward, Julian H.
1936 Economic and social basis of social bands. *In* Essays in
anthropology presented to A. L. Kroeber, edited by
Robert H. Lowie. Berkeley: University of California
Press. Pp. 331–50.
1938 Basin-Plateau aboriginal sociopolitical groups. Bull.
U. S. Bur. Amer. Ethnol., 120: i–xii, 1–346.
1941 Determinism in primitive society. Sci. Monthly, 53: 491–
501.
1947 American culture history in the light of South America.
Southwestern Journ. Anthropology, 3: 85–107.
1949 Cultural causality and law; a trial formulation of the
development of early civilizations. Amer. Anthrop.,
51: 1–27.

1953 Evolution and process. *In* Anthropology today: an encyclopedic inventory. Chicago: University of Chicago Press. Pp. 313–26.

Sumner, William G.
1940 Folkways; a study of the sociological importance of usages, manners, customs, mores, and morals. Boston: Ginn and Co. (First published in 1906.)

Sumner, William G., and A. G. Keller
1927 The science of society. 3 vols. New Haven: Yale University Press.

Sweetman, Harvey L.
1936 The biological control of insects; with a chapter on weed control. Ithaca, New York: Comstock Publishing Co.

Swellengrebel, N. H.
1940 The efficient parasite. Science, 92: 465–69.

Taeuber, Irene B.
1952 British Guiana: some demographic aspects of economic development. Population Index, 18: 3–19.

Taylor, Griffith
1937 Environment, race and migration. Chicago: University of Chicago Press.

Thomas, Franklin
1940 The role of anthropogeography in contemporary social theory. *In* Contemporary social theory, edited by H. E. Barnes, H. Becker, and F. B. Becker. New York: D. Appleton-Century Co. Pp. 143–211.

Thompson, Laura
1949a The basic conservation problem. Sci. Monthly, 68: 129–31.
1949b The relations of men, animals, and plants in an island community (Fiji). Amer. Anthrop., 51: 253–67.
1950a Culture in crisis; a study of the Hopi Indians. New York: Harper and Bros.
1950b Science and the study of mankind. Science, 111: 559–63.

Thompson, Laura, and Alice Joseph
1944 The Hopi way. Chicago: University of Chicago Press.

Thompson, Warren S.
1942 Population problems. 3d ed. New York: McGraw-Hill Book Co.
1944 Plenty of people. Lancaster, Pennsylvania: The Jacques Cattell Press.

1949 Some reflections on world population and food supply during the next few decades. *In* Studies in population: Proceedings of the annual meeting of the Population Association of America at Princeton, New Jersey, edited by George F. Mair. Princeton: Princeton University Press. Pp. 80–92.

Thomson, J. Arthur, and Patrick Geddes
1931 Life: Outlines of general biology. London: Williams and Norgate. 2 vols.

Toynbee, Arnold J.
1947 A study of history. Abridgment of volumes I–VI by D. C. Somervell. New York: Oxford University Press.

United Nations
1949 Demographic yearbook, 1948. Lake Success, N.Y.: United Nations.

United States, Bureau of the Census
1942 Sixteenth census of the United States: 1940. Population. Volume I. Number of inhabitants. . . . Washington: Government Printing Office.

Veblen, Thorstein
1912 The theory of the leisure class. An economic study of institutions. New ed. New York: Macmillan Co.

Vogt, William
1946 Too many mouths. The Land, 5: 259–65.
1948 Road to survival. New York: William Sloane Associates.

Walbank, Frank W.
1953 The decline of the Roman empire in the west. New York: Henry Schuman.

Weaver, J. E., and F. W. Albertson
1936 Effects of the great drought on the prairies of Iowa, Nebraska, and Kansas. Ecology, 17: 567–639.

Wechsler, David
1944 The measurement of adult intelligence. 3d ed. Baltimore: Williams and Wilkins Co.

Weidenreich, Franz
1939 The duration of life of fossil man in China and the pathological lesions found in his skeleton. Chinese Med. Journ., 55: 34–54.

Westermarck, Edward
1932 Ethical relativity. London: Kegan Paul, Trench, Trubner and Co.

Weyer, Edward M., Jr.
    1932 The Eskimos; their environment and folkways. New
        Haven: Yale University Press.
Whelpton, P. K., Hope T. Eldridge, and J. S. Siegel
    1947 Forecasts of the population of the United States, 1945–
        1975. Washington: Census Bureau, U. S. Dept. Com-
        merce.
White, C. Langdon, and George T. Renner
    1936 Geography; an introduction to human ecology. New
        York: D. Appleton-Century Co.
White, Leslie A.
    1943 Energy and the evolution of culture. Amer. Anthrop.,
        45: 335–56.
    1947 Evolutionary states, progress, and the evaluation of cul-
        tures. Southwestern Journ. Anthrop., 3: 165–92.
    1948 Man's control over civilization: an anthropocentric il-
        lusion. Sci. Monthly, 66: 235–47.
    1949a The science of culture; a study of man and civiliza-
        tion. New York: Farrar, Straus, and Co.
    1949b Ethnological theory. *In* Philosophy for the future,
        edited by R. W. Sellars and others. New York: Mac-
        millan Co. Pp. 357–84.
Wilcox, Earley V.
    1947 Acres and people; the eternal problem of China and
        India. New York: Orange Judd Publishing Co.
Williams, Roger J.
    1946 The human frontier: a new pathway for science toward
        a better understanding of ourselves. New York: Har-
        court, Brace and Co.
Wilson, John A.
    1951 The burden of Egypt: an interpretation of ancient
        Egyptian culture. Chicago: University of Chicago
        Press.
Winslow, C. E. A.
    1952 Man and epidemics. Princeton: Princeton University
        Press.
Wissler, Clark
    1914 The influence of the horse in the development of Plains
        culture. Amer. Anthrop., 16: 1–25.
    1924 The relation of nature to man as illustrated by the North
        American Indian. Ecology, 5: 311–18.
    1929 An introduction to social anthropology. New York:
        Henry Holt and Co.

1938a The American Indian; an introduction to the anthropology of the new world. 3d ed. New York: Oxford University Press.

1938b Man and culture. New York: Thomas Y. Crowell Co.

Wright, Sewall

1931 Evolution in Mendelian populations. Genetics, 16: 97–159.

1950 Genetical structure of populations. Nature (London), 166: 247.

Wulsin, Frederick R.

1949 Adaptations to climate among non-European peoples. *In* Physiology of heat regulation and the science of clothing, edited by L. H. Newburgh. Philadelphia: W. B. Saunders Co. Pp. 3–69.

1953 Hot weather and high achievement. Florida Anthrop., 6: 103–20.

Zinsser, Hans

1935 Rats, lice and history. Boston: Little, Brown and Co.

Index